Student's Guide
to the Internet

by David Clark

**alpha
books**

A Division of Macmillan Publishing
A Prentice Hall Macmillan Company
201 West 103rd Street, Indianapolis, Indiana 46290

Dedicated to my wife Toria for her words of encouragement and willingness to share the phone line.

©1995 Alpha Books

International Standard Book Number:1-56761-545-7
Library of Congress Catalog Card Number: 94-79437

97 96   8 7 6 5 4 3 2

Interpretation of the printing code: the rightmost number of the first series of numbers is the year of the book's printing; the rightmost number of the second series of numbers is the number of the book's printing. For example, a printing code of 95-1 shows that the first printing of the book occurred in 1995.

Screen reproductions in this book were created by means of the program Collage Complete from Inner Media, Inc., Hollis, NH.

Printed in the United States of America

Publisher
Marie Butler-Knight

Managing Editor
Elizabeth Keaffaber

Acquisitions Manager
Barry Pruett

Product Development Manager
Faithe Wempen

Production Editor
Mark Enochs

Copy Editor
San Dee Phillips

Cover Designer
Karen Ruggles

Designer
Barbara Kordesh

Indexer
Bront Davis

Production Team
Gary Adair, Angela Calvert, Dan Caparo, Kim Cofer, Jennifer Eberhardt, Rob Falco David Garratt, Erika Millen, Beth Rago, Karen Walsh, Robert Wolf

Special thanks to Martin R. Wyatt for ensuring the technical accuracy of this book.

Contents

Introduction

The Internet: Not Just for Geeks Anymore

Maybe you're a computer geek, but maybe you're not. Maybe you're just an ordinary student who's trying to get your homework done, put in your hours at work, figure out what you want to do with your life, and make it to the big party this weekend. And you've heard talk about this thing called the Internet.

You may have heard some pretty amazing claims about what the Internet can do for you, and actually, they're almost all true. (The one about doing your laundry may be stretching it.) Unfortunately, the Internet is not a very user-friendly environment, and it's hard to find anyone who will help you get through the *newbie* phase. (A newbie is like an Internet fraternity pledge— experienced folks think they can heap all kinds of abuse on the poor soul in the name of initiation.) You don't have to be a newbie and struggle to learn every lesson the hard way. That's where this book comes in.

This book will walk you through from the very beginning—no computer geek knowledge required. You'll learn how to:

- Find out what Internet support your school offers, and lobby to get better service if you're disappointed with what you find.

- Get an Internet account and use it.

- Find your way around at a UNIX prompt.

- Participate in discussion groups all around the world about anything from Princess Di to spitting cockroaches.

- Send and receive electronic mail (e-mail) from friends and enemies alike.

- Download important resource files, cool programs, and the latest in free or cheap games.

- Meet exciting new people who have no way of finding out what you really look like. (Just tell them you're a model!)

And much more. For instance, there's a huge listing of academic resources near the end of the book that can help you do that last-minute research for your paper that's due in two days. It's broken down by academic area, so you can find what you need fast. There's also a chapter on using those flashy online services, such as PRODIGY and America Online, if your school is in the dark ages and doesn't offer Internet access.

Everything You Read May Be Wrong...

My, people come and go so quickly here!
—Dorothy, Wizard of Oz

Before we begin, I need to give you a warning. Things happen fast on the Internet. Computers and addresses come and go and never leave a trace that they even existed. A site that may be the hottest thing you've ever seen one week may be out of business the next.

What am I getting at? That the Internet is dynamic. However, this book you're holding in your hands is static; it represents one moment in time. By the time this book is printed, some of the addresses cited in this book won't work. There will be newer, better software to access the Internet than the programs I've described. There will be fantastic new sites springing up.

The basic tools and strategies, though, are more consistent. For example, I use FTP to download files today, and chances are, that's what we'll all still be using a year from now. The bulk of this book is about those tools and strategies.

By the way, I have used a couple conventions in this book to make it easier to use. For example, when you need to type something, it will appear like this:

Type **this**

Just type what it says to. It's as simple as that. Also I'll need to show you examples of what you'll see on the Internet. These will appear in a special typeface to represent what you see on-screen, like this:

```
This is what you see on-screen.
```

Talk to Me!

I haven't given up on providing you the latest and greatest information about those ever-changing sites and addresses. No, I'm too clever for that. (Ahem. No need to thank me.) That's why I've created a World Wide Web page where you can get the latest updates. Whereas other books offer you free disks with software (usually stuff that is available for free anyway on the Internet), I'm giving you the chance to interact with me and my publisher and to influence future editions of this book.

Look for updates regarding this book at:

http://mcp.com/~dclark/student.html

You can even leave a message for me there and make comments about what you would like to see included on the page. There you will be able to find:

▥ Links to academic sites.

▥ FAQs (frequently asked questions) for students that answer important questions, such as "How can I find a job using Internet resources?" and "How can I meet the person of my dreams over the Net?"

▥ A list of organizations providing Internet access for when you graduate and your digital umbilical cord is severed from your university.

▥ Pointers to software to access the Net.

▥ Anything else I decide to put there. :-)

And just in case you are looking at that address above and don't have a clue about what it means, keep reading. By the time you finish this book, you'll be surfing the net into waters you didn't even know existed.

Acknowledgments

My thanks to the students at Platt Middle School in Boulder, Colorado for checking links and keeping me on my toes.

My appreciation to Libby Black and the Boulder Valley Internet Project for working to provide access to students and giving me a chance to participate in this virtual adventure.

Thank you to Faithe Wempen and the editorial staff at Alpha Books for positive feedback and gently worded criticism.

David Clark

Trademarks

Terms suspected of being trademarks or service marks have been appropriately capitalized. Alpha Books cannot attest to the accuracy of this information. Use of a term in this book should not be regarded as affecting the validity of any trademark or service mark.

Promises, Promises: What You Can Do on the Net

Welcome to the Internet!

If you are starting an education at a major university, college, or even high school, you are going to have to add one more thing to your list of things to do that first week. After you stand in line to sign up for classes, stand in line to purchase your books, and stand in line to get your financial aid check, head over to your computing center and find out about getting an Internet account.

Most colleges and universities make Internet accounts available to students, and some high schools have started doing the same. Don't miss the boat; get your account and start cruising the Net. It could be the best investment in your education that you ever make.

I know—you're probably thinking the Internet is just for computer geeks. Well, it used to be, but that's changing fast. You'll be amazed at the sheer volume and variety of stuff you can find on the Internet, from information about zebras for that big zoology test to the latest Ren and Stimpy wallpaper for Windows.

The Internet—What Is It?

Think of the Internet as millions of computers that can talk and share information. What kinds of computers? Everything from the lowliest 286s and Apple IIes to sophisticated workstations running UNIX, NT, and other hot operating systems. What kinds of information? Well, correspondence certainly (a.k.a. e-mail), but more than just that. Graphics and video clips are making digital trips every second of every day, as are Supreme Court decisions, the latest O.J. jokes, and lots, lots more.

The Internet is run by the people who are on it. That means you and me! We all have a responsibility to ensure that the Internet is used in positive ways. New people are coming online every minute now. That's a lot of people, a lot of new ideas, a lot of potential.

How Big Is It?

How many host computers are hooked up to the Internet? Nobody is really quite sure. The number 3.2 million has been tossed around a bit, and while that number is under dispute, it probably isn't too far off, for the time being. New Internet addresses continue to be added all the time. Keeping up with the changing/growing character of the Internet is a bit like trying to count rain drops. They just keep coming and coming.

What's more, 3.2 million is just the number of host computers—the large computers (usually UNIX-based) that the average users (you and I) hook into as we sit at our desktop computers or the machines in our school labs. At any given school or business, there are probably hundreds of people using the Internet through a single host computer. That means the total number of people logging onto the Internet is a great deal larger than 3.2 million. An educated guess would be around 30 million users around the world at the end of 1994.

These host computers are located in libraries, universities, governmental and corporate agencies, and elementary, middle, and high schools all over the world. They're connected by high speed phone lines. It can take as little as 640 milliseconds for a message to travel from North America to Antarctica.

At the end of 1994, 80 percent of all colleges and universities were linked to the Internet. Chances are pretty good that you can hook in. If, however, you fall into the 20 percent of unconnected schools, make some noise, write some letters, call a few people, and let them know you think this is important. The world is changing and it's time to get on board. While you are waiting for them to act, there are a couple of other ways you can connect to the Internet. You can find the how, where, and whys of those connections in the pages to come.

What Can I Do on the Internet?

A lot. The Internet is defining a whole new culture and you have an opportunity to be part of it, but more than that, you have an opportunity to shape it, to add or detract from it. Be careful. What you do on the Net counts. The most wonderful thing about this is that you will do it all from your personal computer. Shaping cyberspace belongs to those with access to the tools. So get access and learn the tools. I'm not saying it's going to be easy. In fact, some of it's going to be a downright pain in the neck. You'll need to increase your frustration threshold and decrease any tendencies you may have to shrink when confronted with a challenge. Ask a lot of questions and push a lot of buttons.

Here's a sampling of what you can do:

1. Send and Receive E-mail

From the computer in your dorm room or computer lab, you can send electronic mail (e-mail) to anyone in the world who has an e-mail address. Pretty mind-boggling, huh? Check out Chapter 4 to learn all about what e-mail can do for you.

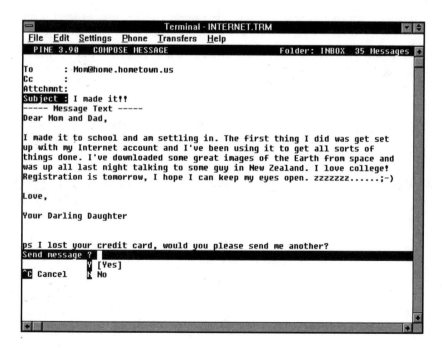

Send mail home to mom or to anyone else in the world.

You can also join in mailing list discussion groups around a variety of subjects, or start your own mailing list around whatever you want to talk about.

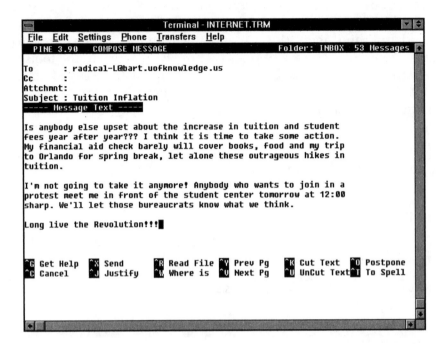

Express your opinions on world peace, financial aid, or endangered species through a mailing list.

Mailing lists are like groups of friends (or enemies, sometimes) who meet through their e-mail mailboxes. When you send a message, a copy of it goes to the mailbox of every group member—kind of like a giant conference call on the phone.

You can also use Internet e-mail to search for information on any topic that interests you. (There are better tools for research than e-mail, though, as you'll learn later.)

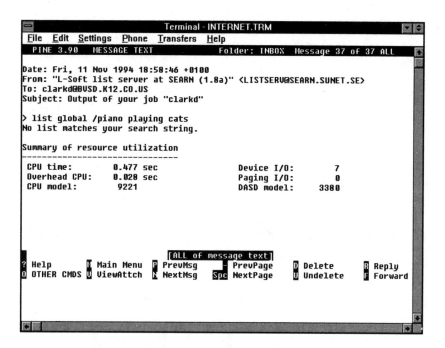

```
┌─────────────────────────────────────────────────────────────┐
│ ⊟                 Terminal - INTERNET.TRM             ▼ ▲│⇕  │
│  File  Edit  Settings  Phone  Transfers  Help                │
│   PINE 3.90    MESSAGE TEXT            Folder: INBOX  Message 37 of 37 ALL │▲│
│                                                              │
│ Date: Fri, 11 Nov 1994 18:58:46 +0100                        │
│ From: "L-Soft list server at SEARN (1.8a)" <LISTSERV@SEARN.SUNET.SE> │
│ To: clarkd@BVSD.K12.CO.US                                    │
│ Subject: Output of your job "clarkd"                         │
│                                                              │
│ > list global /piano playing cats                            │
│ No list matches your search string.                          │
│                                                              │
│ Summary of resource utilization                              │
│ --------------------------------                             │
│  CPU time:      0.477 sec         Device I/O:     7          │
│  Overhead CPU:  0.028 sec         Paging I/O:     0          │
│  CPU model:      9221             DASD model:   3380         │
│                                                              │
│                                                              │
│                        [ALL of message text]                │
│  ? Help      M Main Menu   P PrevMsg   - PrevPage   D Delete   R Reply   │
│  O OTHER CMDS V ViewAttch  N NextMsg  Spc NextPage  U Undelete F Forward │
│                                                              │
│ ◄│                                                        │►│ │
└─────────────────────────────────────────────────────────────┘
```

Do important research for your next thesis or research something totally off-the-wall to amuse your friends.

Well, maybe there's not a group out there for every possibility you can think of. My search for interest groups around piano-playing cats turned up nothing, but that's the breaks. If you look hard enough, you can find something of interest.

E-mail will probably be the first thing you want to try once your account is up and running. Take a deep breath and submerge. It won't be long before you'll be up to your neck in e-mail from friends, relatives, professors, and a lot of people you don't even know... yet.

If you want to get really serious about your e-mail, there's another book you should check out: *The Complete Idiot's Guide to Internet E-Mail* by Paul McFedries. Don't let the title fool you—this book contains plenty of Non-Idiot material, and is also pretty funny, for a computer book.

2. Use Databases All over the World

Where do you want to go? What do you want to know? Chances are, the Internet can take you there. For instance, are you interested in space? NASA regularly makes information available on the Net. Politics? The White House has an Internet site, chock-full of data. A paper due on microbiology? Check out the information provided by any of several major university biology departments.

One of the best ways to access this data is through Gopher, a handy little data retrieval tool that you'll learn about in Chapter 6. With Gopher, you wade through a menu system until you find the information you crave.

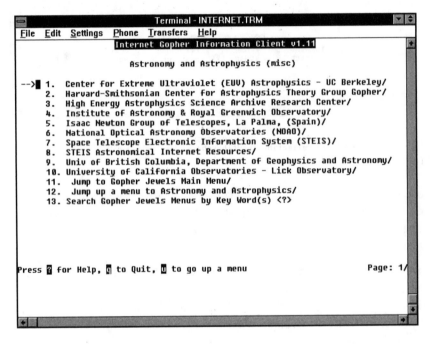

Select a line, and you'll be whisked off to one of many places where astronomy and astrophysics information is housed.

With Gopher, you can also do a word search for your favorite Shakespearean drama or get the latest Supreme Court decision. You can set your searching parameters to look for only the information you want or need, or you can just start roaming. Either way, you'll be bombarded with data.

3. Join In on Discussion Groups

A newsgroup is an online discussion group (kind of like a bulletin board). You post a comment, and someone else posts a comment about *your* comment, and so on. Before you know it, you have a discussion going. Similar to the e-mail discussion groups, these groups give you contact with millions of people around the world who have common interests and passions.

There are well over 6,000 different newsgroups ranging from the subtly profound to the downright ludicrous with the informational and more serious taking up the space in the middle. Are the Simpsons your cup of tea? Then you may want to check out alt.tv.simpsons. Maybe you need information on the latest software updates from Apple Computer; comp.mac.sys.digest is the place for you. Check out Chapter 5 for full details.

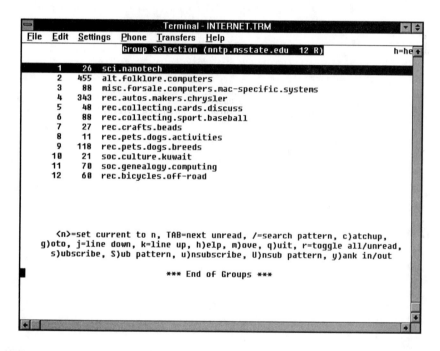

A mere sampling of the newsgroups available. There is literally something for everyone, no matter how strange.

USENET is the most common type of newsgroup on the Internet—so much so that many people consider the terms "USENET" and "newsgroup" synonymous, although they aren't really. You can find a USENET group that discusses any subject you may be studying in school, as well as many more subjects that no school would ever give you credit hours for.

4. Download Programs and Other Goodies

Need the latest in virus protection, the latest compression utility, or the coolest new shareware game? They're all there (somewhere, that is) for the taking. Images from the Hubble Space Telescope and video and sound clips are there as well. You can pull academic papers, FAQs (frequently asked questions), and sources for research papers from the Internet down onto your local hard drive to read and/or print at your convenience.

Sounds too good to be true, but it's real. Stop drooling, and turn to Chapter 8 to learn how to find the files and make them your own.

5. Chat with Other People

Using the Internet Relay Chat or the UNIX utility ytalk, you can have interactive conversations with others around the world. Well, not exactly the same kind of conversation as you would have over the telephone, or face-to-face, but it's the same principle. You type something, which appears on the other person's screen; then they type something back to you. Meet new friends on the Net, ask serious or silly questions from people who know more than you (or are willing to pose as such).

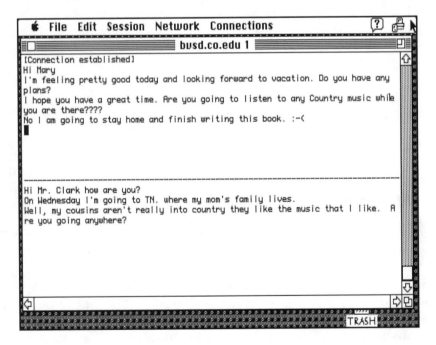

A conversation over the Internet.

In the conversation in this figure, the words I type in the upper half of the screen appear instantaneously (or nearly so) on the screen of the other user I am online with. His or her words appear on the bottom half of my screen. We can write interactively until the cows come home, if that is our inclination. Turn to Chapter 9 to learn how to do it.

Tip ➤ When you're chatting through the Internet, the other person can't see you, and you can't see them. Obviously. So beware; don't assume anyone you meet is really who or what they say they are. That 18-year-old, blonde female aerobics instructor you had such a nice chat with the other night could be anyone: an FBI agent, an international terrorist, or your fraternity brother.

6. Have Fun!

Games abound on the Internet. You can play chess, backgammon, and a variety of other board games with players around the world. Enter a virtual world and meet new friends, attend poetry readings, wander around Narnia and OZ (stop the snow queen if you can!), or transform yourself into an evil dwarf and lay in wait for the newbies who tentatively enter this new world for the first time—but be gentle, remember you were a newbie once.

Not only are there tons of "Live" games to play, but there are also regular computer games you can download, and discussion groups to exchange game tips and tricks.

Spoiler files (text files that tell you how to cheat at certain games or give you unfair hints) abound on the Net. Have you been stuck forever and a day on the main island in Myst? Check out the following World Wide Web home page:

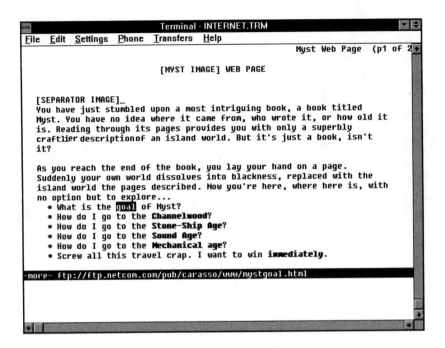

The World Wide Web home page for Myst.

If you read this book closely, you can figure out how to milk this site for the answers to your questions regarding Myst, but wouldn't it be more fun to try and get off the island using your wits?

7. And More...

This is only the start of what you can do on the Internet. The limits to what you can do? Use your imagination. We've only started to tap into what this network is capable of. The biggest limitation (besides lack of imagination) is your physical connection to the Internet—that is, the machine you are sitting in front of and the wires leading out of the back. I can't help you with the imagination part; that's yours to provide. Look in Chapter 2 for information on how to get going with the connection.

This network has the potential to change the way you learn, the way you interact with other people, the way you live your life.

Welcome to the Internet.

Welcome to cyberspace.

Welcome to the future.

Getting Connected

If you're in the process of skimming through this book and deciding which chapters to read, let me give you a bit of advice:

DON'T SKIP THIS CHAPTER!

It may not be as exciting as the chapter on the World Wide Web, or as much fun as the chapter on interactive games, but this is the chapter that will give you the tools to get there. If you really must, skip the chapter on UNIX (at your own risk, of course), but not this one. Connection types aren't exactly up there with Ren and Stimpy in terms of entertainment value, but not everything in life is supposed to be fun. I promise to be as brief as I can.

A Quick Intro to Connection Types

There are two basic types of connections: dedicated and dial-up. Dedicated connections are permanently wired to the server, so you don't have to use a modem to make the connection. (Remember, the server is a computer on campus that all the Internet connections go through.) Dial-up connections are just what they sound like—temporary connections that you make by dialing the server with your modem. When you finish using a dial-up connection, you hang up and the connection is broken. Dial-up connections can be further broken down into two types: direct and terminal.

Dial-up direct accounts usually go by names such as SLIP, CSLIP, or PPP. These accounts let you connect to the server just as if you had a dedicated connection; the only differences are that it's slower than a dedicated connection, and that you have to use a modem to connect to the server. With a direct account, you can use graphical software, such as Cello and Netscape, to make the Internet easier to navigate.

Tip ➤ SLIP stands for Serial Line Internet Protocol. CSLIP (Compressed Serial Line Internet Protocol) is a closely related variant of SLIP. PPP stands for Point to Point Protocol, a newer (and some say better) type of connection.

Dial-up terminal accounts are pretty basic. When you dial into the server with a terminal account, your computer isn't directly "on" the Internet; it's just acting as a terminal for the server. You issue your requests to the server, which issues them on your behalf on the Internet. If you have a really old PC that doesn't run Windows, or some other type of older computer, you are probably stuck using a dial-up terminal account.

Getting Your Internet Account

Almost all big colleges offer some kind of Internet account to students, but not all schools make it easy to get signed up. Call your school's computing center, computer lab, or whatever it's called, and see if they have any clues about what forms you have to fill out or flaming hoops you have to jump through.

Once you get the Internet people on the phone (sometimes known as system administrators, technical support people, whatever), ask them a few questions, and write down the answers. These answers will help you relate what you're going to learn in this chapter to your own situation.

▌▌ Do we have full Internet connectivity? When they ask what you mean by that, say:

FTP
Telnet
e-mail
Gopher
World Wide Web

- Are there machines that are hooked up with dedicated (permanent) connections? If so, where are the ones that I can use located, and what are the hours and restrictions?

- Are there connectors in the dorms so I can use my own PC from my room to connect to the Internet?

- Is there a phone number I can call with a modem from off-campus that will connect me to the server? If so, what's the number, and what's the highest speed I can connect at?

Tip ➤
> What's a server? It's a computer somewhere on campus that makes the actual connection to the Internet. When you connect through your terminal or PC to the Internet, you're going through the server.

- Do you support SLIP (pronounced like the undergarment) or PPP (pronounced pee-pee-pee) connections?

- Can I have the password to access the root directory and destroy all of the files there?

Okay, I just put that last one in to see if you were paying attention.

Whether you can get a direct dial-up account (SLIP or PPP) or have to rough it with a straight dial-up depends on whether or not your school makes these available to students. Get yourself set up with a direct dial-up if at all possible. The advantages of a direct dial-up connection are great. The graphical interfaces make traversing the Net a breeze; they are also fun. The only reason you may want to opt out of this and go for a plain dial-up account is if your computer is too old and weak to run Windows or Macintosh's System 7. If that's the case, it's probably time to look into a new computer; get with the times.

Tip ➤
> If you're given a choice between SLIP and PPP, choose PPP. With PPP, more of the configuration is automatic, so it's often easier to set up your software.

Go ahead and apply for your account now, because it will probably take a couple of days for it to become active. Make sure you get all the information I told you to get in that last list, plus the following:

■■ What will my user ID and password be?

■■ What is my e-mail address?

■■ What is the address of the school's Gopher server (and Web server, if there is one)?

User IDs and Passwords

When you apply for an Internet account, you will be assigned a user ID (sometimes called *username*) and a password. Remember these—they are your keys to the Internet. No password, no access. Well, yeah, you can call up the computer help desk at 2:00 a.m. and try to convince the minimum-wage student worker there that you really ARE yourself, so could they PLEASE give you your forgotten password, but this method is highly unreliable. Just remember them, okay?

Every time you connect, you'll be prompted for your user ID and password. The username is permanently assigned to you and will become part of your e-mail address. You can't change it. Your password, however, is a different matter. The first thing you should do when you log in for the first time is to change your password to something that you can remember but that nobody else can guess.

Picking a Good Password

Passwords for a UNIX system (which is what you're probably dealing with) are case-sensitive (that means upper- and lowercase letters are different) and can include special characters like $ and *. Most systems require you to use a minimum of six characters.

It is not a good idea to write down your password, and you should never give it out to anyone else. Not to be paranoid, but the only way you can make sure that you're the only one using your account is to keep your password absolutely secret. Select something that you can remember but that isn't in the dictionary.

If some evil hacker is trying to guess your password, the first thing he or she will try is your name, your dorm name, your telephone number, and any other facts about you. So don't use any password that's linked to yourself like that. Also *avoid*

- Your birthday or birthdays of family members.
- Your dog's name.
- Your girl/boyfriend's name—find other ways to show them you care.
- Gandolf, Frodo, or any character names from Tolkein, *Star Trek*, or any popular fantasy games.

Now, here are some examples of *good* passwords:

- Blourb6
- scor,pio
- $$tuition$$

Mix up upper- and lowercase letters, add punctuation and symbols, use numbers—you get the idea. You can get weird with your password, and no one will ever know.

Why all of the secrecy? Consider what someone could do with access to your account. In 1994, a hacker broke into a professor's account at the Texas A&M University and distributed 25,000 blatantly racist messages out to the rest of the world. That particular faculty member was left holding the bag and his mailbox was flooded with angry replies. Take steps to protect your password.

Tip ➤

Change your password periodically, every three months or so. Just in case, you never know.

Dedicated or Dial-Up—Which Is Better?

Generally speaking, a dedicated connection is the best way to go (provided someone else, like the university, is paying for it), because it's much faster. Your school probably offers dedicated connections at certain places on-campus, such as a computer lab and maybe in the dorms. However, if your only access to a dedicated connection is through a computer lab, you're not going to find a lot of privacy there, and your usage hours may be limited.

If you don't have access to a dedicated connection, or if you live off-campus or just want more privacy and freedom, you may consider a dial-up connection instead. You'll probably need your own equipment (computer, modem, phone line, and so on) for a dial-up connection, plus some special software. We'll go over this in detail later in this chapter.

Fast and Reliable—Dedicated Connections

With a dedicated connection, your computer is permanently wired to the server; basically, it's permanently connected to the Internet. You have a direct link from your machine to the rest of the world. No poor-quality phone connections, no waiting for the modem to dial—obviously, this is very cool.

You will usually find this type of connection in a lab situation, or maybe in a dorm, if your school is technologically advanced. It's very rare to find a dedicated connection in someone's home since they tend to be outside a student's budget, or just about anybody else's for that matter (around $1,000 a month at the time of this writing). This line is piped into the computer through a local area network (LAN) connection. A dedicated connection looks like this:

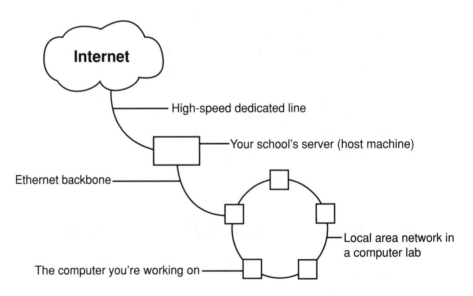

A dedicated connection.

There are several types of dedicated lines, and the main difference between them is the bandwidth. *Bandwidth* is the number of signals a line can process simultaneously; the more bandwidth, the more traffic the line can handle, and the faster your access will be. Bandwidth can also be used to describe a person's mental abilities, for example, "He just doesn't have the bandwidth to handle Calc 202."

If you're working in a lab situation, the hardware and software you'll need are probably already set up. You may not have a choice in the matter, but here's a quick rundown of the requirements, just in case:

- A PC, Mac, or some other type of computing device that has a monitor and a keyboard.

- A cable that connects that computing device to the server. (The school has to provide this.)

- Software that connects you to the server and the Internet. You may hear the term TCP/IP thrown around; it stands for Transmission Control Protocol/Internet Protocol. This is sort of like an Internet "operating system," a language in which all Internet computers have agreed to speak.

- Interface software. The server probably provides some sort of UNIX prompt or menu system that you can wade through, but if you have a Mac or a Windows-compatible PC, there are some wonderful graphics-based programs you can use, such as Mosaic. (More on these later.)

The method that you use for connecting to the Internet through a dedicated connection varies depending on the way the server is set up and on the software installed on the computer or terminal. It could be as simple as clicking an icon in Windows or on a Mac, or you may have to type some commands at a UNIX or DOS prompt. At some point, you'll be asked to type in your user ID and password; then boom, you're in and ready to roll on to the upcoming chapters in this book.

Tip ➤

Need help? Well, if your school has gone to all the trouble of setting up dedicated connections, they probably have some kind of training available. At the very least, instructions should be posted prominently in the computing center, and there may even be a packet of printed information available. Check around!

Software? What Software?

The beauty of a direct connection is that you can use all the really cool software that's available, mostly for free, all over the Internet. What software should you use? Well, the task you want to accomplish determines what kind of program you should run. Here's a quick overview of what's out there:

- Gopher Browsers such as Wingopher and Turbogopher. These programs let you enter the world of gopherspace in a friendly point-and-click environment. Click on the gopher site and you are there. No need to remember long confusing addresses, unless doing so really appeals to you.

- WWW Browsers, such as Mosaic, Netscape, and Cello. These are the Ferraris of the Internet navigational tools. These babies pull down graphics, video, and sound and hop between sites easily, making life on the Net a sheer joy. They also take up a lot of computing power. Don't even try them unless you're in front of a fairly decent computer. See Chapter 7 on the World Wide Web for the specs.

- E-mail programs, such as Eudora and Pine. These are the workhorses that you will use to send and receive e-mail. You'll probably spend more time with these than with any other Internet utilities.

- Internet Relay Chat (IRC) programs, such as Homer, that let you access the IRC and talk interactively with old and potential friends around the world.

- News Readers, such as NewsWatcher and WinVN, that will read newsgroups to let you keep up with the latest developments in over 6,000 subject categories (including rec.autos).

- Telnet utilities, such as NCSA Telnet and telw, that permit active connections with other machines around the world.

This is only the beginning of the software titles available. Look for these on the hard drives in your school lab, or check out the archives at ftp.mcp.com (Macmillan Computer Publishing). Each of these programs and what they can do for you is described in the chapters ahead.

Do-It-Yourself: Dial-Up Connections

A dial-up connection (no surprise) is one where you use a modem to connect to the server through telephone lines, rather than a permanently attached cable. Here's what a dial-up connection looks like:

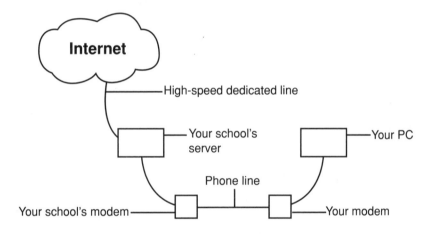

A dial-up connection.

Unlike the dedicated connection, your school will probably not provide you with all the equipment to complete a dial-up connection, which means you'll have to scrounge for the following yourself:

■ An account on your school's server, which is, in turn, hooked into the Internet. (Of course, you need this no matter which kind of connection you use.)

■ A home computer (Mac, PC, or whatever).

- A modem (the faster the better).

- Communications software (that is, a program that will tell your modem what number to dial).

- A roommate who doesn't monopolize the phone line. (Sorry, I can't tell you where to get this item.)

Computers: Any One Will Do

Just about any computer will get you onto the Internet. I've accessed the Internet via a PC Junior and know of a friend who has done the same with an Apple IIe. I can't claim this as one of my more pleasant computing experiences, but it can be done. In essence, anything that runs a communications program and connects to a modem will work.

As you've already learned, there are two different types of dial-up connections: direct and terminal. You can use almost any kind of grungy old computer for a terminal connection, but to take full advantage of the cool graphical stuff that's showing up on the Internet these days, you'll want a direct dial-up connection, and that requires a fairly powerful computer, such as a late-model Mac or a Windows-compatible PC.

Modems: Faster Is Better

What about modems? Technically, you can connect with any modem, even a tired old 300 bps model, but to save yourself some frustration, get the fastest one you can afford. Modem speeds are measured in bits per second or bps. Prices are dropping for 14400 bps modems and you can pick one up for under $150. You can still find 9600 bps or even 2400 bps on the market, and these will do fine for sending and receiving e-mail. If you want to do any serious downloading of files or employ graphical interfaces to the Net, you want a 14400 bps modem. To avoid sounding like a newbie, call it a 14.4; that's pronounced "fourteen-dot-four."

> **Tip ➤** What's a newbie? If you have to ask that question, you are one. A newbie is an affectionate (or not-so-affectionate) term that old-timers use for newcomers to the Internet.

Here's something important to keep in mind: A modem can only run as fast as its slowest link. The limiting factors are:

- Your modem.

- The modem on the other end.

- The telephone line between the two.

That means that if you're using a 14.4 bps modem, but the modem answering your call is only a 2400 bps, the communication will happen at only 2400 bps, and you will have wasted your money in buying the faster modem. Find out what speeds your school's computer supports. (Remember, that was one of the questions to ask. I hope you wrote that down.)

If you've inherited a modem from somewhere, you take what you get, but if you're buying a modem, you need to decide whether you want an internal or an external model. An internal fits into a slot inside your computer; an external sits on your desk in its own casing and plugs into a serial port on the back of your computer. If you're comfortable opening up your computer and you have a slot available for a modem, go for the internal. They tend to be a little cheaper and it is one less device to squeeze onto your desktop.

> **Tip ➤** The speed and quality of phone lines vary from site to site. If you have generally crummy phone service (voice connections dropping for no apparent reason, lines down a lot, static on your connection), you'll probably have trouble connecting—or staying connected—to the server via modem. Start a petition drive to lobby your local phone company to install better lines. You deserve them.

Communication Software

The communications software you need depends on which type of account you chose. If you chose a SLIP or PPP account, you'll dial your modem with special TCP/IP software. If, on the other hand, you're using a terminal account, you can use just about any communications program around.

Even though the computer and modem are similar for terminal and direct accounts, the software you need is different, and the procedures for setting up and using the software is different, too. I'm going to explain the two types separately, so you can avoid reading anything that doesn't apply to you. No need to thank me—it's my job.

Setting Up a Terminal Account

For a terminal account, all you need to do is select a communications program (almost any will do), configure it, turn on your modem, and dial. It's pretty straightforward—direct account users wish they had it so good.

Even if you have a SLIP or PPP account, you can probably use this terminal method if you want to. For example, you may want to test your account before you start the messy business of setting up your TCP/IP software.

Selecting Comm Software

There's a wide variety of communications software available—some of it for free, even. Chances are good that you already have a program on your hard drive that will do the trick for you. If not, there are several good shareware programs that you can buy fairly cheaply.

> **Tip ➤** Shareware is a rather radical concept in software marketing. The author of the program gives it to you for free on a trial basis, and if you use it regularly, you are honor-bound to send him or her a registration fee (usually $5 to $50). Believe it or not, it works—most computer users are actually honest. Go figure.

If you're a Windows user, the terminal program that came with your setup will do an adequate job of getting into the Net. (I don't recommend it for much more than that, but since it's widely available and you already paid for it, you may as well get some use out of it.)

Many computers (Mac and PC alike) come preloaded these days with an integrated software package, such as Claris Works or Microsoft Works. Both of these titles include a communications component and will make the connection as well.

If you want more out of your communications than Terminal or one of these integrated packages can provide, try downloading some shareware from a local BBS or an online service, such as America Online or CompuServe, if you're a member of either. (You can sign up for free for either of these services, and get five hours or so of usage credit, more than enough time to locate a decent communications program and download it.)

If you're thinking, "Okay mister, just cut to the chase and tell me what program to get," fair enough. For Mac users, Zterm is the shareware program of choice. This is a well thought out and solidly designed program. It has many advanced features, including a scripting language. For PC users, Telix is a good program for those who like to stay in a DOS environment. Check out MicroLink 0.90 or Qmodem if that is your operating system of choice. If you choose to use one of these, don't to forget to send in your shareware fees.

Configuring Your Comm Software

First, install your communications software by following the directions that came with it. Then start the program, and get ready to configure it to dial the phone number of your school's server. (You should have gotten this number when you got your user ID and password.) Each package is going to look a little bit different, but many of the variables you'll need to set are consistent among them. You may have to search the menus to find them, but they are there.

Since I can't show you all the programs, I'll show you my favorite: let's take a walk through setting up Zterm on a Mac. First, we need to tell the program what number to dial. I selected **Connection** from the **Settings** menu, and this dialog box appeared.

The important numbers for a dial-up connection.

The important items to set are:

Data Rate   This is the speed of your modem. I have a 14.4 modem, so I'll choose 14400.

> **Tip ▶**
>
> If you own a 14400 modem, you can actually set your data rate higher, up to 57600. You won't actually achieve these speeds, but it feels good.

Data Bits   Set this to 8.

Stop bits   This will be 1.

Parity   None.

Flow Control   Hardware Handshake if you have a high speed modem capable of this, otherwise choose Xon/Xoff.

The other items I have filled in are specific to my account. You'll enter your own name and password.

> **Tip ▶**
>
> At this point, there's no reason you have to fill in the Account and Password fields. Zterm won't log you in automatically unless you create an automatic login script. (You can find instructions for doing that in the Zterm docs.) If you're not planning to create a script, just leave those fields blank.

Almost done. Let's select **terminal** from the **Settings** menu.

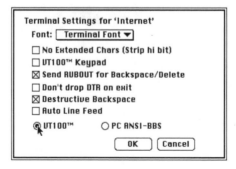

Proper terminal settings can make or break your day.

The important thing here is to set your terminal type to VT100. This is an almost universal terminal emulation mode for the Internet in dealing with text-based screens. You may also want to check that the backspace is set to act as a delete key. This means that when you hit **Backspace**, it will delete. This is very useful, especially when you're working from a keyboard without a separate delete key. (Are you listening Mac Plus users?) When you're done, close the dialog box, and you're ready to roll!

Connecting with a Terminal Account

Okay, are you ready to dial? Anticipation building? Actually, it's rather anti-climactic; dialing in is a simple procedure if everything is set up correctly.

Some communications programs give you a blank screen and let you type commands. Qmodem and Zterm are examples of that. For programs like that, type the following command, substituting the number you're supposed to dial for the *555-5555*:

```
atdt 555-5555
```

What does that mean? Well, typing **at** gets the attention of the modem, and **dt** means to dial in the tone mode. If you are using a rotary phone, substitute **dp** (dial pulse).

Tip ➤

There's a vast variety of modems and software out there, and not every model works with every program right out of the box. Your modem or software may require some special initialization codes to be typed before you type the dialing command. Check the documentation for those codes.

Other programs don't let you type a number directly like that; they make you open a dialog box and type the number there. Still other programs allow you to type commands directly but also offer an automatic dialing feature that lets you dial by choosing a menu item or a keystroke. Qmodem offers this. Use it if you want to.

Once you enter the number, press **Enter**, and you should hear the modem dialing and then some obnoxious noise at the other end that sounds like your hardware is about to self-destruct. Don't panic; it's suppose to sound like that. A connect message should appear next and you are on your way.

Here is the entirety of my dialin/login. The bold part is what I typed, and the rest is what got spit back onto my screen.

```
atdt 4475200
CONNECT 9600
ULTRIX V4.3A (Rev. 146) (bvsd.k12.co.us)

login: clarkd
Password: (I typed my password here)

You have 2 new bulletins on /usr/local/lib/pubbs/bvsd. See pubbs(local).
David, you have mail.
bvsd.k12.co.us~%
```

Pretty simple. I fill in my login name and password, and I'm ready to surf the Net.

Login procedures will vary from site to site and you may have another hoop to jump through before you come to your login and password prompts. If that's the case, the person who signed you up for the account should have filled you in on it.

What to Expect with a Terminal Account

When you dial into a UNIX machine with a terminal account, your computer screen will think, look, and act like that UNIX machine. It won't be pretty. Everything is text-based, and your mouse won't work for moving or selecting text in the middle of a paragraph; you have to use the arrow keys to move around. However, the mouse *will* work with most of the menu items in your communications program, so you can do some basics, such as cut and paste. For example, let's say I receive the following e-mail message:

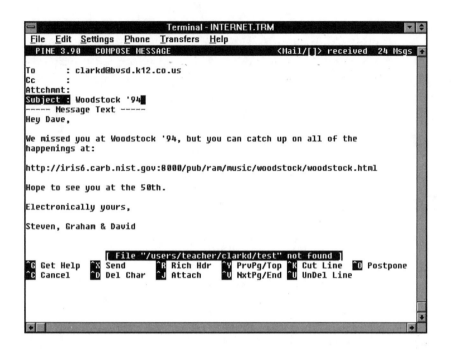

```
┌──────────────────────────────────────────────────────────────────────┐
│ ▭              Terminal - INTERNET.TRM                         ▼│▲│
├──────────────────────────────────────────────────────────────────────┤
│ File  Edit  Settings  Phone  Transfers  Help                          │
│    PINE 3.90    COMPOSE MESSAGE              <Mail/[]> received  24 Msgs▲
│                                                                        │
│ To      : clarkd@bvsd.k12.co.us                                        │
│ Cc      :                                                              │
│ Attchmnt:                                                              │
│ Subject : Woodstock '94█                                               │
│ ----- Message Text -----                                               │
│ Hey Dave,                                                              │
│                                                                        │
│ We missed you at Woodstock '94, but you can catch up on all of the     │
│ happenings at:                                                         │
│                                                                        │
│ http://iris6.carb.nist.gov:8000/pub/ram/music/woodstock/woodstock.html │
│                                                                        │
│ Hope to see you at the 50th.                                           │
│                                                                        │
│ Electronically yours,                                                  │
│                                                                        │
│ Steven, Graham & David                                                 │
│                                                                        │
│                                                                        │
│               [ File "/users/teacher/clarkd/test" not found ]          │
│ ^G Get Help  ^X Send     ^R Rich Hdr  ^Y PrvPg/Top ^K Cut Line ^O Postpone│
│ ^C Cancel    ^D Del Char ^J Attach    ^V NxtPg/End ^U UnDel Line        │
│                                                                        │
│                                                                        │
│ ◄│                                                                   │►▼
└──────────────────────────────────────────────────────────────────────┘
```

A note from a few buddies of mine.

You'll learn more about e-mail in Chapter 4, but bear with me for the moment. Notice that there's a World Wide Web address in the middle of it (the line that starts with http://). If I wanted to connect to that address using the WWW (see Chapter 7), I could spend all day trying to type it into my WWW program without a typo. UNIX is very unforgiving of typos. However, I could select it with my mouse and copy it to the Clipboard, and then paste it into the appropriate place in my WWW program to connect up with the Woodstock information.

In almost every other case, you'll need to stick with the keyboard to navigate your way around. The keys will take on a different meaning depending on what Internet utility you're running at the time (e-mail, netnews, Gopher, and so on).

Setting Up a Direct Account

For a dial-up direct account, you need a different kind of software: a TCP/IP
dialer program. You'll find out more about that shortly. You also need application software, such as Mosaic, Netscape, and such, to let you surf the Net
graphically (which, after all, is the whole point of getting a direct account
instead of a terminal one).

Picking Your TCP/IP Software

TCP/IP stands for Transmission Control Protocol/Internet Protocol. It's the
standard that all the computer-owners have agreed on for exchanging information on the Internet. Without it, the Internet couldn't operate.

Here's how it works. The TCP/IP software is a translator; it converts whatever your computer has to say into Internet language. There is TCP/IP software for just about every operating system, thereby allowing different kinds
of computers to share information.

Mac users will want to get hold of MacTCP. This software is available from
Apple Computer, Inc. Older versions are frequently packaged with commercial Internet starter kits.

Windows users have it a bit easier. There is a shareware program called
Trumpet Winsock that you can get from a variety of places—start by asking

your school's computing center folks. (It's readily available for downloading all over the Internet, but of course, you're not connected yet.) You may also be able to locate a demonstration version of a product called Chameleon that comes with TCP/IP software.

If you're setting up a SLIP or PPP account, you are about to go through a wonderful learning process. (I know, that can be good or bad, but let's try to stay positive, shall we?) There are some additional pieces of information you're going to need when your account becomes active.

Here are the questions to ask:

- ▌ What is the domain name and TCP/IP address of my host?

- ▌ Do I have to worry about my own IP address or will that automatically be assigned to me every time I log on?

- ▌ What is the IP address of the Domain Name Server?

- ▌ Do we support compressed or uncompressed SLIP or PPP?

Wow, that's a lot of techno-babble, but it may be necessary. There could be hope however. Try these questions:

- ▌ Do you have a TCP/IP program I can use? Is it preconfigured? (Please say yes, please say yes). If not, what do you recommend and where can I get it?

- ▌ Where can I get prewritten scripts for using that program to connect and disconnect from our server?

If your school provides software and scripts for you (bless their hearts), you are one lucky student. You can skip all this stuff, because all you'll need to do is install and surf. If not, stay tuned.

Direct Dial-Up Techno-Babble and What It Means

Let's take the questions above one at a time, and I'll walk you through setting up Trumpet Winsock (a TCP/IP program for windows).

What is the domain name and TCP/IP address of my host?

Pretty simple stuff this. Basically, the address of the host you connect to. Mine is **bvsd.k12.co.us**

Do I have to worry about my own IP address or will that automatically be assigned to me every time I log on?

For some SLIP users, your IP address will always be the same. You set it; that's it. That's not the norm, however. Most use what is called *dynamic addressing*. With dynamic addressing, the host sends a message to your machine when you log on. Thus, your IP address will be different each time you are active on the Net. Your IP address (for those who have forgotten) is your machine's address on the Internet.

What is the IP address of the Domain Name Server?

The IP address of your name server is the name of a machine that will translate the addresses you type into something the computer can understand. There are two types of addresses: numeric and alphabetic. People like alphabetic (such as bvsd.k12.co.us); machines like numeric (like 128.138.129.177). When connecting with another computer, I can use the alphabetic address. My request passes through a name server program on another computer, which converts the alphabetic address to the numerical form. The computer is happy; the people are happy.

Do we support compressed or uncompressed SLIP or PPP?

Yes or no here. Compressed adds some speed to the connection but is not supported everywhere.

Setting Up Your TCP/IP Software

Install your TCP software on your hard drive and start it up. How you do this depends on the TCP/IP program you have and the type of computer you're using, but it's usually fairly simple. Just follow the instructions that came with it.

In Trumpet Winsock, you select **Setup** from the **File** menu and fill in the blanks, as shown in the figure. The numbers that go in the blanks should have been provided for you by the person at the campus computing center who gave you your password and user ID. (If you don't have it yet, it's time for a follow-up call.)

```
┌─────────────────────────────────────────────────────────────┐
│ ─                    Network Configuration                   │
│                                                              │
│  IP address       ┌───────┐                                  │
│                   │0.0.0.0│                                  │
│  Netmask           255.255.255.0    Default Gateway  128.138.213.21 │
│  Name server       128.138.213.21   Time server              │
│  Domain Suffix     bvsd.k12.co.us                            │
│  Packet vector     00    MTU 1500   TCP RWIN 4096  TCP MSS 1460 │
│  Demand Load Timeout (secs) 5                                │
│                                                              │
│  ┌──────────────────────────────────────────────────────┐   │
│  │ ⊠ Internal SLIP              Online Status Detection  │   │
│  │                                                       │   │
│  │ SLIP Port    2               ◉ None                   │   │
│  │ Baud Rate    19200           ○ DCD (RLSD) check       │   │
│  │ ⊠ Hardware Handshake         ○ DSR check              │   │
│  │ ☐ Van Jacobson CSLIP compression                      │   │
│  └──────────────────────────────────────────────────────┘   │
│                                                              │
│  ┌──────┐  ┌────────┐                                        │
│  │  Ok  │  │ Cancel │                                        │
│  └──────┘  └────────┘                                        │
└─────────────────────────────────────────────────────────────┘
```

Getting your TCP software set up right is the first step toward dial-up Nirvana.

Since my server uses dynamic addressing, I'll leave the IP address set at 0.0.0.0. Winsock will take care of this for me. The MTU, TCP RWIN, and TCP MSS settings can also be left as you found them. My name server is 128.138.149.23, so those numbers fill in the appropriate holes. SLIP Port refers to what comm port your modem is attached to. Probably either 1 or 2.

Set the baud rate to match the speed of your modem (or higher if you have a 14.4). Check Hardware Handshake—if your modem and the modem on the other end can handle it. (If you're running at 14.4, give it a whirl.) Finally, there's Van Jacobsen CSLIP, which stands for compressed SLIP. Use this if your site supports it.

That's enough to get you started. If you really want to get technical and find out about MTUs, TCP RWINs, and the other stuff, read the documentation that comes with your TCP software.

Of course, you're not expected to know all these numbers off the top of your head. Ask the people who gave you your user ID and password, and they'll tell you what numbers to use.

You may also be asked to specify the phone number you're dialing, the type and speed of your modem, and other communications info. You should get the phone number from the person who gave you your ID and password.

For the modem type and speed, look on the box the modem came in, or if you don't have it, look for a sticker or label on the modem. If all else fails, guess Hayes-compatible and cross your fingers. (See the information on modems later in this chapter for other hints.)

Logins and Scripts, Oh My!

Okay, now it's time to log in, but before you do, there are a few more things you need to know. Didn't I tell you this was going to be a learning experience? Are we having fun yet?

Your login sequence will be slightly different with a SLIP or PPP account. You will be accessing different software on your host machine than if you were on a straight dial-up connection. If your site supports direct dial-up and they also provide you with the software, ask them about providing you with a script. A script is a text file of the commands used for logging into a computer. Your TCP/IP software reads this script and automatically logs you in. No mess, no fuss. This script must be aware of all the oddities and particulars of your sequence. That is, it must be customized to fit your login sequence. When properly configured a script can:

▐ Initialize your modem.

▐ Dial your host's number.

▐ Fill in your login and password (if you choose).

▐ Jump through any other hoops your system expects.

In short, it does all the work of logging in for you. Here is a partial example of what a script looks like:

```
#
# initialize modem
#
output atz\13
input 10 OK\n
#
# set modem to indicate DCD
#
output at&c1
input 10 OK\n
#
# send phone number
#
output atdt242284\13
#
```

```
# now we are connected.
#
input 30 CONNECT
#
#  wait till it's safe to send because some modems hang up
#  if you transmit during the connection phase
#
wait 30 dcd
#
# now prod the terminal server
#
output \13
#
#  wait for the username prompt
#
input 30 username:
username Enter your username
output \u\13
#
# and the password
#
input 30 password:
password Enter your password
output \p\13
#
# we are now logged in
#
```

Looks rather foreboding, doesn't it? It is, and it isn't. Look at it this way. The computer reads this script and sends the commands. Every line that begins with # is ignored by the computer. Those are just comments to let you (as a reader of this script) know what the commands mean. So the following sequence:

```
# send phone number
#
output atdt242284\13
```

tells us that output atdt242284\13 is the command for sending the phone number.

Tackle this if you want to. Check the documentation that came with your TCP/IP software; it should have some instructions about how to write a script. If you can get a prewritten script for your system, you won't have to deal with this TCP/IP script-writing hell—a pit of flames which has driven even great computer geeks to their knees. (Well, okay, it's not *that* bad, but it is beyond the scope of this book to go into more detail.) Don't let them get away with telling you that no scripts exist; ask for one to be written, or ask them for names of expert users who can help you.

What Do I Do with the Script Once I Have It?

The script (remember it is just a plain text file) will be placed in the same directory on your hard drive as your TCP/IP software, so the software has access to it. To run a script using Trumpet Winsock, (a TCP/IP software package for Windows), I choose the **Login** option under the **Dialler** menu, like so:

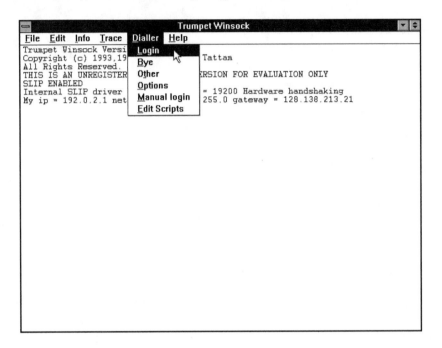

Setting up a script in Winsock.

The login command is linked to a script entitled login.cmd (which just happens to be the script used here). If the script is present, Winsock will follow the commands, and I'm ready to run my SLIP or PPP software (Netscape, Fetch, Wingopher, whatever).

When I'm ready to leave the Internet, I'll choose **Bye** from the same menu. This calls up another script that sends the appropriate commands to log me out of there.

Manual Login—An Alternative to Scripts

While waiting for that script to be written (or if you'd just really rather not bother with the whole scripting mess), use the **Manual login** option shown in the preceding figure. If you make this selection, your TCP/IP software will act like a terminal program. You type in the commands to dial up just as if you were in a communications terminal program, such as Qmodem. (See the section on dial-up connections.)

You fill in the prompts as the computer requests them, and you can get to the same place as if you used a script. If your system has a fairly simple SLIP or PPP login procedure, you may not even need a script. After you have dialed in, you'll want to minimize the TCP/IP software, or you can move the window to the background and open your Internet applications, such as Turbogopher or Mosaic.

> **Tip ➤** If you've made up your mind to write your own script, don't say I didn't warn you. Pick up The Complete Idiot's Next Step with the Internet, a great book that'll tell you, among other things, exactly how to write your own script for almost any TCP/IP program.

The Internet Adapter: Graphics for Terminal Accounts

The Internet Adapter (TIA) is a strange and wonderful little program. If you're stuck with a terminal account, you can use it to add some graphics into your life. TIA will let you run graphical interfaces over a dial-up connection. To use TIA, you need:

- ▥ Everything required for a dial-up connection.
- ▥ TCP/IP software.
- ▥ A TIA software and license code installed in your UNIX account.

Installing TIA adds another step of complexity and I won't go into the details here, but reading the UNIX and FTP chapters closely will help the process make sense when you decide to tackle it. TIA is a commercial product and has a modest price tag attached to it. You can order it through e-mail. You also have the option of ordering a demo version that will work for two weeks. For more information on how to obtain and set up TIA, send e-mail to:

    tia@marketplace.com

or gopher to:

```
gopher.marketplace.com
```

or ftp to:

```
marketplace.com
```

Any of these sites will provide you with the information you need to get TIA up and running.

Taking Your Account for a Test Drive with Telnet

Everything set? Your connection is in place, your login and password are embedded in your memory, and you're ready to roll. Great, let's get the tel(net) outta here.

Telnet is a way of making a connection with another computer. For dial-up (direct or strict) customers, this happens after you have dialed into your host computer. (Telnet may even be one of the commands you need to issue in your login sequence.) Telnetting on a direct connection is done a bit differently, but it all amounts to the same thing; you are hooking up with another computer.

First, for the dial-up folks: Once you have filled in your password, your login name, your mother's maiden name, and your visa number (just kidding, if they ask you for the latter, drop out), you'll come to your UNIX prompt. More about this is in the UNIX chapter, but for now, I will tell you this is where you type in commands to bend the computer's will to your own. The command we're interested in here is **telnet**. Type in **telnet**, like this: **csh>(or whatever appears on your screen)telnet**. Don't hit return, not yet.

Typing **telnet** is sort of like picking up your phone. You want to connect, but you haven't told it where. Following **telnet**, type an address of where you want to connect to. How do you find these addresses? Look in Chapter 11 of this book for some Telnet addresses specific to your academic area. For now, here's one you can use. We'll see what's shaking at the Library of Congress. The address to connect there is **locis.loc.gov**.

```
csh> telnet locis.loc.gov
Trying 140.147.254.3 ...
Connected to locis.loc.gov.
Escape character is '^]'.
```

```
L O C I S :  LIBRARY OF CONGRESS INFORMATION SYSTEM

         To make a choice: type a number, then press ENTER


   1    Library of Congress Catalog      4    Braille and Audio

   2    Federal Legislation              5    Organizations

   3    Copyright Information            6    Foreign Law


   *    *    *    *    *    *    *    *    *    *    *

   7    Searching Hours and Basics
   8    Documentation and Classes
   9    Library of Congress General Information
  10    Library of Congress Fast Facts
  11    * * Announcements * *     New Interface for Some Files]
  12    Comments and Logoff
        Choice:
```

Type your choice at the bottom for the area you're interested in, hit **Enter**, and wait. In a matter of seconds, the information will flash on your screen. This Telnet site was a pretty simple one to connect to. Many Telnet sites will require a login name and password. Often, this information will be presented when you log in:

```
Welcome to Disneyland
Use 'mickey' as your login
Use 'donald' as your password

login:
```

If presented with a request for a login name and none is suggested, try:

```
newuser
visitor
guest
```

If none of these work you are probably out of luck. Here are a few more tips when making a Telnet connection. If you see a prompt that asks you to fill in a terminal type, such as this:

```
TERM(VT100)
```

type **VT100** or just hit **Enter** if you see it in parentheses.

When disconnecting from a Telnet session, each site has a different setup. In the preceding example, you would type **12** as your choice and hit **Enter**. If exiting is not apparent from looking at the screen, try typing **Q**, **q**, or **^q**.

If you just can't figure any way to get out or your Telnet connection hangs on you, type ^](ctrl-right bracket). This will pop you back to a Telnet prompt (`telnet>`). Type **close** at this point, and you'll be back to the familiar ground of your UNIX prompt.

Telnetting from a Dedicated Connection

I've got good news and bad news. The good news is that it's a simple procedure to telnet from a dedicated or direct dial-up connection. You simply fire up your Telnet software (some examples are NCSA telnet and Wintel; look for them on your school lab's hard drives), type the address, and away you go. Following is an example:

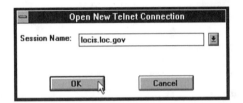

Telnetting made easy.

The bad news? Even with a dedicated or dial-up connection, telnet sessions remain strictly in the land of text-based information. That is, it won't look any different than if you were to come in over a phone line and modem. It'll run a little faster, but as soon as you telnet, you're hooked up to another computer—the commands you issue are to that machine, not yours.

Are you ready for some more good news? Telnet is falling out of favor with many sites as a means of making their information available. There are less and less sites that you can telnet to. That would be bad news if there wasn't something better to take its place. Fortunately, there is. You can read about them in the chapters on Gopher and World Wide Web. Stay tuned.

By the way, I wasn't really serious about skipping the UNIX chapter. Do it now or do it later, but sooner or later you're going to find a need for some basic UNIX commands.

Do it now; turn the page.

Chapter Two Test

I lied. There's no test. I just said that to get your attention. (Don't you just *hate* that?)

The Least You Need to Know About UNIX

I remember how I felt when I first encountered UNIX over the Internet—a little shy, somewhat foolish, and definitely awkward. I had endured my digital adolescence in a Macintosh environment, and now it felt like I was going to have to go through it all again. I was used to pointing and clicking where I wanted to go. I wandered happily from icon to icon, never thinking about what exactly those clicks meant.

That doesn't mean I didn't experiment a bit with other operating systems. I tried DOS. Played with my c> behind closed doors, fiddled with my autoexec.bat and config.sys. However, it didn't take me long to chuck all that in the trash and head back to the GUI-land (GUI is short for Graphical User Interface) of the Macintosh operating system. Then along came the Internet. I desperately wanted to exploit the resources there. It took but a few seconds of looking at bvsd.k12.co.us% (my UNIX prompt) to know that I had seen something like this before.

I feared the worst, and after a few experiments, my fears proved true. UNIX is like DOS; you have to know the commands to type to get the results you want. Yech. I resolved to learn enough UNIX to make my way through the Internet, and gradually, over the next few weeks, I picked up enough commands to do just that.

If you're a DOS user, you'll probably have an easier time than I did. Windows and Mac users will have to make some initial adjustments. Once you get over the shock, it really isn't all that bad. There's a bit of a learning period you have to go through, and while it may feel clumsy at first, keep telling yourself that it's just a stage you're going through.

> **Tip ➤** UNIX has a graphical user interface of its own. It's called X Windows. If you ever get a chance to access the Internet from a UNIX workstation, give it a try; it's quite a ride.

There are a few similarities between UNIX and DOS, such as a few commands in common, but the similarities end there. UNIX is a much more powerful operating system than DOS can ever hope to be. One thing that sets UNIX apart is that unlike DOS (or Macintosh System 7), UNIX is a multiuser system. Basically, that means that a whole bunch of people can be using the same machine at the same time. You, your mother, your girl/boyfriend, along with a bunch of people you don't even know can be logged on, happily going about your business, oblivious of the fact that just next door, someone is doing the same thing.

Enough of this, let's get into the meat of UNIX. UNIX was not created with you or me in mind. It was created to be functional, not friendly. It survived and thrived in an environment filled with nerds—computer scientists, engineers, and mathematicians, people who weren't thinking too much about how to create a helpful system that ordinary people could use, at least not at first. And it shows.

UNIX never got much attention outside of schools and labs, and it may well have died out without a fuss eventually, if it weren't for the mass public discovery of the Internet. You see, UNIX is the operating system of choice of the Internet.

Is it necessary to become a UNIX guru to get on the Internet? Absolutely not. New interfaces are being developed that mask UNIX's shortcomings altogether. Working from a dedicated connection or with a SLIP or PPP connection, as mentioned in the last chapter, will help you avoid UNIX, and I imagine that future books on the Internet will probably exclude the topic of UNIX altogether. We're not there yet, however; a great many people still dial in with a terminal account, and still need UNIX. So rather than wait for the computer industry to hurry up and accommodate our needs, let's get started.

> **Tip ➤** Want to know more about UNIX? Pick up The Complete Idiot's Guide to UNIX by John McMullen.

Prompt? What Prompt?

With a dial-up terminal account, once you have logged in with your user ID and password (see the previous chapter), you will see your *UNIX prompt*, provided that your system administrator hasn't set you up with a menu to choose from. Even if he has, there may be an option to get to the prompt. Prompts will look different from machine to machine. Here are some examples:

```
$
csh>
sparc%
bvsd.k12.co.us>
```

Yours will look different, but they all serve the same purpose. This is the place you type commands to tell the computer to do something.

Commands for Basic Survival

Learn these commands, if you learn nothing else. They may save your sanity someday.

Changing Your Password

Use **passwd** to change your password. (What did you think it stood for, log off?) Do this often—every other month or so. When you issue this command, you'll first be prompted for your current password. Type it, and you're asked for the new one twice, to make sure you aren't making a spelling error that you'll regret later.

Getting Help

The **man** command stands for "manual," UNIX's help system. (No, that wouldn't have been my first guess either. I would have thought the command would be something like Help, but that's UNIX for you.) To bring up a help file on a certain topic, use **man -k** *keyword*. For example, if you wanted to know about directories, you would type:

```
man -k directory
```

That would bring up information regarding commands that have to do with directory structure.

Using a Tutorial

The **learn** command brings up a handy program that helps you learn UNIX. (You won't find it on all UNIX machines, but most have it.) Give it a try.

Commands for Getting to Know Other People

Besides the vast array of interesting people you can talk to on the Internet, there are probably several fairly cool people you can talk to via computer on your own school's server. Use these commands to make new friends.

Seeing Who's Around

Type **finger** at your prompt to find out who is online at the same time as you are on your host machine. The **finger** *name* command will list every one by that name who has an account on the same machine as you do. For instance, typing **finger david** would bring up a list of all of the Davids on my host machine, along with each person's login name, the last time they logged in, and anything else they've elected to tell you about themselves.

The **finger** command can be very useful to help you find a login name of someone when all you know is the first or last name. If I were to finger myself, like so:

```
finger clarkd
```

this is the information I would get back:

```
Login name: clarkd      (messages off)  In real life: David Clark
Office: Columbine    443-0792           Home phone:
Directory: /users/teacher/clarkd        Shell: /usr/local/etc/CNSlogin
On since Oct 18 19:36:53 on ttyr1 from tco15.Colorado.E
No Plan.
```

Messages off means that other users can't request talk sessions with me (more about that later).

I choose what to include in my finger information by using the **chfn** command. I could tell people that my real name was Peter Pan. (See the extended UNIX discussion to learn what No Plan means.)

Seeing What Everyone Is Up To

Like **finger**, the **who** (or **w**) command will also show you who is online at the same time as you. It goes one step beyond **finger**, though, in that it also shows you what they're doing. For instance, I typed **w** and got the following results:

```
User       tty from         login@ idle   JCPU  PCPU  what
mminerva   p0 cns956.Colorad 5:58pm          18    18  -csh
johnsd     p2 tco5.Colorado. 7:13am 12:27  1:42  1:42  kermit
mismith    p3 tco9.Colorado. 7:07pm           3     3  pine
sconvers   pa tco5.Colorado. 7:32am 11:48                -
clarkd     q9 tco13.Colorado 7:09pm                    w
```

The login name is on the left. The far right column tells what command that person last issued. Notice that my own last command was **w** (of course).

Using this command is a good way to learn new tricks. If you see someone trying a UNIX command that you've never seen before, type it and see what happens.

Sending an Instant Message

The **write** command will let you send a message directly onto the screen of another user. For instance, after you used **w** to see who was online, you could pick one of those people and write a message.

First, issue the **write** *username* command, where *username* is the person's login name (the name in the far left column of the list you got with the **w** command). Then type your message, and press **Ctrl-D** to send the message. It doesn't get much easier.

Chatting Away the Hours

ytalk is a fun little command that will allow you to enter into an interactive chat session with one or more users who are online. That means you type a message, which appears on their screen (sort of like **write**), and they type a message back to you, which appears on your screen.

You request a talk session with someone else with the command **ytalk** *username*. If someone requests a talk session with you, then a message similar to this will pop up on your screen:

```
Message from Talk_Daemon@bvsd.k12.co.us at 20:01 ...
talk: connection requested by msmith@spot.Colorado.EDU.
talk: respond with:  talk msmith@spot.Colorado.EDU
```

To respond, I would type **talk msmith@spot.Colorado.EDU** at my prompt, and we would be thrown into an interactive chat session where everything that I type on my screen would appear on hers and vice versa.

With **ytalk**, it's possible for more than two people to be in a chat session together. You can have as many people as your screen can hold. When you're in a chat session, press **Escape** to bring up an options menu that will let you invite more people. **Ctrl-C** exits a **ytalk** session.

> **Tip ➤** Before you request a talk session or send a written message, use the **w** command first. Don't interrupt somebody who is in the middle of sending e-mail or otherwise occupied. Look for the folks for whom the right column reads: `-csh`, `lcsh`, `tcsh`, or the like. This means that they're hanging out or in between jobs—ripe for a talk request.

Hold My Calls, Please!

Use **mesg n** to block any incoming write or talk messages so you can work uninterrupted. Don't forget this one. I wrote this one into my .login after being interrupted so many times. Grrr...

Ready to Be Social Again

Use **mesg y** to turn permission back on when you're in a more social mood.

File and Directory Commands—In Case You Care

That UNIX prompt you see is your link to the host computer, which has its own hard disk. This much you probably already know, but did you know that you have access to that hard disk and can work with files and directories on it? Keep reading.

Finding Out How Much Space You Have

When you log in, you start out in your home directory on your host machine's hard drive. Along with a UNIX account can come a certain amount of space on that machine that you can use in a variety of different ways. If you want to find out how much space you have, type **bvsd.k12.co.us% quota -v**. Here's my information:

```
Disk quotas for clarkd (uid 10983):
Filesystem      usage  quota  limit
/home4           3052   5000  15000
```

Here is the interpretation of what all this means:

usage	3052	I currently have 3052K of files in my home directory.
quota	5000	This quota is a *soft quota*; it's more of a request than a real quota. I can exceed this quota if I need to. This is handy for when I need to download files and want to bring down a monster. The trick is to remember to delete it after I transfer it to my hard disk. Use the command **rm file_name** to delete a file.
limit	15000	The limit of how far I can push the limit. That far. The system will not let me put more than 15000K of files in my directory. If I exceed my soft quota (5000) on a regular basis, I receive....

Tip ➤ Different machines may have different commands to discover your quota. If typing **quota** doesn't work, try **quota -v** or **checkquota**. If none of these work, don't worry about it. They'll let you know if you're using up too much disk space.

If I exceed my limit on a regular basis, I receive threatening notes from the system administrator telling me that my account will be "cleaned up" for me if I don't do it myself. I usually try and be a good citizen. After all, I'm sharing this disk with many other users. If the disk becomes full, we all lose.

What can you do with that 5MB? What can you put there? Actually, there are probably several things there already. Which leads me to the next set of commands.

Directory Commands: ls, cd, and more

You can view the contents of your home directory by typing the UNIX **ls** command. Doing so at my prompt brought up the following:

```
stories/
Mail/               docs/
News/               training/
bin/                resources/
book/
```

Notice that all of these end with a /. This indicates that they are directories. To see what's inside them, I would first have to tell the computer to switch to that directory. **cd** is the command to do that job. For example:

```
cd training
```

will switch me to that directory. Then I use the **ls** command to show what's held in that directory. The result is

```
email   smiles
```

Since these are not followed by a /, I know that they are files that I can read. The command **more smiles** will show me the contents of the file, and **cd ..** will take me up a directory. Let's review the commands we just learned.

Command	Effect
ls or **dir**	Lists what's in the directory.
cd	Changes directories.
more	Prints a file to the screen.
cd ..	Moves up one directory.

Tip ➤ **dir** will also work to show the directory contents. This command will give you more information than **ls** but will take longer to display on your screen (a pain when you're viewing contents of a large directory).

When you first start out and you type **ls** at your prompt, you probably will not have much of anything visible in your directory. So, just for an experiment, type **ls -a**. That will show us every file in our directory. Here's what came up:

```
./              .mailrc         .shell*
../             .msgsrc         .sig*
.accounts       .ncrecent
.addressbook    .netrc
.cshrc          .newsrc
.elm/           bin/
.exrc           .nn/
.gopherrc       training/
```

```
.pinerc                resources/
.hushlogin             stories/
.ircmotd               .pubbs/
.profile               .readmotd
.kshrc                 News/
.login                 docs/Mail/
.logout                tmp/
.lynx_bookmarks
.lynxrc
```

Notice that *a lot more* showed up. All of the files that begin with a period didn't show up with the regular **ls** command, because they're hidden files. Why are they hidden? Because you usually don't need to deal with them. They're system files, the files that tell the computer how to deal with you. Here's what some of them mean:

.login   The computer reads this each time you log in. Environmental settings, such as your prompt and terminal type, are set here.

.cshrc/.kshrc   Another initialization file called up when entering your UNIX shell account.

.pinerc   Settings for the Pine mailing program are created here. If you want to create a signature file, you will need to tell Pine where to look for it by altering this file.

.newsrc   A list of newsgroups provided by your server.

.hushlogin   Keeps the **mod** (message of the day) from flashing on my screen every time I log on. I can view them at my leisure by typing the **pubbs** command at my prompt.

.lynxrc   Settings for the World Wide Web browser **lynx**.

You can look at any of these hidden files without doing any harm by using the **more** command. For example, **more .login** will show you the contents of your .login.

It can't hurt to look at the files. Just use the **more** command. You'll see a lot of cryptic looking lines and symbols. Is it important to understand what all these symbols and signs mean? Not necessarily—only if you like to tweak and customize. Leaving all these files just as they are will do you no harm.

Who, Me? Edit a File?

If you want to play around and alter the settings of a file (for example, your login), you have to enter the changes using an editor program. pico is a good one.

Before altering an important file, make a copy of it with the **cp** (copy) command, like this:

```
cp .login .login2
```

This command copies the file .login and calls the copy .login2. I can play with .login2 to my heart's content without fear of destroying my access. Now open up .login2 in your text editor. Try this:

```
pico .login2
```

Your .login2 file appears on-screen, ready for editing. If you make a mistake, don't panic. You can discard all of the changes you've made easily. Simply type ^x (**Ctrl-x**). You'll see the following:

```
Save modified buffer (ANSWERING "No" WILL DESTROY CHANGES) ?
```

Put an **n** here, and the computer will forget everything you just told it to do. If however, you like what you see, plop down a **y** and you're ready to see what you have done.

> **Tip >**
>
> Don't be stupid. Don't make indiscriminate changes to important files like .login. You can mess up your account to the point where you won't even be able to log in. I have personally done this on several occasions, and it's no picnic trying to explain to the helpdesk person just what I was doing and be snickered at.

.plan is one file that you may want to edit (or create) with pico or some other editor. Remember earlier in the chapter where I fingered my name? At the bottom of my information was the line .plan. Your .plan is information about yourself that you want other people to know. People often use this to post a favorite quote, a piece of ASCII art, or their wishes, hopes, and dreams. To make a .plan, you need to create a file using your favorite UNIX editor. Again, I'll use pico as an example, since most systems have it.

> **Tip >**
>
> Don't have pico? Try vi or emacs.

At my prompt, I type **pico .plan**. I am then thrown into my editor, where I can design my .plan. I save my work, exit, and whoomp, there's a .plan file in my home directory. (I can tell it's there by using the **ls -a** command.) You're also going to have to grant other people the rights to look at your .plan. You can control who has access to your directory and the files in it. I don't want to go into an extended discussion about UNIX file permissions here (which is the only way to do it), but the command to issue at your prompt is

```
chmod +r .plan
```

chmod means change mode. +r means add reading privileges to the rest of the world. .plan is the file you are granting these privileges for. Whenever anyone fingers my name or login, they'll see the contents of the .plan file.

If you want more information about UNIX file permissions, you can type **man chmod** at your prompt, because that's all I'm going to tell you about them.

Making a Directory

The **mkdir** *directoryname* command lets you create a new directory. Make sure you're in the directory that you want the new directory to branch off from. For example, if you want to create a directory called 1995/ off the clarkd/ directory, change to clarkd/, and then type **mkdir 1995**.

> **Tip ➤** A note for DOS users who use a backslash (****) when dealing with directories. UNIX uses the forward slash (**/**).

Moving with mv

mv stands for move (good guess). You can use it either to move files or to change their names. To move a file from place to place, start out in the directory where the file is currently residing. Then type **mv** *filename new_location*. For example, **mv .plan docs** will move my .plan file into the directory called **docs**.

To change the name of the file, use **mv** *filename new_filename*. How does UNIX know that the new filename is not a directory where you want to move the file? Well, it doesn't. If you specify a name after the *filename* that matches an existing directory, UNIX moves the file to that directory. If the name after the *filename* is something unfamiliar, UNIX renames the file to that name, and leaves it in the current directory. For instance, **mv .plan 3pigs** will retitle my .plan as **3pigs** since there is no directory called 3pigs. Clever, huh?

Copying Files

You ran into this command earlier, if you've been following along with the chapter. The **cp** *filename location* command will make a copy of a file in a new location. Typing **cp .plan docs** will make a copy of my .plan in the docs directory but leave the original intact.

The **cp** command can also be used to create a duplicate in the same directory. Just use **cp** *filename newname*. Like **mv**, **cp** can determine whether or not a directory exists that matches what you type after *filename*. If no directory exists, **cp** will assume that you want to make a copy in the same directory. For instance, typing **cp .plan 3pigs** will create a duplicate file in the same location, and name it **3pigs**.

Changing What They Can Find Out About You

chfn is the ticket. Use this command to change the information others see when they finger your account. It works like this: **bvsd.k12.co.us%chfn**. Doing so will bring up prompts that will allow you to make changes:

```
Changing finger information for clarkd
Name[Clark David]:
Office[Columbine]:
Office Phone[443-0792]:
Home Phone[]:
```

Each of these lines will be displayed one at a time and will allow me to make changes to it. The information contained in [] is the information that is shown whenever my account is fingered. To leave it untouched, I can just hit **Enter**, but as long as I'm here, let's have some fun.

```
spot> chfn dclark
Changing finger information for dclark
Name[Clark David]: Captain Picard
Office[Columbine]: Enterprise
Office Phone[443-0792]: 1-800-trek
Home Phone[]: 1-800-space
```

Now anyone who fingers my account will see the following:

```
bvsd.k12.co.us% finger dclark
Login name: dclark        (messages off)   In real life: Captain Picard
Office: Enterprise, 1-800-trek        Home phone: 1-800-space
Directory: /home/dclark              Shell:/usr/local/etc/CNSlogin
On since Jan  7 12:13:46 on pts/40 from cns945.Colorado.EDU
No Plan.
```

Maybe you want people to know who you really are; maybe you don't. Either way, the option exists for you to be someone else for those special connected moments. Most people don't realize that when they dial into a UNIX system, they're entering a whole new world of computing power, complete with stupid little tricks to amuse friends and provoke enemies.

Changing Your Prompt

The bland, inscrutable UNIX prompt, for example, can be changed to say anything you want. There are those of us who delight in little changes we can make in our accounts, changing our prompts to read

```
What is your wish, master?
```

rather than the boring old

```
bvsd.k12.co.us>
```

Depending on what flavor of UNIX your system is running, this may or may not work, but try typing **set prompt** = *"whatever your heart desires>"*. Your prompt will immediately change to that. This will only last for that session however. Next time you login in, you will be back where you started. If you want to change it permanently, add that line to your .login.

Find out what day of the week you were born on by typing **bvsd.k12.co.us% cal** *1972*. This brings up a calendar for the year 1972.

Just in case you forget, type **whoami** at your prompt for a reminder. Write a personalized greeting message to yourself when you login. Add a line something like this to your .login:

```
echo "Hello David, nice to see you again."
```

This will appear each and every time you log in. When you get sick of that message, change it. Is it functional to make such changes? Not very. Fun? You bet.

And Finally, My Favorite UNIX Command

When I'm so fed up with the machine and I feel like tossing it across the room, I issue this command:

```
bvsd.k12.co.us Make sense
```

The computer responds with:

```
*Make:  Don't know how to make sense.  Stop.
```

It makes me feel a little bit better to know that the computer is aware of its own limitations and is willing to admit them.

Chapter 3

> **Tip ➤**
>
> For techies: Use the **make** command to maintain a list of the components of executable files. Use the **makefile** command to create an executable file from archived files on a UNIX machine.
>
> For nontechies: You can substitute other words in here as well. Try **friends**, **jelly**, or **love** depending on how you feel at the moment.

E-mail

There wouldn't be an Internet without e-mail.

I'm serious. You can browse all of the databases you want. Play all of the interactive games that are out there, download all of the newest and neatest software, but without the communications aspect, the Internet is nothing but a big shopping mall. The ability to communicate with anyone who has an e-mail address—immediately—is a revolution. It will change the way we do business, and the way we study and go to school.

So what's the big deal? The sophistication and speed of our personal communications have steadily increased over the years. Less than 100 years ago, a letter home to mom could have taken weeks. Push that back a few more years, and getting that package of cookies delivered could have cost some poor Pony Express rider his life. Mere mortal danger didn't stop us; from the invention of the telegraph right on through to the formation of Federal Express, we've looked for ways to move our thoughts across space faster than the next guy.

Enter computer mediated communication. A message can travel from North America to Antarctica in less than a second, and it doesn't take much longer than that to bounce the same message all around the world. So how does that change how we write? Or does it?

It does.

Some say that CMC (computer mediated communication) is more akin to face-to-face communication than to mail sent via "snail mail" (the internauts unkind reference to the Postal Service). With CMC, you get immediate receipt and immediate response. You can send off a quick message:

```
Dear mom,
Send money.
Love,
Your darling daughter
```

Such a short message via regular mail would seem a waste of thirty-two cents. If you're going to write two words, you may as well write two hundred. A full page of text costs no less to send than a half-empty page, and besides there's the guilt factor to contend with. (Mama loves to hear about your life.) However, with e-mail, sending off a quick note is analogous to taping a note to the refrigerator door—the details can wait. Of course, so can Mom:

```
Dear darling daughter,
Send last semester's grades.
Love,
Mom
```

Well, maybe a longer letter wouldn't hurt. She *is* your mom, after all. You can balance the brevity of your messages by more frequent communications, since e-mail is more convenient. Your letter doesn't have to sit for days while you procrastinate about that trip down to the corner to buy stamps. You can mail it from your dorm—or from your school's computer lab.

Have I sold you on e-mail yet? Good.

What All Mail Programs Have in Common

Mail programs are the least standardized of any Internet utility. You'll probably just use whatever system has been set up by the system administrator. However, there are some similarities, no matter which program you use.

E-mail Addressing

Before you can send e-mail, you need to know the address of the person it's going to. Just as you can't address an envelope to "Dear Old Mom" and drop it in the mailbox, you can't expect an e-mail address to be delivered unless you include the full address of the recipient.

Tip ➤

Don't know anyone else on the Internet yet? No problem. If you just want to test your e-mail to see if it's working, you can address the message to yourself. In fact, that's what we'll be doing shortly in this chapter.

An e-mail address is a combination of letters, numbers, and symbols. They almost always include an @ sign (an "at" sign) and some periods. For instance, here's mine:

```
clarkd@bvsd.k12.co.us
```

It breaks down this way:

clarkd	My login name. When I log onto my UNIX host, this is the name I use.
@	The "at" sign. Every internet address has one of these in it. If someone gives you their e-mail address and it does not contain one of these, clear your throat and declare there must be a mistake. Watch them turn red.
bvsd	The name of the machine I log onto.
k12	I work in a school district that services Kindergarten through 12th grade.
co	That school district happens to be in the state of Colorado.
us	Colorado just happens to be one of the big 50.

See, I told you it makes sense. The information before the @ sign is the user name. The information after gives the location where his account resides. The periods separate the various parts of the location. There will never be a space in an e-mail address and it is generally safe to stay with lower case.

You can tell a lot from an e-mail address. For instance, sometimes you can tell what country someone is from by the last two characters in the address. Here are some examples:

au	Australia
at	Austria
ca	Canada
de	Germany
dk	Denmark
fi	Finland
fr	France
it	Italy
jp	Japan
no	Norway
uk	United Kingdom
us	United States

And there are more. There is a two-letter code for almost every country with e-mail access. Of course, not all addresses end in a country code. Some addresses tell you the function of that particular site. For instance,

```
fwempen@mcp.com
```

is a valid e-mail address. The .com at the end tells us that mcp is a commercial site. (In this case, it's the site of my publisher's parent company, Macmillan Computer Publishing.) If your connection is through your school or university, there is a good chance that your e-mail address ends in .edu, which stands for Education. Here's a list of other functional endings:

gov	government
com	commercial organization
mil	military
net	network resources
org	nonprofit organizations (usually)

Making sense of these addresses cannot only give you information about who you're mailing to, but can also help you remember your own e-mail address. Always a good thing to know.

Your First Message

Okay, time to mail yourself a letter. I'm going to be using the UNIX program Pine for this example. Pine is a popular program carried at many sites. It is reasonably easy to use and you can invoke it by typing **pine** at your Unix prompt. Pine will then come up with the following screen:

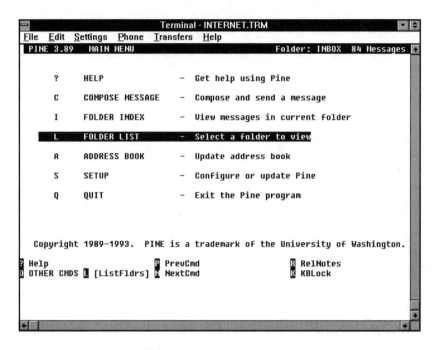

The Pine main menu, your gateway into the world of e-mail.

As you can see, Pine is menu driven. If I want to compose a message, I can either type a **c** (for compose) or use my arrow keys to highlight the **Compose** command and press **Enter**. Either way will take me to the next window.

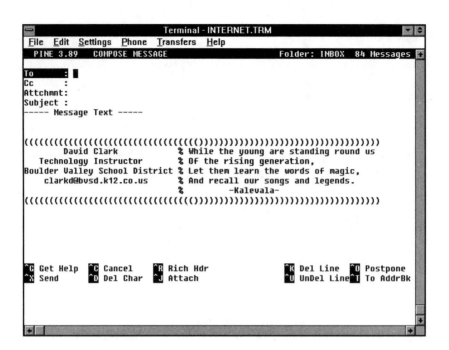

Ready to write that first piece of e-mail.

The **to** line is where I type the e-mail address. Since this may be your first message, send it to yourself. No sense in letting someone else see it, just in case you goof up.

If your domain name (everything after the @ sign in the e-mail address) is the same as the person you are sending to, you need only use their login name when sending e-mail. For example, if my address is clarkd@bvsd.k12.co.us and I wanted to send a letter to my son whose e-mail address is clarkj@bvsd.k12.co.us, I need only fill in clarkj in the **to** line since we have the same domain. The other lines that may need to be filled in are as follows:

Cc: is for carbon copy. You can put another e-mail address in here if you want to mail a copy of this letter to another person.

The Attchmnt: line is useful if you want to include a file that's in your UNIX home directory. This attachment can be a text file or a binary file, such as a graphic or executable file. You can also leave this blank.

The **Subject:** line is important. You can see by looking at the upper right corner that I have 84 e-mail messages waiting for me to read. Since I choose to have a life away from my computer, I won't read every one of these. I will decide by the subject headings accompanying the e-mail which ones to read. Something like

```
Your house is on fire
```

is bound to get more of my attention than a subject heading like

```
Peas for dinner tonight
```

Make your subject headings concise, to the point, and enticing. Since this letter is just to yourself, it doesn't really matter so let's just fill it in with **test message**. (Or be creative if you want; nobody will know.)

The place below all these lines is where you can type your message. My completed, ready to mail e-mail message looks like this:

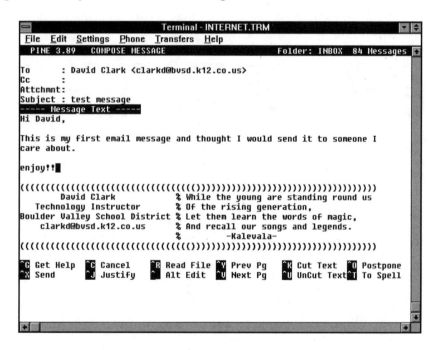

Just a ^x away from sending my first e-mail!

The stuff below my typed message is my signature file. It's automatically appended to every e-mail message I send. I'll show you how to make one of those later.

On the bottom of the screen is the commands menu. ^ is the symbol for the Ctrl (control) key. Learn where this key is; you'll be using it a lot on the Internet. To send your message using Pine, type ^x and follow the prompts on the bottom of the screen. You'll be asked if you really want to send (of course, that's why I typed ^x, not an easy combination to hit by accident!). Just press **Enter** a couple of times and your first e-mail message is on its way. Within seconds, it will appear in your mailbox.

Checking Your Inbox

Now that you have something in your mailbox, you can open your mailbox and deal with an actual message. It doesn't matter that it's just from yourself. There are few things more depressing than an empty mailbox and I didn't want to take you in there until I was sure you had some mail waiting for you. Keep reading this chapter if you don't want those empty-mailbox blues. I'll teach you ways to get more e-mail than you can possibly deal with.

When e-mail comes into your box, you'll see a listing of the messages, and you can decide which ones you want to read. Take a peek at my inbox:

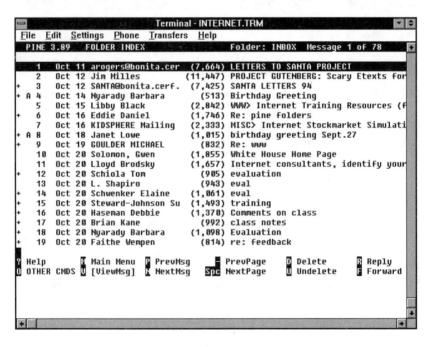

Nothing feels better than a mailbox full of mail.

There are many funny symbols that may be a part of your mailing program or not, but a few main elements are standard in most mailing programs, such as the following:

■ Name of the sender

■ Length of the posting

■ If you're using the Pine mail program, this will be represented in bytes.

■ Subject of message

See, I told you the subject heading was important. There's no need to be linear in your reading—it's possible to jump back and forth in selecting what messages to read. If time is short, the subject headings that jump out and grab me get my attention first.

To read a message, I select it by typing the number or using the arrow keys to select it and press **Enter**. The message will appear on my screen. Here's message 19:

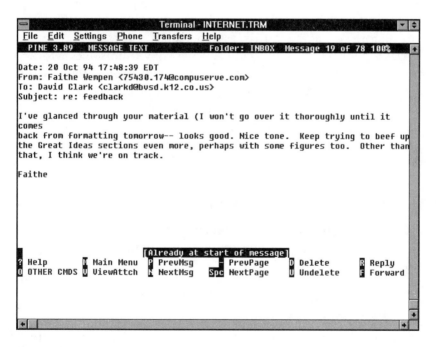

```
┌─                   Terminal - INTERNET.TRM                  ▼ ▲
  File  Edit  Settings  Phone  Transfers  Help
   PINE 3.89   MESSAGE TEXT        Folder: INBOX  Message 19 of 78 100%

 Date: 20 Oct 94 17:48:39 EDT
 From: Faithe Wempen <75430.174@compuserve.com>
 To: David Clark <clarkd@bvsd.k12.co.us>
 Subject: re: feedback

 I've glanced through your material (I won't go over it thoroughly until it
 comes
 back from formatting tomorrow-- looks good. Nice tone.  Keep trying to beef up
 the Great Ideas sections even more, perhaps with some figures too.  Other than
 that, I think we're on track.

 Faithe




                       [Already at start of message]
 ? Help         M Main Menu  P PrevMsg    -   PrevPage   D Delete    R Reply
 O OTHER CMDS   V ViewAttch  N NextMsg    Spc NextPage   U Undelete  F Forward
```

Encouragement from my editor.

To return to my inbox, typing **i** will do the trick. Alternatively, typing **m** will pull me all the way back to the main menu. Or if I want to give up completely, typing **q** will dump me out of Pine altogether.

Replying, Forwarding, Deleting, and So On

Once you've read your message, you need to make some choices. Of course, you can just leave it there and face it each and every time you enter your mailbox as a constant reminder of your ineptitude in answering your mail. (I don't recommend this one; it really grates on you.) Or you can do one of the following.

Reply to the Author

This is a nifty feature that lets you reply to the author without having to actually remember the e-mail address. In Pine, simply type **r** from within the message and you're on your way.

You will be asked if you want to include the original message as part of your reply. Before you agree to this, ask yourself if it is really necessary. Does your correspondent really need to know what they themselves wrote to you? Sometimes, it's good to include it, especially if you're referring to some delicate point in their original posting, but if in doubt, type **n** for no and continue on your way. The subject heading will then be filled in for you as

```
re:<whatever the original subject was>
```

Now you can type your message and send it.

Forward the Message to Another Person

Perhaps you know someone who would benefit from seeing this e-mail. Forward a copy to them by typing **f** in Pine. Add your own comments if you want and send the message on its way.

Save the Message to a Folder

Most mail programs have a way of saving mail into folders for future reference. You can file a message in a folder and dispose of it later. This is great for saving an important message for reference, or filing away mail from friends that you want to mull over before you respond.

In Pine, the command for saving a message to a folder is **s**. You will then be asked for a directory name. If the directory doesn't exist, Pine will create it for you.

Delete the Message

The other options are all well and good, but when you get down to the bottom line, what are you going to want to do with most of the stuff in your mailbox? Delete it, of course.

Mail can accumulate in your mailbox very easily if you let it, especially if you subscribe to any discussion groups via e-mail. (You'll learn more about these fine discussion groups later in this chapter.) Until you delete them, your mailbox messages take up space on a hard drive somewhere (probably on your service provider's computer). Your measly few dozen messages may not add up to much, but if everyone keeps every piece of mail they ever receive, that poor hard disk will fill up quickly. When a disk becomes full, services slow down for everyone; no one can receive any mail, and the system administrator has to take some drastic action to free up disk space, which may include deleting the entire contents of your mailbox without your consent!

Don't let that happen. Be a good citizen and delete your old mail. This is accomplished easily in Pine, by simply typing a **d**. You can do this either when the message is on-screen or in your message index. The mail will remain in your mailbox until you quit the mailing program, and even then, you will be asked if you really want to delete the mail with the following message at the bottom of the screen:

```
Expunge the 6 deleted messages from "INBOX"? (y/n) [y]:
```

Tip ➤ **Expunge** means delete, by the way. Try that word out on an English major sometime—they're generally impressed by that sort of talk.

Typing **n** here will leave your mailbox untouched should you panic at the last moment. Once it's gone, it's gone.

Who Is Eudora?

Eudora is the other mailing program you are going to hear a lot about. If you're looking for a program that will let you avoid the ^x and ^cs of Pine and you want to stay within your own operating system (Mac or Windows), Eudora may just be for you. You need a direct connection (dial-up or dedicated—see Chapter 2) to use Eudora, so don't waste your time if you're stuck with a Terminal account.

When you get into Pine, all of the leg work has already been done for you; it's set up and ready to go. That's because Pine is a UNIX program, already on the System. With Eudora, you'll need to acquire it and set it up yourself, unless you're working in a computer lab where they already have it installed.

When starting up Eudora, you'll see a blank window.

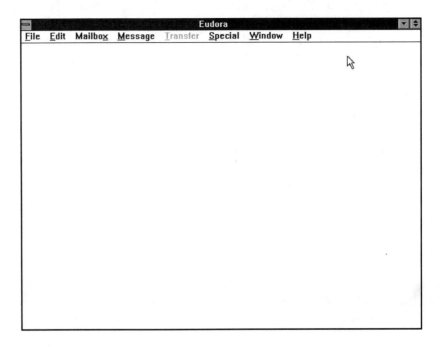

The Eudora Menu Bar.

Exploring around in the menu will teach you a lot, but the first stop you need to make is under the **Special** menu item. Look for **Configuration**.

```
┌──────────────────────────────────────────────────────────────┐
│                        Configuration                         │
├──────────────────────────────────────────────────────────────┤
│ ┌─Network Configuration─────────────────────────────────────┐│
│ │ POP Account:      clarkd@bvsd.k12.co.us                    ││
│ │ Real Name:        clarkd                                   ││
│ │ SMTP Server:      bvsd.k12.co.us                           ││
│ │ Return Address:   clarkd@bvsd.k12.co.us                    ││
│ │ Check For Mail Every   0    Minute(s)                      ││
│ │ Ph Server:                                                 ││
│ └───────────────────────────────────────────────────────────┘│
│ ┌─Message Configuration─────────────────────────────────────┐│
│ │ Message Width: 80   Message Lines: 20   Tab Stop: 8        ││
│ │ Screen Font:  Courier New      Size: 9                     ││
│ │ Printer Font: Courier New      Size: 12                    ││
│ │ ☐ Auto Receive Attachment Directory:                      ││
│ └───────────────────────────────────────────────────────────┘│
│                                    Cancel        OK           │
└──────────────────────────────────────────────────────────────┘
```

Pretty straightforward, don't you think?

Pretty easy to fill out. Just follow my example; only fill in your own information, of course. The thing you need to notice is where it says POP Account. Eudora is a pop mail program. That means with its default configuration it will download your mail onto your local hard drive and remove it from your UNIX account. This can be an advantage in that by having the mail on your hard drive, you can read your mail and type your replies offline. If you have to pay for your connection by the hour, you'll save yourself some money by using Eudora.

Once configured, sending and receiving mail with Eudora is only a click away. To bring up the compose window, I choose **New Message** from under the **Message** menu item.

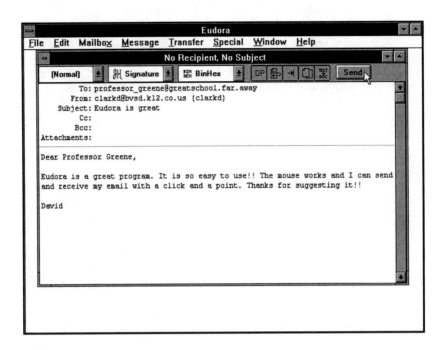

Click on the **Send** button and the message is on its way.

Checking your mail is just as easy. Select **Check Mail** from under the **File** menu. Eudora will:

■ Connect to your host.

■ Download your mail to your local hard drive.

■ Disconnect.

You can then leisurely read your mail and compose your replies in a friendly point-and-click environment.

Unfortunately for the dial-up user, Eudora was initially developed to be used in labs with dedicated connections to the Internet. It works best in that environment. It can be used with a dial-up direct connection (SCIP or PPP), but it is difficult to configure. In addition to the setup described above, you'll need to write a login script that will inform Eudora of where to look for your mail. This scripting can be challenging to write. It is possible that a stock script for your site already exists, and in that case, why reinvent the wheel? Check with your system administrator. If that isn't the case and you feel up to a challenge, get the documentation from the address below and start hacking.

```
ftp.qualcomm.com
```

Look in the pceudora/quest directories. The binary files as well as complete documentation are available. Check out Chapter 8 for FTP help.

Creating a Signature File

> **Tip ➤** **Signature files** are commonly referred to as *.signature*, pronounced dot-signature. Beware! If you call it period-signature, everyone will think you're a complete geek.

A *signature* is a standard bit of verbiage that you include at the end of every message you send, telling something about yourself. It's kind of like an electronic bumper sticker.

Long signatures can irritate your recipients and hog precious system resources. Out of courtesy, you should limit your .signature to 4–6 lines. In that short space, you'll make your own personal statement.

What to put? The infinite possibilities boggle the imagination. You could start with your name and e-mail address. Your school or fraternity name, maybe, if you're feeling loyal. Many people also include their favorite quote or piece of ASCII art. (ASCII stands for the American Standard Code for Information Interchange. It's a standard for computer-generated characters.) ASCII art is artwork that is created by using only the symbols found on your keyboard. Here is my rendition of the rocky mountains:

OK, so I'm no great artist, but you get the idea. There is a good supply of examples to be found at:

```
gopher twinbrook.cis.uab.edu
```

Look in the **continuum/ascii art bazaar** directories. Some of these are absolutely fantastic! If you've read ahead to Chapter 6 (the one on Gopher), this address should make sense. If you haven't, write down the address for future reference. This Gopher server, located at the University of Alabama/ Birmingham has a large collection of ASCII art. A good place to get some ideas.

When you're ready to create your .signature, open a new document using a UNIX text editor from your UNIX prompt. I generally use an editor program called pico, like so:

```
%pico .signature
```

pico is the text editor program, and **.signature** is the name of the file I am creating.

> **Tip ➤** If you're using Eudora, select **Signature** from the **Window** menu, and create your signature file in the blank window that pops up.

You'll then be faced with a blank page, and it's time to let your creativity flow. Create your file, and when you're done, type ^x to exit pico. When you send mail through Pine, it automatically looks for a file called .signature. If it finds one, Pine appends the contents of that file to the bottom of each and every piece of mail you send. Pretty cool, huh?

These are just a couple of the more common e-mail packages you might run into. There are many more, and they may have a very different look and feel to them. UNIX mail is a very popular program. Type **man mail** at your UNIX prompt for the commands.

Elm is another program you might run into. It has similarities to Pine (which, by the way, is an acronym for "*Pine is not elm*"). Here is what you will see:

```
Mailbox is '/usr/spool/mail/clarkd' with 55 messages [ELM 2.4 PL22]
  N 1  Dec 19 Mail Delivery Subs (42)  Returned mail:  Host unknown (Names
  N 2  Dec 19 Jim Milles         (77)  Re: Censoring 'Net for K12 access
    3  Dec 19 Web66 Mailing List (28)  WWW Traffic up 48%!!
    4  Dec 18 Eddie Daniel       (21)
    5  Dec 18 Haseman Debbie     (36)
    6  Dec 18 Peter Scott        (39)  Update <FRE022> CapAccess: National
    7   Dec 17 Jim Milles        (46)  Censoring 'Net for K12 access
  O 8  Dec 16 Jim Milles        (117)  Time for Success Stories, #3!
  O 9  Dec 16 Jim Milles         (63)  Re: What happened to the Amtrak sche
   10  Dec 16 To David Clark     (13)
```

```
¦=pipe, !=shell, ?=help, <n>=set current to n, /=search pattern
a)lias, C)opy, c)hange folder, d)elete, e)dit, f)orward, g)roup reply,
m)ail,
   n)ext, o)ptions, p)rint, q)uit, r)eply, s)ave, t)ag, u)ndelete, or
e(x)it
```

It is not quite as simple to use as Pine, but it is fairly straightforward. To read a message, select it using the arrow keys and hit return; to compose a message, type **m**. There is a large variety of mailing programs available and yours may look entirely different. Ask for documentation when you establish your account if your mailing program is different from these.

E-mail Smiles and Other Basic Netiquette

The trouble with e-mail is that you can't see the person's body language. Plain text can easily be confusing or misinterpreted—you may say something ironic, and your recipient might take it as deadly serious. Before you know it, you've got some disgruntled psycho looking you up in the student directory and hunting you down with a chain saw... well, let's hope it doesn't come to that. At any rate, it's important to remember the limitations of plain text.

Smiles

Your basic smile looks like this:

```
:-)
```

It may look like so much garbage until you look at it sideways, and the smile is revealed. You can use this to let the reader know that:

- ▌ You are happy about what you just said in your last statement as in: `I'm coming home for the holidays. :-)`

- ▌ You don't want to be taken too seriously, as in: `Don't wait up for me, I'll be coming down the chimney with Santa. :-)`

Either way, the smile lets the reader know how you feel about what you said. Contrast this one with the one above:

```
I'm coming home for the holidays. :-(
```

The writer of this message is telling us that he'd rather be on a ski trip, or hanging out on campus. Other smiles you may want to use include:

;-)	Used when a sarcastic remark was just made (winking)
:-o	Wow
:-x	A kiss

You can make up your own or check out the ones at:

```
gopher rescomp.stanford.edu
```

and follow the path:

```
Temporary Items
Larry's Public Files
dchef/open.house
The_Rosebud_Pub
text
smile
```

You can find smiles there for every occasion including one for a buck-toothed vampire, the Pope, or a person with glasses. (Although what difference it makes whether someone is wearing glasses, I don't know. I don't make these things up—I just write about them.)

DON'T SHOUT and Other Courtesies

IF YOU WANT TO SHOUT AT SOMEBODY, TYPE YOUR MESSAGE IN ALL CAPITALS. OTHERWISE AVOID DOING THIS. IT IS VERY ANNOYING AND DIFFICULT TO READ. SOME PEOPLE FIND IT OFFENSIVE.

There, glad I got that out of my system. Here are a few other suggestions to make your e-mail messages more palatable to the person on the other end:

- Be clear and concise.
- Always include your name and e-mail address at the end of your message.
- Check your spelling and grammar. Pine has a built-in spell checker; to use it, press **Ctrl-t**.
- Don't waste computing power. Keep your attachments only to what's necessary.
- Use basic common sense and courtesy. These are real people on the other end of your communication.

Follow these few rules and you are off to a great start communicating on the information super highway.

Exchanging Mail with Online Service Users

If you know someone who has an account with an online service, such as CompuServe or America Online, it is possible to send mail to those people. Here are the addressing conventions:

Service	Addressing	Example
America Online	username@aol.com	david2@aol.com
CompuServe	usernumber@ compuserve.com	12345.678@compuserve.com
Delphi	username@ delphi.com	SuperSurf@delphi.com
GEnie	username@ genie.geis.com	SuperSurf@genie.geis.com

Tip ➤ In a CompuServe address, change the comma to a period. For example, 75430,174 becomes 75430.174.

To send from one of these services:

Service	Addressing	Example
CompuServe	INTERNET: internet address	INTERNET:fwempen@mcp.com
America Online	internet address	fwempen@mcp.com
Delphi	internet "internet address"	internet"fwempen@mcp.com"
GEnie	internet address	fwempen@mcp.com

Mailing Lists—A Different Kind of E-Mail

A *mailing list* is a topic-oriented discussion group that uses e-mail as its means of communicating. There are hundreds of such lists around on any topic you can think of. These lists are managed in different ways. For example, let's say there are twenty people who want to exchange information on a topic (they're all in the same class and want to share their notes). In this case, the twenty folks swap addresses and write a common alias in their mailing program or ask the system administrator to establish an e-mail address that will deliver mail to all the members. This type of mailing list can work well for a small, stable group.

On the other side of the spectrum are the monster lists, the international discussions with constantly changing membership and mission. There are three major types of mailing lists out there you may encounter. They have a lot of similarities in the ways they work; in fact, most of the commands are the same. They are as follows:

listservs	This is the dominant list processing software you'll encounter. These discussion groups originated with BITNET (the Because It's Time Network, another large computer network) and have pretty much been absorbed into the Internet. listserv@address is the way to recognize this one.
Majordomo	majordomo@address is the look of these lists. Majordomo lists are relatively simple to set up. We may be seeing more of these in the future.
Listproc	Guess how this one looks. listproc@address is right!

All of these automate the process of subscribing and unsubscribing to the list. Here's how it works: Each mailing list has two addresses, a list management address and a posting address. The list management address is for administrative purposes only; it handles subscription requests and such. The posting address is the real meat of the mailing list. When you send mail to the posting address, everyone who has subscribed to the mailing list gets a copy of that mail in their mailbox.

Tip ➤ A word of caution: If you're going to subscribe to a mailing list, you need to make a commitment to check your mail every day. Mailboxes can fill up very fast when you start subscribing to lists, and your system administrator may get very grumpy with you if hundreds of messages sit idle in your inbox for a long time. I'd suggest using the Delete key generously and reading only those messages with subject headings that are of interest.

Finding a Mailing List to Subscribe To

The most common type of mailing list is a LISTSERV group. LISTSERV is a popular mail server program; the lists administered by this program are called LISTSERV groups. (Duh.) There are about 4,000 LISTSERV groups at the moment—something for almost everyone. Since LISTSERV is the big, mainstream mailing list system, let's focus on it.

There are several ways to get a list of LISTSERV groups. You can FTP (see Chapter 8) to ftp.sura.net and look in the /pub/nic directory for a listing, or you can use World Wide Web (see Chapter 7) to go to http://www.ii.uib.no/~magnus/paml.html.

You can also request a list by mail, but be warned: this is a very long list. Here's how to do it: From your e-mail program (Pine, for instance), compose a message to listserv@listserv.net. Leave the subject blank. In the body of the message, type **list global**. Nothing else, just that. Go ahead and send your message.

It'll take several minutes, but eventually you'll receive two pieces of mail. The first one will have the subject heading: Output of your job. This message is a rather dull note that lets you know how much computing energy it took to process your request. Take a look at it, wonder what all the numbers mean, and delete it.

The second one is the one you are looking for. The subject heading of this one will be: File: "LISTSERV LISTS". This is the one that contains your list. At last check, this file was 553k in size, but you asked for it, so here it is. It'll start with "A" and lead you right through to the end.

If you already have some idea of what you want, you can limit the search to certain keywords. Send the same e-mail message to listserv@listserv.net, but in the body of the message, type **list global /*keyword*** where *keyword* is the subject you're looking for. Send your message.

The file you get back will be noticeably smaller and easier to handle. That one word can make the difference between a monster file and a manageable one. The keyword can be anything you want. I sent off the following request, looking for lists on computer related topics.

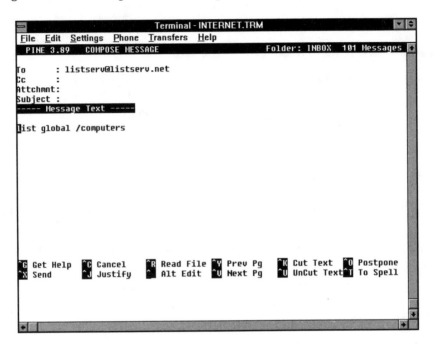

Searching for the right group.

Here's part of the list I got back:

```
Network-wide ID  Full address and list description
---------------  ---------------------------------
'NEW-SUPERCOM... S-COMPUT@UGA.BITNET (Peered)
                 SuperComputers List (UGA)

ACHNEWS          ACHNEWS@UCSBVM.UCSB.EDU
                 Newsletter of the Association for Computers and the
                 Humanities
```

```
ACORN-L          ACORN-L@TREARN.BITNET
                 ACORN computers Discussion List
ACWNYS-L         ACWNYS-L@UBVM.BITNET
                 NY State Alliance for Computers and Writing

CAEE-L           CAEE-L@SEARN.BITNET
                 SEFI-CAEE: SEFI Working Group on Computers And Engineering
```

This is just the first screen of lists. There were about 25 available on this subject.

Tip ➤

Interested in other mailing lists besides LISTSERV? There is a reasonably good list to be had, though, of the ones that are open to the public: FTP (see Chapter 8) to **pit-manager.mit.edu**, and look in the /pub/usenet/news.announce.newusers directory for files that begin with Publicly_Accessible_Mailing_Lists.

Subscribing to a Mailing List

Once you've found one you like, it's time to subscribe. Subscribing to LISTSERV groups is pretty easy, so let's look at that procedure first. For an example, I'll pick one of the LISTSERV groups I found when I requested the list, and go with ACHNEWS.

In your e-mail program (such as Pine), compose a message to listserv@listserv.net. Leave the subject blank. (Is this starting to look familiar? I hope so.) In the body of the message, type:

```
subscribe ACHNEWS your name
```

Send your message. Where it says *your name*, it really means your first and last name, not your e-mail address. Here is what my subscribe request would look like:

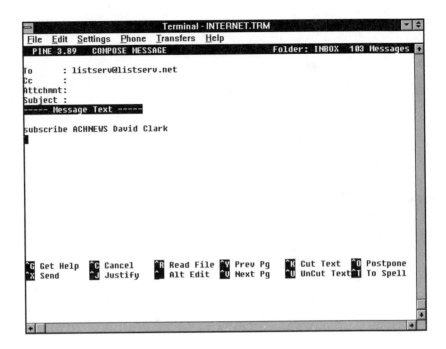

Subscribing to a mailing list.

 Tip ➤

Notice that in all these subscription and list requests, I have eliminated my .signature. Leaving it would only confuse the poor computer, which would subsequently send back error messages to me. So delete your .signature from your e-mail before sending it.

That's it. In a short while, you should get a message back telling you that you are subscribed. In a few cases, with LISTSERVs that are more tightly controlled, you may get a message back telling you of another hoop to jump through. Just do what it says—after all, it's only a piece of machinery and there's no need to take it personally.

If you get tired of a LISTSERV group or decide it's not for you, you can unsubscribe by sending the same message, but using:

```
signoff ACHNEWS your name
```

To subscribe to a non-LISTSERV group, the procedure varies, depending on whether the list is manually or automatically administered. The automated variety work much like a LISTSERV group—send a message to the mail server program. If it's not LISTSERV, it's something else; just substitute the "something else" for LISTSERV in the previous example.

If it's a small, manually administered mailing list, you can often reach the administrator by sending e-mail to

listname-request@hostname

where, of course, *listname* is the list name and *hostname* is the host name.

Posting to a Mailing List

Once subscribed, you can start posting to the group (although it's generally a good idea to be a *lurker* for awhile and not post right away). Read what other people are saying and get a feel for the tenor of the group before adding your two cents.

To post to the group, you'll have to use the posting address I told you about earlier. It's different (usually) from the address where you sent your subscription request. The posting address will be in the message sent back to you informing you that you are subscribed. If you can't find that message, perhaps you can pull it off the list where you originally discovered it. For instance, in

ACHNEWS   ACHNEWS@UCSBVM.UCSB.EDU

the address on the right is the one I want to use. This will send my mail to the whole group.

Great Ideas for Using E-mail

▮▮ Write home for money. Many computer-literate parents are delighted to learn that they can send e-mail to their kids. Point out to them how much they are saving on long distance and have them cut you a check for the difference.

▮▮ Get your reports and assignments in on time without leaving your dorm. E-mail the report in and go back to sleep.

▮▮ Keep in touch with friends and teachers back home.

- Hunt for a job. Look for a list discussing your major. Make some intelligent remarks, get your name out there, and drop subtle hints about graduation coming up and not knowing what you're going to do next with your life.

- Make some new friends, and create some key-pal relationships with people in other lands, other cultures.

- Pursue your hobbies—golf, fly fishing, bonsai, whatever. If it's a hobby, there's probably a listserv for it.

- Let the President know why you are/are not going to vote for him in the next election by sending mail to: **president@whitehouse.gov**. (Don't expect a personal reply, but sometimes it just feels good to get it off your chest.)

- Send your most profound questions to the Usenet Oracle. "When will I be loved?" "Who is buried in Grant's tomb?" "What is the meaning of Spam?" All e-mail will be answered. If you're in the mood, you can even become one of the oracles yourself and answer questions from other confused souls. For information, send e-mail to: **oracle@cs.indiana.edu** and put the word **help** in the subject line.

- Find that one true love. Send e-mail to **perfect@match.com**. You'll receive back a 155 multiple choice questionnaire that will then be cross-referenced with other respondents once you send it back in.

- No more trips down to the corner to send a fax. Send e-mail to **faxmaster@pan.com** for more information. Note, this isn't cheap.

- Play games. Send mail to judge@u.washington.edu or judge@shrike.und.ac.za, with "help" as your subject to find out about playing core ware, a game of computer programming skill.

- Check with your system administrator and see if he will let you be a list manager of your own listserv. You could create one just to discuss your triumphs and successes!

USENET: The Global Bulletin Board

Remember that first day at a new school? The disorientation. Cryptic signs hanging from the ceiling and you wondering which one applied to you. Conflicting directions from different people about what you were supposed to do. The frustration. The desire to turn around and go home. USENET is a little bit like that.

On that first day, however, you knew that if you stuck it out, it would all be worth it. So instead of turning around and catching the next bus, you faced your apprehensions and went forward. In the end, that first day became a blur, shadowed by the successes you've had since. USENET is like that, too.

So read carefully, follow step by step, and the first-day blues can be, well, if not avoided, then certainly minimized. That is, unless you are one of those people who never read the introductions to chapters.

So, What Is USENET, Anyway?

USENET is a series of public bulletin board-like discussion groups, called *newsgroups*. Anyone with access can post to these newsgroups, and anyone can respond to anything that is said in any of the groups. You can even suggest the formation of a new newsgroup, and considering that roughly 90 megabytes of information are exchanged each day, USENET works amazingly well. (90 megabytes of information would fill over 3,000 books the size of this one.)

Like most of the Internet, USENET (also referred to as netnews) is managed by the people who use it. That's you and me. Pretty scary, huh?

Anatomy of a Newsgroup Name

Don't be intimidated by the long, cryptic names of newsgroups—yes, I *know* there are oddly placed periods and dashes, but it's really quite simple. All newsgroups use a similar syntax in choosing their names. For example, the group comp.sys.ibm.pc.games.flight-sim breaks down this way:

> **comp** tells us that this group is in the computer subcategory.
>
> **sys.ibm.pc** tells us that the operating system we're working with is for IBM and compatible PCs.
>
> **games.flight-sim** lets us know that the discussion will revolve around games, specifically around flight simulators.

There are roughly 6,000 different newsgroups and they are organized into seven major and several minor categories:

> **comp** Groups in this category contain discussions relating to computer science, computer games, different operating systems, artificial intelligence, and so on. If you want to know about computers, you can find it here. Some of the groups you will find there include:
>
> > comp.sys.mac.announce
> >
> > comp.ai.edu
> >
> > comp.graphics.animation
> >
> > comp.unix.wizards
>
> **news** This refers to netnews. You can find information relating to USENET here. These groups are good places to start looking when you have questions regarding the news. Some examples:

news.announce.newsgroups

news.announce.newusers

news.newusers.questions

news.groups.reviews

rec   As in recreation. Music, hobbies, the arts, skiing, and more, such as:

rec.arts.startrek.reviews

rec.humor.funny

rec.skiing.alpine

rec.arts.theatre.plays

sci   Groups relating to the various disciplines of science. Offerings include:

sci.research.careers

sci.space.news

soc.history.science

sci.astro.amateur

soc   Groups of sociological concerns. There is a soc group for just about every country to discuss political and sociological concerns there. Some examples:

soc.penpals

soc.rights.human

soc.women

soc.culture.cuba

talk   Here is where debates on controversial (and noncontroversial) topics can take place. Discussions can become quite heated in these newsgroups. Groups in this category include:

talk.abortion

talk.bizarre

talk.politics.mideast

talk.politics.misc

misc Everything else that doesn't fit into one of the other categories. Examples:

> misc.jobs.misc
>
> misc.misc
>
> misc.forsale.computers.pc-clone
>
> misc.education

These are the major categories; you will most certainly see others at your site. Some of these will include:

alt A wide variety of groups ranging from Barney to the supernatural.

bionet Discussions among biologists.

bit Many bitnet LISTSERVs are piped into newsgroups under this heading. Subscribing to these groups is an alternative to having these discussions come into your mailbox.

biz Newsgroups relating to topics of interest to business.

clari Groups from Clarinet. This is a subscription service that brings information from UPI into newsgroups.

k12 Groups relating to K12 education.

Seeing What's Available

Don't panic when you see the huge mass of information that awaits you on USENET. Depending on your site, you probably have anywhere between 1,500–3,000 different newsgroups you can read. That's more information than you want. When you enter the world of USENET for the first time, you will more than likely be subscribed to every one of them. The computer has no idea of your interests and leaves it up to you to decide. Everything from alt.simpsons.itchy.scratchy to soc.bosnia.news is waiting for your inspection.

That is, unless your school has already created a customized list for you. In that case, you'll be subscribed to between five and ten introductory groups. If so, you don't know how lucky you are, and you can skip the next part on clearing the newsgroup list, unless you want to see what I'm going to put the rest of these people through.

When you first start up a newsreader, a file called .newsrc will be created. If you have never used a newsreader before, I'm going to take you through it very briefly just so we can create this file. At your prompt, type:

```
nn
```

You'll see some introductory pages. Read this stuff and scroll through it by hitting the **Spacebar** until you come to a screen that looks reminiscent of your e-mail inbox. At that point, quit by typing **Q**, or if you really want to hit some other buttons and play around until you get so frustrated that you want to chuck the computer out the window, then go for it. USENET can do that to you. Watch out.

Once you have quit, type:

```
more .newsrc
```

First, let's find out what newsgroups your site has to offer. From your UNIX prompt, type:

```
more .newsrc
```

The file .newsrc is a listing of every newsgroup available for you to read. The **more** command will pass them across your screen one page at a time. Here is an example of what you will see:

```
(1b)news.admin: 1-16159
news.admin.misc: 1-10363
news.admin.policy: 1-12847
news.admin.technical: 1-557
news.announce.conferences: 1-4416
news.announce.important: 1-21
news.announce.newgroups: 1-3940
news.announce.newusers: 1-703
news.answers: 1-20677
news.config: 1-1162
news.future: 1-4102
news.groups: 1-73550
news.lists: 1-1691
news.lists.ps-maps: 1-1194
news.misc: 1-6093
news.newsites: 1-1390
news.newusers.questions: 1-23600
news.software.anu-news: 1-4991
news.software.b: 1-9805
news.software.nn: 1-5094
news.software.nntp: 1-6850
```

```
news.software.notes: 1-183
news.software.readers: 1-9035
news.sysadmin: 1-2596
comp.admin.policy: 1-4910
comp.ai: 1-13003
comp.ai.digest: 1-1
comp.ai.edu: 1-1525
comp.ai.fuzzy: 1-2000
comp.ai.genetic: 1-2550
comp.ai.nat-lang: 1-1421
comp.ai.neural-nets: 1-13010
comp.ai.nlang-know-rep: 1-204
```

This is just a few of them. Press the **Spacebar** to advance to the next page. Notice that each newsgroup name in the list is followed by a colon. The colon means that you are subscribed to that particular newsgroup. Newsgroups that you aren't subscribed to will have a ! at the end of them.

Clearing the Newsgroup List

Notice that, at least in my list, there isn't a single ! in sight. (There probably won't be in yours either.) So the challenge is to change all of the : to !. (Yes, I know, you want to keep some of them, but this way we can begin with a clean slate and work from there.)

Luckily there is an easy way to unsubscribe all of them at once. Unluckily, you have to use the vi editor to do it. Don't get me wrong—I realize that vi is a powerful text editor, but it can also be powerfully intricate and confusing. So follow along and I promise this is the only time I will ask you to do this.

First, you have to open your .newsrc using vi. At your UNIX prompt, type this:

```
vi .newsrc
```

and press **Enter**. Your .newsrc appears on-screen just like it did when you used the **more** command, except now you can make changes to it. Follow these directions:

1. Press **Esc**. This takes you out of editing mode and into command mode.

2. Type :%s/:/!. The :%s means "substitute," the /: shows what to find, and the /! shows what to replace it with.

3. Press **Enter** to execute the command.

4. Type **:wq** to exit vi.

5. Press **Enter**.

This is a global replace command that will substitute every : with a !, unsubscribing you from every newsgroup.

> **Tip ➤** If you inadvertently hit another key, or your cat jumps on the keyboard in the middle of the procedure, don't panic—just press **Escape**, and then type **:q!**. That will take you out of vi without saving any of the inadvertent changes you've made and you can start from scratch.

Now that you are unsubscribed from all the groups, it's time to start building a .newsrc that will meet your needs.

Choosing Your Newsgroups

For picking the newsgroups you want to subscribe to, you have a couple of options. You can either browse through your .newsrc for a newsgroup that looks good to you, or you can search through it for keywords. You can do a search like this from your UNIX prompt:

```
grep keyword .newsrc
```

I'm using the UNIX **grep** command to search through my .newsrc for newsgroups relating to my interest as defined by my keyword. If I was looking for a newsgroup relating to computer games, for example, I would type:

```
grep games .newsrc
```

Such a search brought the following results on my server:

```
comp.sources.games! 1-765
comp.sources.games.bugs! 1-372
comp.sys.amiga.games! 1-47535
comp.sys.ibm.pc.games! 1-62417
comp.sys.ibm.pc.games.action! 1-30867
comp.sys.ibm.pc.games.adventure! 1-20229
comp.sys.ibm.pc.games.announce! 1-449
comp.sys.ibm.pc.games.flight-sim! 1-14799
```

```
comp.sys.ibm.pc.games.misc! 1-15608
comp.sys.ibm.pc.games.rpg! 1-21396
comp.sys.ibm.pc.games.strategic! 1-18144
comp.sys.mac.games! 1-49855
rec.games.chess! 1-33879
rec.games.moria! 1-15023
bit.listserv.games-l! 1-25366
comp.os.os2.games! 1-800
comp.sys.acorn.games! 1-108
comp.sys.ibm.pc.soundcard.games! 1-25
comp.sys.ibm.pc.games.marketplace! 1-1384
```

If you did such a search on your server, you would probably see some of the same groups and some different ones. Not all hosts carry every newsgroup that's out there.

Let's pick one that looks interesting and see what it has to offer. However, before we do that let's look at our options.

Newsgroup Reading Programs

Before we go any further, you're going to have to decide on a newsgroup reading program. There are four basic newsreading programs you can use from your UNIX prompt. They are as follows:

rn (read news)   This is one of the older programs and doesn't have the features of the newer programs but still gets the job done.

trn (threaded read news)   A new and improved version of rn that allows you to view the differing conversations in a threaded version.

nn (netnews)   It's fairly easy to use and configure.

tin   The newest of all programs and probably the easiest.

Of all these, I would recommend either tin or nn if you're just getting started with USENET. Since nn is the most common program, I'll be using it for most of the examples in this chapter.

Finding out which program your school supports is easy. Try typing in the commands at your UNIX prompt: **nn** or **tin**. If either works, you are in luck and on your way, if not, try **rn** or **trn**. Any of these will get you into USENET. If none of these work, check with your campus computer people and find out what your options are for reading the news.

Reading and Subscribing—The First Time

Ready to check out what USENET has to offer? Good. Remember that we cleared out our .newsrc and are not currently subscribed to any newsgroups. Now it's time to subscribe. Let's try it using **nn**. Invoking **nn** from the UNIX prompt is going to bring us this message:

```
No News (is good news)
```

It's only right. When you cleared out your .newsrc list, you indicated that you didn't want to read any groups, but now, you want to check out a newsgroup to see whether it's interesting enough to subscribe to. To check it out without subscribing, use the following command:

nn -X *newsgroup*

where newsgroup is the name of the group you want to check out. (Make sure the -X is uppercase.) Once you've subscribed to one or more newsgroups, you can read them anytime by just typing **nn**—this -X business is only for reading newsgroups that you haven't subscribed to yet.

Which group should you check out first? Absolutely your call. Turn back to the list you created with the **grep** command a few pages ago for some ideas. Personally, I like rec.games.chess, so I will type:

nn -X rec.games.chess

I'll get the following response:

```
Newsgroup: rec.games.chess                          Articles: 469 UNSUB
a Ian Torwick       22  >Star Trek 3D board now so
b Elliott Winslow   26  >>Estrin
c Kevin Gowen       13  >chess is stupid.
d ed.knowles        13  >>1 d4 Nf6 2 c4 e6 3 Nc3 Bb4 4 Bg5!?
e Glen Newbury       9  Chess Books
f LewisP4909        10  >
g Timothy Takach     6  >>
h Glen Newbury       3  Time Clocks
i Darrin Bond       13  >
j crawf             23  >>
k Jordan S. Berson  13  >
l Peter Stein       53  >Chess Databases: my decision: Chess Assistant
m Herb Wolfe        12  >E-MAIL CHESS
n Ramjet            24  -
o cowboy2           43  >
p Robert Hams Jr.   30  :tHE gAME rOOM The Game Room THE GAME ROOM
q Herb Wolfe        30  >>>>Weakest GM's Ever
r J E H Shaw        14  >>
s Jeffrey Golds     29  >>>>
-- 21:28 -- SELECT -- help:? -----Top 3%-----
```

This screen shows 19 messages relating to the game of chess. The 3% at the bottom lets us know that we are only seeing the top 3% of all the messages available for us to read. So if 19 messages is only 3%, that means there is a total of, um... well... you can figure that one out yourself. There's a whole bunch of them.

The names in the left column indicate the author of the posting. The number in the middle shows us the length of the message and the right column gives us the subject. Notice there are a fair amount of >s and >>s and >>>s and so on. These signs indicate that posting is a follow-up to the message directly above it. For instance, in the sequence:

```
e Glen Newbury     9  Chess Books
f LewisP4909      10  >
g Timothy Takach   6  >>
```

Glen had something he wanted to say regarding Chess Books. LewisP4909 found it of enough interest that she/he wanted to add his/her two cents worth. Then in comes Timothy who responds to whatever it was that Lewis said. Got that? Good.

We have tricked the computer into thinking that we are subscribed to this group, but we're not yet. Being subscribed means that this group (or groups) will automatically come up onto our screen when we invoke **nn**. To formally get yourself into the group, type **U** (uppercase again). This will bring up the message:

```
Already unsubscribed.  Resubscribe to rec.games.chess ?
```

Answer with a resounding **y**, and you have just subscribed to your first newsgroup.

Newsgroups with nn: The Cliff's Notes Version

Let's review. Here are the steps you need to follow to get set up with nn:

1. In vi (or some other text editor), edit your .newsrc file to change all the colons (:) to exclamation points (!). This unsubscribes every newsgroup.

2. Inspect your list of available newsgroups by typing **more .newsrc** at the UNIX prompt.

3. To read a newsgroup, type **nn -X** *newsgroup*.

4. Once in the newsgroup, type **U**, and then answer **y** to subscribe to it.

Simple as that.

Subscribing to More Newsgroups

From this point on, subscribing to new newsgroups is easy. From inside nn, type **G** (uppercase). nn will ask you what newsgroup you want to read. For example, let's see how the job market looks in Michigan. I type **G** and see the following message at the bottom of the screen.

```
Group or Folder (+./~ %=sneN)
```

I type **mi.jobs** and press **Enter**. The mi.jobs newsgroup comes up:

```
Newsgroup: mi.jobs                          Articles: 23 of 3389/29 UNSUB
a Fred Bosch         1   Telecommunications recruiters, sales, managers
b Jimbo98086        20   ****MUMPS Programmers (Search Firm)
c Jimbo98086        20   -
d Brady Hartman      49   ATEGRA NEEDS SQL RDBMS DE<>S/SYSTEM ARCHITECTS NATIONWIDE
e Brady Hartman      49   -
f Arbor I Systems    45   Smalltalk and Gemstone de<>nted Ann Arbor MI and New York
g KHANSEN@suvax1     24   Your Cover Letter Critiqued Online and Free
h Khris Hruska        6   Looking for people who found a job through the Net...
i James Downward     23   Job opening for Macintosh/Newton Programmer
j PEKKAN             54   URGENT JOB OPENINGS!
k MISTHWEST2         19   SAP R/2 and R/3 Positions for Consideration
l Patrick Lademan    42   >>---> Software Jobs >>--->
m johnrody@onramp    36   BROADCASTING JOBS-free sample!!
n Dan Karbal         18   Computer Operations Manager
o JAMES GARY         12   Sales to Physicians/Chiropractors
p Jim Dakin          15   Tandem Non Stop SQL, Pathways
q Jim Dakin          19   MS C++, GUI, DOS, Windows 3.1, contract
r Charles Garces     21   freelance work/experience requested
s Patrick Lademan    18   >>---> Oracle w/Forms Exp. >>--->
-- 18:05 -- SELECT -- help:? -----Top 81%-----
```

At this point, I type **U** to subscribe to this group.

> **Tip ➤**
> Don't let it confuse you that you use the **U** command to subscribe as well as unsubscribe. Yes, I know, there should be an S command for Subscribe, but let's just leave it alone and go with what works, okay?

Reading and Posting to a Newsgroup

Let's take a look at some of the postings in the mi.jobs newsgroup, now that we're here. The bottom line tells me that I am looking at 81% of all of the postings available to me at this time to read. This means there are just a few more on the next page. I can handle that.

I choose the postings that look interesting to me and type the letter next to each one to select them. The posting

```
i James Downward    23  Job opening for Macintosh/Newton
```

looks good. So does

```
n Dan Karbal        18  Computer Operations Manager
```

I type **i** and **n** (the letters in front of these messages) and those two postings become highlighted (selected for later reading). I can check out the message summaries on the next page by pressing the **Spacebar**.

Once I have selected all of the postings I want, I type **Z** (uppercase) to read the messages I've marked. Let's look at one:

```
Macintosh/Newton Programmer/Analyst Position
Innovation Associates, Inc. has an immediate opening for a full
time programmer/analyst to assist in completing a six month
development project to develop a mobile, pen-based graphic
interface to a database system for medical applications.  If the
project is successful, this position may lead to permanent
employment.  Applicants should have a BS in Computer Science or
Engineering and some experience in developing applications for
Macintosh computers and Newton PDA's in C/C++ and NewtonScript.
Experience in developing database applications and graphic user
interfaces is desirable.  For immediate consideration, please
send your resume in confidence to:
James Downward
Innovation Associates, Inc.
P.O. Box 1506
Ann Arbor, MI 48106
Tel:    (313) 997-9338
FAX:    (313) 997-9338
E-mail: Downward@Sphinx.Biosci.Wayne.com
```

Tip ➤ Note to desperate job seekers: This is not a real job. Out of fairness to Innovation Associates, I've altered their info just enough so they aren't inundated with résumés from the readers of this book. After all, this is an Internet manual and not an employment agency.

If I find a message that interests me, there are a couple of ways that I can respond. Of course, I can use the phone or "snail mail" to get my résumé to them, but it would make me look a lot more technologically saavy if I can get a snappy reply off to them via the Internet. That not only demonstrates my mastery of the Internet, but my résumé will get there before all of those bozos who are still in the dark ages communications-wise. Who would *you* rather hire?

My options for responding to this posting are:

- ▌ Posting a follow-up.

- ▌ Responding to the author via e-mail.

- ▌ Saving the posting for future reference.

I'll show you how to do each of these, but first, a word about text editors.

Time Out: Change Your Default Text Editor

Before you compose a message for USENET, you may want to consider changing what editor you will be using. (A text editor is nothing more than a simple word processing program.) On many systems, vi is the default editor. The frustrations of using vi have turned a lot of people off to USENET; avoid vi if you can.

How do you know what your choices are? Check with your system administrator. Most systems have at least a few text editor choices. If you have another text editor available, let nn know that you want to use it instead. From within nn, type **:set editor** *editorname* where, of course, *editorname* is the name of the text editor program you want to use.

Pico is a common editor and fairly easy to use. To install pico as my editor on my system, I entered:

```
:set editor pico
```

From here on, pico (or whatever) will be your editor. Other editors you could try instead of pico include emacs, elm, or med. I like pico the best, though.

...and now, back to our regularly scheduled program.

Posting a Follow-Up

To post a follow-up article, with the article on my screen, I type **F**. After being asked if I want to include the original article in my posting, I am thrown into my editor (pico, in my case), then I make my response and send it off just as if I were sending e-mail. My posting will appear in the newsgroup as a follow-up article, for the whole world to read:

```
i James Downward   23  Job opening for Macintosh/Newton
j David Clark      45  >
```

This may not the best choice to deal with this particular posting, especially if I did a fair amount of groveling and some creative résumé stretching in this message to impress these potential employers. In this case, you would want to consider the next option: responding via private e-mail.

Responding Via E-Mail

Type **R**, and you'll be thrown into the editor as before. Only this time when you send it, it will go directly into the author's mailbox. This will feel much like sending e-mail. And for good reason. It is.

Saving the Message

If you're not ready for that degree of commitment or don't have your résumé ready to zip off via e-mail, you'll want to save this posting for future reference. Send a copy to yourself by typing **M**. Doing so will bring up an option for you to type in an e-mail address. You can then mail a copy to yourself.

If you prefer, you can save the file in your UNIX account. Type **S** and nn will ask you where you want to put it. Type a path (a directory and a file name); if the directory doesn't exist, nn will create it. You can then read the message whenever you want using the **more** command (remember, just like you did with the .newsrc file at the beginning of this chapter).

Posting Your First Message

Can you feel the excitement building? Yes, it's time to make a contribution to the general welfare and post an original message to a newsgroup.

With most groups, it is a good idea to read some of the traffic before jumping right it. Spend some time and get the feel for the personality of the newsgroups. Doing so will keep you from being spotted as a newbie. When posting, all of the etiquette discussed in the e-mail chapter applies here as well. It may be a good idea to review those before making your first posting.

You can post to USENET either from within a newsgroup (within nn) or directly from your UNIX prompt. To post from your UNIX prompt, type:

nnpost *newgroup*

where *newsgroup* is the name of the newsgroup (of course). To post from within a newsgroup, type:

:post

You will be asked which group you want to post to. At this point, you can fill in the name of the group, or if you leave it blank, it will post to whatever group you are in at the moment.

Before you can actually type your message, there are several hoops you will have to jump through. Included are the following:

subject   Filling in the subject line is pretty important, just as it was with e-mail. This line is what will make people want to read what you have to say, so make it interesting.

keywords   Some news programs can use these to help the reader determine whether or not they want to read your posting. This can be left blank.

summary   Same as for keywords.

distribution   Distribution refers to how far and wide you want your article to be posted. By leaving it blank, it will be distributed out to newsfeeds all over the world. Ask yourself if this is really necessary before hitting return. Other options you can type in here include the following:

can	Canada
usa	United States
na	North America
eunet	Europe
CO, FL	State within the US

This can be handy if you are posting something for local eyes only.

Quick Summary of nn Commands

Are you one of those types who reads the Cliff's Notes rather than the whole book? Then this section is for you—a handy reference of nn commands.

There are two types of commands in nn: *selection commands* and *reading commands*. When the newsgroup menu is on the screen and you are choosing which articles to read, you're issuing selection commands. When you have an actual message on your screen and you're deciding how to dispose of it, you're issuing reading commands.

> **Tip ➤** Watch out for case sensitivity! Those of you who are DOS users may not be accustomed to "a" meaning something different than "A." But you're in UNIX now, and the rules have changed. Make sure you type letters exactly as they're shown.

Selection Commands

Use these when choosing what articles to read in index mode.

a-z	Select article for reading.
space	Move to next page.
?	Bring up the Help menu.
G	Go to another group.
N	Move to next newsgroup.
Q	Quit nn.
U	Unsubscribe or subscribe.
X	Mark all articles as read.
Z	Read selected articles.

Reading Commands

Use these commands when article is on-screen.

Space	Move to next page in selected article.
?	Bring up the Help menu.
F	Post a follow-up to selected article.
M	Mail copy of article to anyone.
R	Reply via e-mail to selected article.
S	Save article to a local file.
Q	Quit nn.
U	Unsubscribe/subscribe to newsgroup.

A Look at tin

tin is the newest of all the news reading programs. It's not as common as the other programs, but we will probably be seeing more of it. Start tin by typing **tin** at the UNIX prompt. When it starts, you'll see your list of subscribed newsgroups in a menu.

```
                Group Selection (nntp.msstate.edu  14 R)           h=help
 1 75840  misc.jobs.offered
 2  4765  misc.jobs.resumes
 3   258  news.announce.newgroups
 4    31  news.announce.newusers
 5    46  news.lists
 6   964  rec.arts.drwho
 7 11161  rec.motorcycles
 8 26525  rec.music.gdead
 9    15  sci.nanotech
10 19402  soc.culture.japan
11    50  alt.exotic-music
12 21606  alt.folklore.computers
13   171  rec.juggling
14   216  comp.mail.pine

<n>=set current to n, TAB=next unread, /=search pattern, c)atchup,
g)oto, j=line down, k=line up, h)elp, m)ove, q)uit, r=toggle all/unread,
s)ubscribe, S)ub pattern, u)nsubscribe, U)nsub pattern, y)ank in/out
*** End of Groups ***
```

Where nn will take you through your newsgroups one at a time, tin gives you the option of choosing which newsgroup you want to read first. The commands are listed at the bottom of the screen. To read a newsgroup, I can type the number in front of it and hit return. Doing so will bring up another menu of all the postings in that particular group. You can then go through them and read the ones that are of interest to you. If you haven't subscribed to any groups yet, typing **y** will bring in all the groups available to you (expect several hundred). You can then use **s** to subscribe to the ones you want.

tin is moving in the right direction of providing us a program that is intuitive and easy to use. It is worth keeping your eye on and asking your campus computer folks if they can put it on, if it's not there already.

Great Ideas for USENET

- Subscribe to news.lists. This group periodically lists the top 40 newsgroups for the month. You can find out where the hot discussions are taking place.

- Sell your aging computer system in misc.forsale.computers.

- Ask advice in comp.sys.*your favorite operating system* to get more recommendations than you want on what you should buy next.

- Learn some new tricks in comp.unix.wizards. Amaze your friends with your mastery of UNIX.

- Keep up with the latest Mac shareware. Subscribe to comp.mac.sys.digest, or comp.sys.ibm.pc.digest for the other side of the tracks.

- Check out where you are going to get that next degree to avoid going out into the real world. Read some of the following:

  soc.college

  soc.college.grad

  soc.college.gradinfo

  soc.college.teaching-asst

  soc.college.graduation

- Type **grep jobs .newsrc** from your UNIX prompt to find out what newsgroups relating to jobs your host offers. Do this after you find out how much that next degree is going to cost.

- Avoid the bar scene and stay home. Find a friend and conversation on soc.singles.

- Keep up with *The Young and the Restless* on rec.arts.tv.soaps.

- Read alt.alien.visitor, but not before you go to bed.

Gopher

As far as college mascots go, I'd have to give the Gopher a C-. I personally have a bit of trouble gaining athletic inspiration from a rodent. However, the University of Minnesota (home of the Golden Gophers) gets an A+ for their development of Gopher, the Internet navigation utility. Gopher was one of the first attempts to make the Internet accessible to the general population, and it did a very good job.

To understand how cool Gopher is, you need to understand how heinous the situation was before it was developed. Before Gopher, you needed to know the exact address of the site you wanted to connect to—the whole, long, tedious address. Once you got to the site (usually via a Telnet session), you'd be faced with a request for a login and password. If you were missing those, you were out of luck. Further, once you got into the site, there were seldom any directions—if you were lucky, you might get a few lines of information along with the UNIX prompt.

Gopher changed all of that. First of all, Gopher gives you a menu system to find your way around. No more typing long addresses! Today's Gopher sites allow anonymous use: no more passwords! But wait, there's more. Add to that a searching utility called Veronica, organization by subject and geographical headings, the ability to download text and binary files, and we have ourselves one hot program.

Tip ➤

If you have a connection that supports graphical programs (see Chapter 2), you can use one of the many graphical Gopher programs out there, such as WinGopher. These programs are so intuitive and easy to use that I won't waste your time explaining how to use them—just point and click, and go exploring.

To access Gopher, type **gopher** at your UNIX prompt. If your UNIX host has its own Gopher server or is set up to connect you to another server elsewhere, you should see a menu that resembles the following figure—the menu from the University of Minnesota, the *original* Gopher.

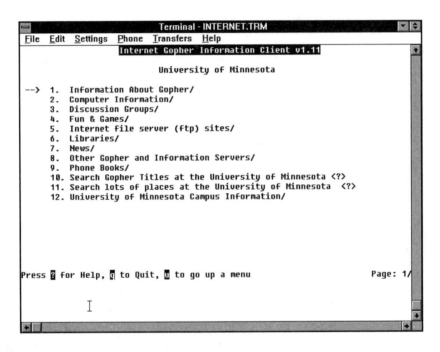

```
┌─────────────────────────────────────────────────────────────────────┐
│ ═                        Terminal - INTERNET.TRM                 ▼ ▲ │
│ File  Edit  Settings  Phone  Transfers  Help                         │
│              ┌─────────────────────────────────────────┐          ▲  │
│              │Internet Gopher Information Client v1.11  │             │
│                                                                       │
│                       University of Minnesota                         │
│                                                                       │
│  --> 1.  Information About Gopher/                                     │
│      2.  Computer Information/                                         │
│      3.  Discussion Groups/                                           │
│      4.  Fun & Games/                                                 │
│      5.  Internet file server (ftp) sites/                           │
│      6.  Libraries/                                                   │
│      7.  News/                                                        │
│      8.  Other Gopher and Information Servers/                        │
│      9.  Phone Books/                                                 │
│      10. Search Gopher Titles at the University of Minnesota <?>      │
│      11. Search lots of places at the University of Minnesota  <?>    │
│      12. University of Minnesota Campus Information/                  │
│                                                                       │
│                                                                       │
│                                                                       │
│                                                                       │
│ Press ? for Help, q to Quit, u to go up a menu          Page: 1/      │
│                                                                       │
│                I                                                   ▼  │
│ ◄ ═══════════════════════════════════════════════════════════════ ► │
└─────────────────────────────────────────────────────────────────────┘
```

The U of M Gopher main menu.

If typing **gopher** at your prompt does nothing for you, your school may not have Gopher set up. If that's the case, you'll have to connect to Gopher via Telnet. (Don't worry, it's not as bad as it sounds.)

Here are a couple of sites to try:

consultant.micro.umn.edu   The University of Minnesota (the same site as in the preceding figure).

infoslug.ucsc.edu   The University of California/Santa Cruz.

To use them, just type **telnet** and the address at the UNIX prompt. For example:

telnet consultant.micro.umn.edu

If asked for a login, type **gopher**.

Each Gopher menu you encounter will look a little different, because they're all set up by different people. However, there is one menu item you will see on most every top level Gopher menu:

```
8.   Other Gopher and Information Servers/
```

This is one of the choices that will take you out into the world, hurtling through gopherspace. Perhaps you want to check out offerings at the University of Nebraska in Lincoln. (Okay, maybe not, but if you did, this would be your best way of getting there.) Perhaps Oxford University in the U.K. is more your cup of tea (no pun intended, all you tea-drinking English types). Either way—or any way—you choose to go, you can swing from continent to continent, country to country by making a menu selection.

How to make the menu selection? Simple enough. Use the arrow keys to move the arrow down to the item you want, and then press **Enter**. Easier still, just type the number of the item you want and press **Enter**. Gopher will then get to work.

Once a connection is underway, you'll notice the message connecting in the lower right corner of your screen and then the message retrieving directory. These let you know that Gopher is working for you, tunneling through the wires of cyberspace at your command. Once the directory (the list of what's there) is retrieved, you'll get a new menu with new choices.

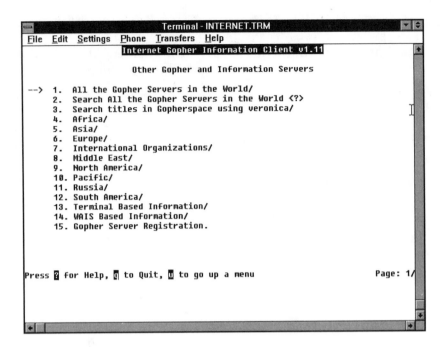

```
 ⎓                  Terminal - INTERNET.TRM               ⏷ ⮝
 File  Edit  Settings  Phone  Transfers  Help              ⮝
 ┌─────────────────────────────────────────────────────┐
 │      Internet Gopher Information Client v1.11         │
 │                                                       │
 │         Other Gopher and Information Servers          │
 │                                                       │
 │  --> 1.  All the Gopher Servers in the World/         │
 │      2.  Search All the Gopher Servers in the World <?>│
 │      3.  Search titles in Gopherspace using veronica/  │
 │      4.  Africa/                                      │
 │      5.  Asia/                                        │
 │      6.  Europe/                                      │
 │      7.  International Organizations/                 │
 │      8.  Middle East/                                 │
 │      9.  North America/                               │
 │      10. Pacific/                                     │
 │      11. Russia/                                      │
 │      12. South America/                               │
 │      13. Terminal Based Information/                  │
 │      14. WAIS Based Information/                      │
 │      15. Gopher Server Registration.                 │
 │                                                       │
 │                                                       │
 │                                                       │
 │ Press ? for Help, q to Quit, u to go up a menu   Page: 1/│
 │                                                       ⮟│
 └─────────────────────────────────────────────────────┘
 ⬅                                                      ➡
```

Most Gopher systems will have an Other Gopher and Information
Servers listing.

Exploring Geographically

Most of the menus are set up hierarchically, from general to specific. With
each menu selection you make, you narrow down what you want to see. For
instance, if we wanted to check out employment opportunities at the University of Hawaii, we would move through the following menus: **North
America, USA, Hawaii**, and finally **University of Hawaii**. Once there, we'd
see this menu:

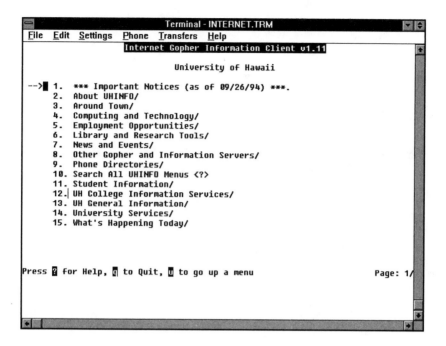

University of Hawaii—Surf's up, dude.

Then we'd select

    5. Employment Opportunities/

which would give us a listing of jobs related to the University of Hawaii. If you have the stomach for beautiful sand beaches and delicious sky, this site may be your ticket to an island paradise upon graduation. If not, there are similar listings at many other sites; I'm sure you can find one to fit your needs and temperament.

Exploring by Subject

It's just as easy to wade through Gopher by subject. There is a wonderful index called **Gopher-Jewels** that'll give you a menu organized into subject areas to work with. Lots of different sites have Gopher-Jewels on their menus—it may even be on your school's home Gopher menu. If not, you can get there with the following path:

```
Other Gopher and Information Servers
North America
USA
California
University of Southern California - USCgopher
Other Gophers and Information Resources/
```

You will then see this menu:

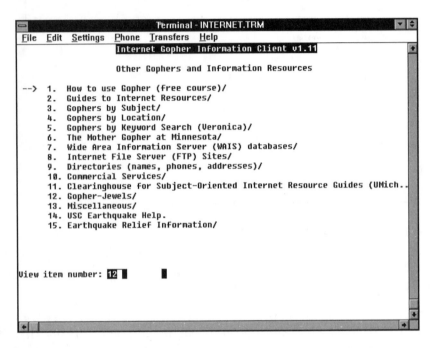

The USC menu of Other Gophers and Information Resources. Notice that Gopher-Jewels/ is option number 12.

> **Tip ➤** Gopher-Jewels is #12 on the menu (at least it was when I wrote this), but don't rush right there. Take a look at some of the other choices USC has to offer. There's a wealth of resources here. If you have the time, stop and browse a bit. Choose a few menu items, and see where they take you. I've found many of my favorite sites on the Net by mistake.

Ready to go on? Okay, let's go. Selecting the Gopher-Jewels menu item will give you this:

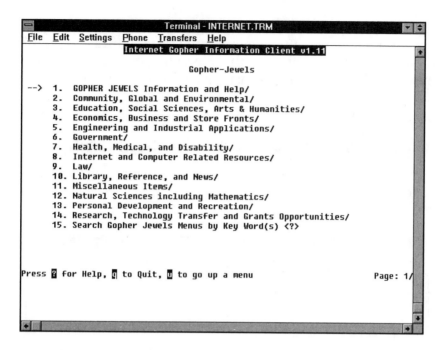

Gopher-Jewels, a treasure chest (sorry about the pun) of information.

Where you go from here is up to you; it's not called Gopher-Jewels for nothing. A few leisurely hours spent tunneling through gopherspace will bring you more information than you can digest in a lifetime. So dive into something that looks interesting to you and start hitting keys.

More Help Getting Around

Here are a few more commands you can use to navigate Gopher:

Command	Effect
-	Go up a page within the same Gopher menu.
space	Go down a page within the same Gopher menu.
u	Go to the previous Gopher menu.
q	Quit Gopher.
m (main)	Go back to the original Gopher menu you started from.

Using these commands, it's virtually impossible to get lost in Gopher. You can browse through menu after menu from Alaska to Africa and on to Costa Rica—it doesn't matter. Typing **m** will always take you home. Now don't you wish that it had been that easy navigating around campus your first week there?

What to Do When You've Found Something Good

You've waded through a dozen different Gopher menus; you've been pushing buttons for an hour and finally you've found it: the recipe your mom used for chewy chocolate chip cookies.

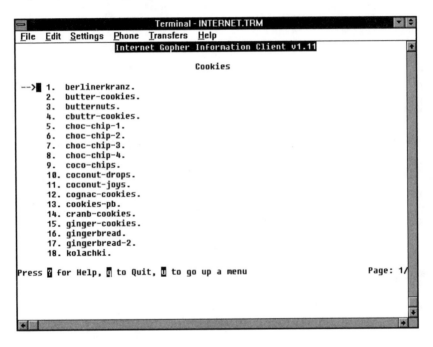

Cookies just like mom used to make (well, somebody's mom).

> **Tip ➤**
>
> Here's the path for those cookies, just in case you want to make them yourself:
>
> ```
> Other Gopher and Information Servers
> North America
> USA
> Minnesota
> University of Minnesota
> Fun and Games
> Recipes
> Desserts
> Cookies
> ```
>
> You'll find lots of other good stuff along the way.

Setting Bookmarks

Thanksgiving is still two months away, and the cookies that have spent a week in the care of the United States Postal Service just aren't the same. Don't start salivating all over your keyboard just yet however; let's take a minute and set a bookmark for it so you can always come back whenever you want.

To set a bookmark, type **a** when you have your selection made (when you've moved the arrow to the menu item or typed its number), but *before* you hit **Enter**. You'll see something like the following figure:

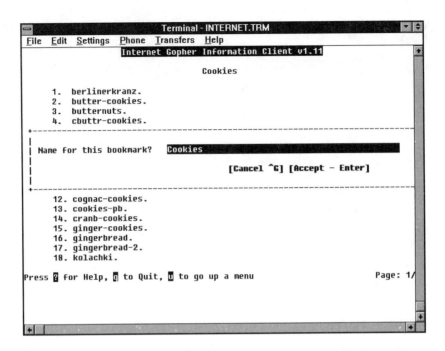

Making an (inedible) cookie bookmark.

If the name that shows up is okay for the name of the bookmark, press **Enter** and your bookmark is set. If you prefer to name it something else, such as **mom's best**, type it before you press **Enter**. Then, next time you want to see that recipe (or whatever else you've put on your bookmark list), type **v** at any time from within Gopher. This will bring up your own customized Gopher bookmark menu.

Mailing Text Documents to Yourself

Another option for hanging onto this jewel is to mail a copy of it back to yourself. The file would then show up in your inbox the next time you checked your e-mail. You can even mail the copy to someone else—like maybe your Aunt Ruth (if she's on the Net), whose cookies never were worth a darn. Here's how it works:

1. Bring up the document you want to mail to yourself (or to anyone else) onto the screen.

2. Move to the end of the document by hitting the **Spacebar** to go down page by page, or type **q** as if you wanted to quit (which I did in the next example).

3. You'll then see the message at the bottom of the screen.

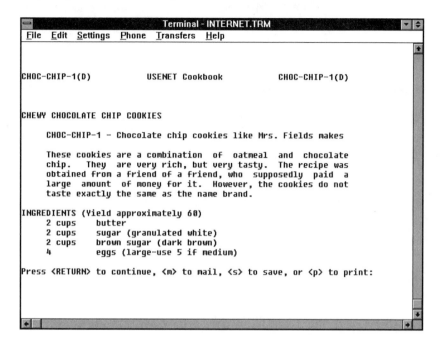

```
┌──────────────────────────────────────────────────────────────────────┐
│ ─         Terminal - INTERNET.TRM                              ▼ ╪│
├──────────────────────────────────────────────────────────────────────┤
│ File  Edit  Settings  Phone  Transfers  Help                         │
├──────────────────────────────────────────────────────────────────────┤
│CHOC-CHIP-1(D)            USENET Cookbook          CHOC-CHIP-1(D)      │
│                                                                      │
│                                                                      │
│CHEWY CHOCOLATE CHIP COOKIES                                          │
│                                                                      │
│     CHOC-CHIP-1 - Chocolate chip cookies like Mrs. Fields makes     │
│                                                                      │
│     These cookies are a combination  of  oatmeal  and  chocolate    │
│     chip.   They  are very rich, but very tasty.  The recipe was    │
│     obtained from a friend of a friend, who  supposedly  paid  a    │
│     large  amount  of money for it.  However, the cookies do not    │
│     taste exactly the same as the name brand.                       │
│INGREDIENTS (Yield approximately 60)                                 │
│     2 cups     butter                                               │
│     2 cups     sugar (granulated white)                             │
│     2 cups     brown sugar (dark brown)                             │
│     4          eggs (large-use 5 if medium)                         │
│Press <RETURN> to continue, <m> to mail, <s> to save, or <p> to print:│
│                                                                      │
└──────────────────────────────────────────────────────────────────────┘
```

A recipe that you probably will not be able to make in your dorm microwave.

Typing **m** at this point will bring up a window where you can type in your e-mail address and mail the thing.

Saving Documents to a Local File

If you just want a copy of the recipe on disk, mailing it to yourself is the long way around. You can just save the recipe directly with the **s** command. Type **s** and the file will be dumped into a file in your UNIX directory (remember your UNIX directory from Chapter 3?). You can then use the **more** command from your UNIX prompt to view it.

Notice that there is also an option to print. Sounds simple enough—if only it were that easy. With the proper setup, the print command probably works for someone, somewhere, but there are a lot of variables involved, any of which can prevent the printing from happening. What the heck; give it a try—it can't hurt. We're nothing if not brave explorers on the Net, willing to take a chance now and then. Just don't get your hopes up too high on this one.

If you really need a hard copy, sending the file to yourself through e-mail is the way to go; then you can print the message the same way that you print normal e-mail. (Look back to Chapter 4 where I talked about printing e-mail off the screen.)

Downloading with Gopher

It's possible to download software, graphics, and other binary files from all over the world using Gopher. When it works, it's pretty slick. (Notice the veiled warning there—it doesn't always work very well, for a variety of reasons.)

Let's try it and gopher over to the Merit Software Archives in Michigan. To get there, I followed this path:

```
other gopher and information servers/
North America
USA
Michigan
Merit Software Archives
```

You'll be greeted with this menu:

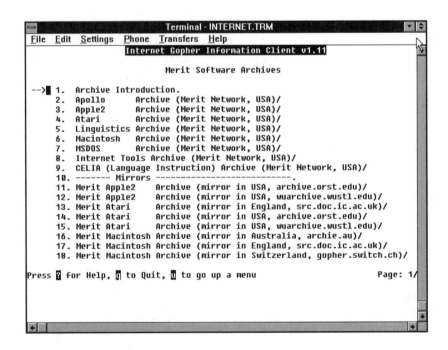

The Merit Software Archives—Mind-boggling, isn't it?

As you can see, there's quite an offering for just about anyone looking for software for any operating system. I selected **msdos** as my first choice, then **communications**, and finally **telix** to take me to the following:

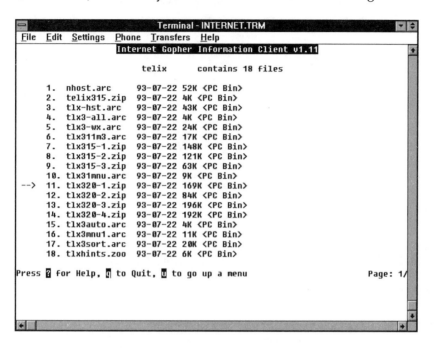

You can download the Telix communications package for DOS from here.

Tip ➤ If you aren't particularly happy with the program you're using to dial up, you may want to give Telix a try.

To download Telix, I have two paths I can take. Option number one is to type **D**. By doing so, I will see the following dialog box that asks me to pick a protocol:

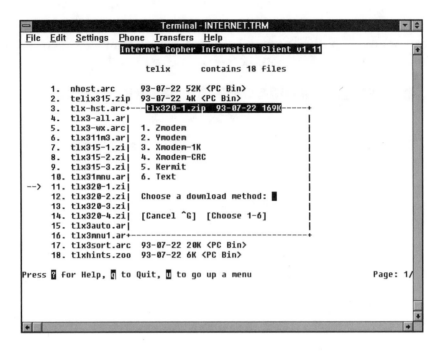

```
 □                  Terminal - INTERNET.TRM                      ▼ ▲
 File  Edit  Settings  Phone  Transfers  Help
              Internet Gopher Information Client v1.11                 ▲

                  telix      contains 18 files

       1.  nhost.arc      93-07-22 52K <PC Bin>
       2.  telix315.zip   93-07-22 4K <PC Bin>
       3.  tlx-hst.arc+---[tlx320-1.zip  93-07-22 169K]-----+
       4.  tlx3-all.ar|                                     |
       5.  tlx3-wx.arc|  1. Zmodem                          |
       6.  tlx311m3.ar|  2. Ymodem                          |
       7.  tlx315-1.zi|  3. Xmodem-1K                       |
       8.  tlx315-2.zi|  4. Xmodem-CRC                      |
       9.  tlx315-3.zi|  5. Kermit                          |
      10.  tlx31mnu.ar|  6. Text                            |
  -->  11.  tlx320-1.zi|                                    |
      12.  tlx320-2.zi|  Choose a download method: █        |
      13.  tlx320-3.zi|                                     |
      14.  tlx320-4.zi|  [Cancel ^G]  [Choose 1-6]          |
      15.  tlx3auto.ar|                                     |
      16.  tlx3mnu1.ar+-------------------------------------+
      17.  tlx3sort.arc  93-07-22 20K <PC Bin>
      18.  tlxhints.zoo  93-07-22 6K <PC Bin>

 Press ? For Help, Q to Quit, U to go up a menu          Page: 1/
                                                                      ▼
 ◄ ▌                                                              ►
```

Pick a protocol, any protocol. Zmodem is best, if your software can support it.

I select the downloading protocol that my communications software supports and the file is transferred directly to my hard drive—that is, if the phone lines aren't too noisy and if my computer isn't having a bad hair day, and so on. Just as with printing from Gopher, there are a lot of variables, and the word on the Internet is that file transfer with Gopher is flaky at best. But hey, it's a step in the right direction and gives us hope for the future.

The second option is a bit more complicated, but for the strong of heart, it'll prove a bit more reliable. Here goes. Use the arrow keys to move the arrow to the program you want to download, and then press **Enter**. You'll see the following dialog box, asking for a filename.

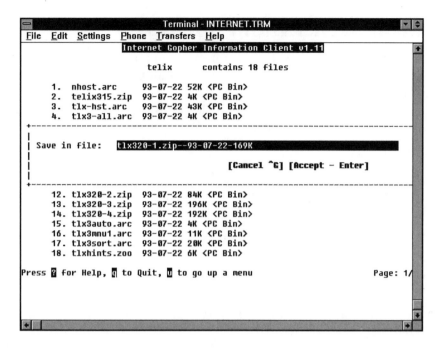

This name is ridiculously long; you'll want to shorten it to something you have a reasonable chance of typing correctly.

You can accept the filename, or specify a different one. I recommend shortening the filename a bit. This file will be transferred into your UNIX directory, and long filenames can be a bit of a pain to work with. Just press the **Delete** key and get rid of some of the garbage. I would shorten this file to:

```
tlx123.zip
```

When you have the name as you want it, press **Enter**, and the file will be moved to your UNIX directory. However, you can't use it yet; you still have to get it from your UNIX directory to your desktop machine. I'm going to keep you in suspense about that little trick until Chapter 8, so stay tuned.

Searching Gopher with Veronica

You can spend many hours sifting through menu after menu in Gopher looking for what you want with no success. It's all well and good to go a gophering with no particular goal in mind, but when your midterm take-home is due and you've waited until the last minute, you need information and you need it quick.

Enter Veronica.

Veronica is a utility that searches gopherspace. It's straightforward, easy to use, and extremely over-utilized (and therefore agonizingly slow to use). You can access Veronica by selecting

    Other Gopher and Information servers/

then

    Search titles in Gopherspace using veronica/

On the menu that appears, you'll see Veronica listed. In fact, you will see several Veronica servers listed.

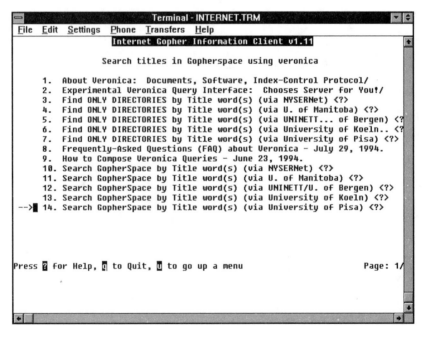

Notice that there are *several Veronica servers you can use and several ways you can use each one. Talk about flexibility.*

As you can see, you have many options to choose from. The choices that read **Find ONLY DIRECTORIES by Title word(s)** will lead you on a search for top level directories only. This can be a good selection if you're doing a search on a general subject and you don't want to be inundated with information. Your other option is to make a selection from one of the items that reads: **Search GopherSpace by Title word(s)**. This will give you a much broader search and, in many cases, give you more information than you ever could use, depending on your search.

So which Veronica server do you choose first? Here's my thinking: It's always best to choose the server nearest to you geographically. This is done as a matter of courtesy since a closer connection will utilize fewer computing resources. You'll commonly (often, frequently, repeatedly) end up looking at this message:

```
1.   *** Too many connections - Try again soon. ***.
```

Too busy in Dallas (my closest server). My next line of reasoning is this: If the closest doesn't work (you tried to do the right thing), go for the one farthest away. Dallas is busy because it is the middle of the day in Texas. People are at work and doing whatever they need to get their job done and many are using Veronica. However the good folks in Pisa are enjoying their sleep and that server may be a little quieter. Try there next. Be patient; it may take awhile before you are able to connect. (Of course, all of this assumes that you are a day trekker. If 2:00 a.m. is more your cup of tea, reverse the logic above.)

Let's look at a Veronica search. We'll select

```
17. Search GopherSpace by Title word(s) (via University of Pisa) <?>
```

The <?> at the end of the line lets us know that we're dealing with a searchable index. The box that appears is where we type our search request. The simplest type of request is a single word. Let's do a search for Shakespeare to give us a hand on the essay due for ENG 450 tomorrow. We type in Shakespeare like so:

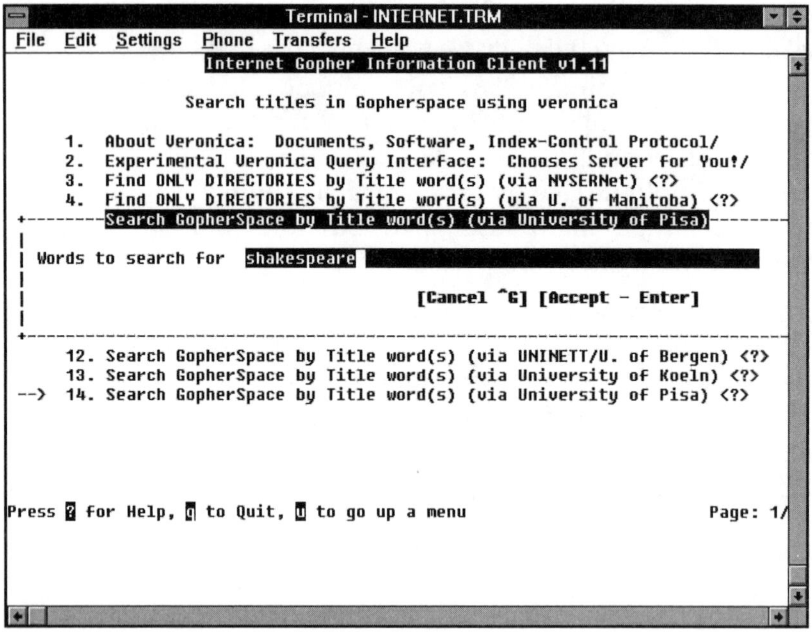
Terminal - INTERNET.TRM
File Edit Settings Phone Transfers Help
Internet Gopher Information Client v1.11
Search titles in Gopherspace using veronica
1. About Veronica: Documents, Software, Index-Control Protocol/
2. Experimental Veronica Query Interface: Chooses Server for You!/
3. Find ONLY DIRECTORIES by Title word(s) (via NYSERNet) <?>
4. Find ONLY DIRECTORIES by Title word(s) (via U. of Manitoba) <?>
Search GopherSpace by Title word(s) (via University of Pisa)
Words to search for shakespeare
[Cancel ^G] [Accept - Enter]
12. Search GopherSpace by Title word(s) (via UNINETT/U. of Bergen) <?>
13. Search GopherSpace by Title word(s) (via University of Koeln) <?>
--> 14. Search GopherSpace by Title word(s) (via University of Pisa) <?>
Press ? for Help, q to Quit, u to go up a menu
Page: 1/

Searching for Shakespeare in Pisa.

My search returned 418 references to Shakespeare. Among those files were:

- A complete text of all Shakespeare's work.
- Image files of the bard.
- A listing of the bill from the Wisconsin Shakespeare festival.
- A Trekkers guide to Shakespeare which contains a listing of all references to Shakespeare found in Star Trek movies, TV, and books.

All of these selections are in the familiar Gopher menu format and it's just a matter of choosing where you want to go, applying slight pressure on the **Enter** key, and you're there. Surely you can find *something* in all of this to help you with your report. But don't wait until the last minute next time, okay?

Gophering Via a Direct Connection

There are several wonderful Gopher software packages that you will encounter in a lab with a dedicated connection, or that you can acquire for use through your own SLIP or PPP connection. A couple of these are

Turbo-Gopher and PC-Gopher. When you're using these, Gopher works basically the same way, but there are some special advantages. What special advantages? Well, it'll depend on which software you're using, but you may have:

■ Capability to view image files immediately via a slave application.

■ Capability to send text documents directly to your printer.

■ Point-and-click interfaces.

■ Easier and smoother transfer of binary files.

It doesn't get any easier than that.

 Tip ➤ A slave application is a separate piece of software on your hard drive that works in cahoots with your Gopher software. Gopher can call on this software, if needed, to do nifty things like display graphics.

Here's a shot of what you'll see when you fire up one of these babies:

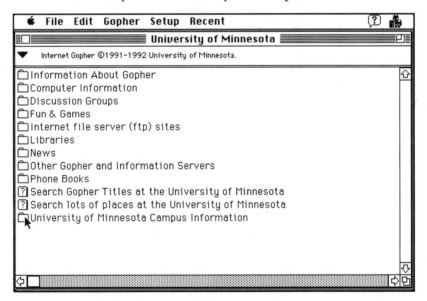

Point-and-click your way through gopherspace with TurboGopher over a dedicated connection.

Great Ideas for Gopher

Want some ideas for cool sites to check out with Gopher? Well, you've come to the right place.

I'm about to give you a bunch of site names. To access them from your UNIX prompt, just type **gopher** and then the address. If "gopher" is part of the site name, you still have to type **gopher** at the beginning of the name anyway. It might look something like this:

> **gopher gopher.well.sf.ca.us**

If you have a burning desire to discover the real path to any of these addresses, you're going to have to become adroit at taking apart Internet addresses. For example, gopher.well.sf.ca.us is an easy one. (Really!)

us is so easy, I'm not even going to print it. For ca, think states, and for sf, a city maybe? (san fr***co, do some thinking on your own here, come on.) Go geographically to that area of the world, and I bet you a nickel the well can be found there.

For sites ending in .gov or .com, you'll have to hunt for governmental agencies or commercial entities in some of the subject-oriented Gopher menus. However, why bother, unless you enjoy this sort of thing. (I know I do.) Ready? Gopher it. (Sorry.)

- Check out the weather in Ft. Lauderdale to know what to wear for Spring break or discover snow conditions in Vail. Gopher over to:

  weather.Colorado.edu

- Browse the ASCII art exhibit at

  twinbrook.cis.uab.edu

  to get ideas for your signature file (turn back to Chapter 4 if you've forgotten what that is).

- Download digital art from

  alt.et.tudelft.nl 1251

Tip ➤ The number you see following some Gopher addresses is the port number on that particular machine. Some require that you include the port number, most don't. Rule of thumb: If it's included in the address when you find it, use it. If not, don't worry about it.

▪ Prepare for your afterlife (after college, that is) by gophering to

gopher.msen.com 9062

This address will take you to the Career Center Online Gopher.

▪ To find out how your legislator voted on key issues relating to the environment, gopher to

gopher.igc.apc.org.

▪ Learn how to "Mutate and Take Over the World" (among other things) at the WELL Gopher. Hop over to

gopher.well.sf.ca.us

▪ Take a study break at the Electronic Newsstand. Gopher to

cns.cscns.com.

or

usa.net

and browse through such journals as *Field and Stream*, *Guitar Player*, and *Growing Edge*. Something there for everyone.

▪ Read the latest news releases from NASA and find out what's going on above your head. Gopher to

spacelink.msfc.nasa.gov

▪ Curl up with your computer before the fire and read from *Moby Dick*, *Aesop's Fables*, *The Legend of Sleepy Hollow* and others, by gophering to the Gutenberg Project site at

spinaltap.micro.umn.edu

▪ Read reviews from *Star Trek: Deep Space Nine*. Gopher to

chop.isca.uiowa.edu

and look under General Information/.

▪ To decide which movie to see tonight, gopher to

spinaltap.micro.umn.edu

Look in the **fun/movies/** directories for a searchable index of recent movie reviews.

■ Read reviews of your favorite computer games at the Games Pavilion in Xanadu, Australia. Gopher to

www.glasswings.com.au

■ Heading out of town soon? Don't go clueless; get some travel information. Gopher to

cwis.usc.edu

and follow the Gopher-Jewels menus `Recreation/Travel`.

■ Find out how you can do something good for the planet. Gopher to

gopher.greenpeace.org

Check out their World Wide Job vacancies; maybe there's something there for you.

The World Wide Web

You may not know it yet, but *this is the chapter you've been waiting for.* The World Wide Web has done for the Internet what Marcel Marceau did for mime, what Orville and Wilbur did for the airline industry, what Woodstock '94 did for mud wrestling... well, you get the idea. The Internet existed for years before the Web, but since the Web has caught on, the Internet has grown exponentially. Why? Well, mostly because the Web makes the Internet friendly and fairly simple to access.

Through the World Wide Web, you can do almost everything you've learned in other chapters so far. (The notable exception is sending and receiving e-mail, which still requires a separate utility.) Using a WWW browser, you can:

- Download files easier than with FTP.
- Access Gopher sites.
- Read newsgroups.
- Do keyword searches easier than with Archie...
- ...and more.

Interested? I thought you would be.

So, What Is the Web?

The World Wide Web (a.k.a. WWW, or "the Web") has a totally different organizational structure than anything else on the Internet. (It just figures, doesn't it?) It presents itself as a page of text with hyperlinks you can select to take you to resources on the Internet—good stuff, such as photos and other graphics, weather satellite images, sounds, music clips, and full-motion video.

Here's a basic Web page:

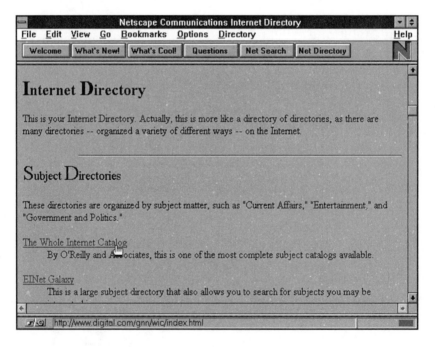

The World Wide Web takes you out into the Net the easy way.

The highlighted/underlined words are links. For example, if I were to click on **The Whole Internet Catalog**, Netscape would spirit me off to that site where I would find more options to explore. Clicking there brings up this:

Chapter 7

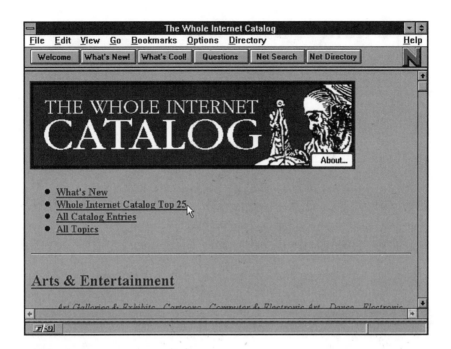

Links to more links.

Obviously, this is the coolest way to travel the Internet, and after using WWW for awhile, most people come to regard every other Internet tool as second-rate.

So why would anybody use anything else? Why waste your time reading chapters on FTP, Gopher, and so on? Well, as with any great idea, there are still a few details to work out. To make full use of the Web, you need a pretty good connection (dedicated or direct dial-up) and a fairly decent computer. Not everybody has that, not yet. Computer labs all around the nation are still filled with (can you believe it?) 286s, Mac pluses, and other such pieces of junk, er, I mean hardware. When you take a gander at what people have on their desks at home, the situation is even more dismal.

Don't despair and don't stop reading if you have a less than optimal system on your desk. There are other options for retrieving the information available over the Web, and we'll get to those soon.

What You Need to Use WWW

Technically speaking, you can use WWW with any Internet connection. All you need is a Web browser program to work with. There are simple, no-frills Web browser programs for every type of computer. For example, Lynx and SlipKnot work even with a dial-up terminal connection. You'll learn about them later in this chapter.

But—and it's a big ol' but—be prepared. You may not like the Web very much if you have to suffer through a terminal account and a slow modem connection. To cruise the Web at a decent velocity and snag all the sounds and pictures that make it worthwhile, you need a fast, direct connection. A SLIP or PPP dial-up direct connection will do, but a dedicated connection is better. (Now may be a good time to check out your school's computer lab, if it has one.) You also need graphics-based browser software, like Mosaic Netscape (or Cello, or Mac Web, or any of the other popular ones).

> **Tip ➤** Don't forget TIA, the utility you learned about in Chapter 2 that will trick your dial-up terminal connection into thinking that it's a dial-up direct connection, thereby enabling you to use all the cool software you crave, like Netscape.

Later in this chapter, I'll show you how to get around in several different browsers (including Lynx, SlipKnot, and Netscape), so no matter what your situation is, you're covered.

A Word About Web Addresses...

If you thought regular Internet addressing was confusing, wait until you get a look at a Web address.

> **Tip ➤** The good news is that it's not always necessary to know the exact address of a site; more often than not, you'll get to a site by going through a hyperlink, where the address is already typed for you. Even so, there will be times when you'll want to enter the address of a Web site directly.

Web addresses are known as URLs. (That's pronounced "U-R-L," not "url" as in "hurl.") URL stands for Uniform Resource Locator, a fancy phrase designed to scare the hell out of new users. It looks something like this:

```
http://magpie-bvsd.beatman.net/~clarkd/Home.html
```

Wait. Don't run screaming yet. I can explain. The `http` at the beginning tells you that you are connecting to a World Wide Web home page.

Tip ➤ It is also possible to connect up with Gopher and FTP servers via WWW browsing software. You'd just replace the `http://` with `ftp://` or `gopher://`, as in:

```
ftp://bvsd.k12.co.us
gopher://bvsd.k12.co.us
```

---

http stands for Hypertext Transfer Protocol. It's the protocol for connecting to World Wide Web pages on the Net. The `://` may look like computer garbage and you may certainly consider it that if you want—just don't leave it out! The next part is the name of the machine where the page is housed. In this case, `magpie-bvsd.beatman.net`. `/~clarkd` tells the WWW browser to look in that directory for a document entitled `Home.html`.

It sort of makes sense if you think about it long enough. Web addresses can be very, very long if the page is nested deep in directory after directory. It's not uncommon to see a URL that never seems to end when you're typing it out for those times when you need to connect directly.

Wandering onto the Web

Okay, it's time to take a look at the Web. So as to not be anticlimactic, we'll look at the various ways of accessing WWW from plainest (Lynx) to prettiest (Netscape).

Lynx—The Terminal Alternative

Lynx is a UNIX text-based browser for the Web. Since it's a UNIX program, you run it from your school's UNIX computer, not from your own PC. (If it's not installed on your school's computer, beg someone to install it.) Type **lynx** at your UNIX prompt to get started.

Tip ➤

If you know the exact address you want to connect to, you can type it at the same time you type lynx, as in:
lynx http://bvsd.k12.co.us.

If you don't specify the address you want to connect to, you'll connect to whatever address your school has set up as its home page. It'll look different from the examples below, but the basic setup will remain constant.

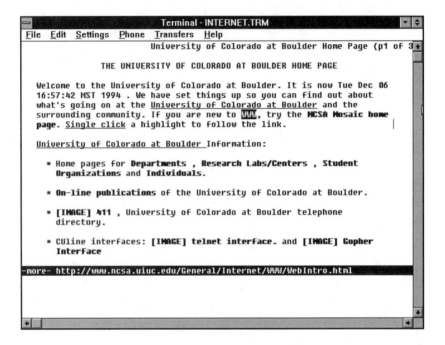

University of Colorado at Boulder Home Page, through Lynx.

The words in bold represent links to other sites. I can move between these words by using the arrow keys on my keyboard. If there is a site I want to explore, I select it and hit **Enter**. For example, if I wanted to check out the online publications at CU, I would tap my down arrow key to highlight that link, then press **Enter**, and the following would fill my screen:

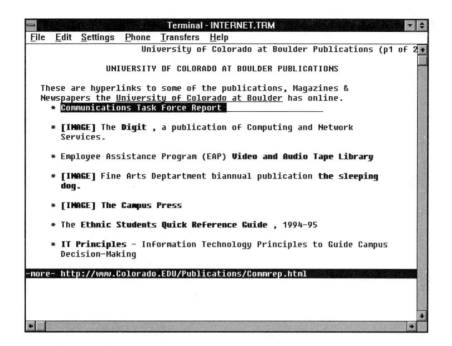

Lynx strikes again: publications at the University of Colorado.

This is only a listing of what's available—there's no real information yet. So let's continue. If I want to see what's happening with the computing services department, I could select the Digit link. I would then see another page with links to articles. Selecting one of those would bring up the article and all of the wisdom contained therein. Basically, you just keep selecting links until you find what you're looking for.

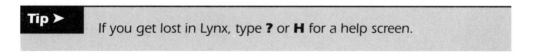

Tip ➤ If you get lost in Lynx, type **?** or **H** for a help screen.

Ready to go off to a specific location? You remember the addressing stuff we talked about earlier; well, it's time to put it to use. If you have the address of a site you want to check out, retrieve it now. If not, use **http:// www.mcp.com**, home of Macmillan Computer Publishing and a great site to browse.

Type **g** to tell Lynx that you want to go to a specific site. You'll see this at the bottom of your screen:

```
URL to open:
```

Fill in the address of a site:

```
URL to open: http://www.mcp.com
```

and you will connect with that site.

> **Tip ➤** If you ever get lost, you can type **m** to start over at the beginning. However, I find most of my best sites when I'm lost, so don't be too eager to hit that **m** key.

Find something you want to save? Type **p** for Print. (Yes, I realize printing and saving aren't the same thing, but Lynx considers them similar.) You'll get these choices:

```
Save to a local file
Mail the file to yourself
Print to the screen
Specify your own print command
```

Treat these commands as you would any other WWW link. Use the arrow keys to select one, and then press **Enter**. For instance, selecting the Mail link will bring up a prompt for an e-mail address. Fill in your own, and the file will be in your mailbox the next time you open it.

Another way to save yourself if you get lost is to use the **Backspace** key. Pressing it brings up your session history—that is, a list of all the places you've been since you started Lynx. You can go back to any of them from there.

If you're in the middle of retrieving a page and it's taking forever, you can press **z** to tell Lynx to give up and forget it. This is especially useful when you're retrieving something obscene and your roommate's mother comes in.

If you find a site that you want to return to (like maybe when your roommate's mother leaves), you can create a link to it in your bookmark file. Bookmark files are just lists of addresses of all the cool places you've found. Just type **a** to add the currently displayed site to your bookmark list. You'll see this:

```
Save D)ocument or L)ink to bookmark file or C)ancel? (d,l,c):
```

Type **l** to create a bookmark. Then later, when you want to view your bookmarks, type **v** (of course, you have to be in Lynx). Your bookmarks will pop up as selectable links. Select one of them and press **Enter** for an instant connection. It's like having your own customized menu for navigating the Web. Last but not least, you can type **q** at any time to quit.

Images, Sounds, and Other Things Lynx Doesn't Support

Notice that on some of the pages there are references to images, like so:

```
* [IMAGE] The Digit , a publication of Computing and Network Services.
```

The [IMAGE] reference means that there's a graphic included as part of this page, which would be automatically displayed if you were using a fancier browser program that supported graphics. (Lynx doesn't.) You could interpret this as a cruel reminder that you don't have the right kind of connection—or you could see it for what it really is—just another link.

Depending on how the graphic is placed in the document, you may still be able to view it, but there are a couple of steps involved. It's probably not worth the trouble (most graphics on WWW pages are incidental), but if you're determined to try, follow these steps:

1. Select the image as you would any link.

2. Press **Enter**. You'll see a message like this:

```
This file cannot be displayed on this terminal:  D)ownload, or C)ancel
```

(Rub our noses in it, why don't you.)

3. Press **D** to bring the document down into your UNIX directory.

4. Download the file as described in Chapter 8.

5. View it using a graphics viewing program on your hard drive.

To repeat, unless you know that this graphic is something you really want, or unless you're in a graphics archive and you're looking for something specific, you shouldn't bother with getting the graphic. There are a lot of graphics worth bringing down to your hard drive, but the ones on these upper-level WWW pages are there mostly for show. Then again, you may want to try it once or twice just to let the computer know who calls the shots around here. It may make you feel better, or it may not.

By the way, images aren't the only thing you can download using Lynx. Video and sound clips are available as well. You can pull these down in the same way as images. You'll need to have the viewing or sound software installed on your hard drive to take advantage of them once they are transferred.

MultiMedia Formats on the Net and What You Need to View or Play Them

Pulling down these wonders does you no good at all if you don't have the software on your hard drive to open them. Here's the scoop on the file types and the software you'll need. All of these are shareware and are available on the Net. Check the Appendix in the back of the book for the appropriate addresses.

File Extension	Type of File	Software Needed
.jpeg/.jpg .gif/tga	Graphics	Lview(Windows) Jpeg View (Mac)
.au/.snd .voc/.wav	Sound	Wham (Windows) Sound Machine(Mac)
.mpeg	Video	MPEG Player 3.2(Windows) Sparkle(Mac)

SlipKnot—Graphics for Dial-Up Terminal Users

The best way to view the wealth of the World Wide Web is to use a dedicated connection, such as in a computer lab. Failing that, the next best way is by dialing up through a SLIP or PPP account. A SLIP connection will let you run the latest and greatest graphical WWW browsers, such as Mosaic Netscape, over your modem. Flip back to Chapter 2 for details.

Some schools may not offer SLIP accounts to students. If that's your situation, check out TIA (The Internet Adapter) covered in Chapter 2. It'll trick your regular dial-up terminal account into thinking that it's a SLIP account, although it can be a pain to set up. (For that matter, SLIP accounts in general are a pain to set up.)

What if you're stuck with a dial-up terminal account and you don't want to mess with TIA? There's one other place you can turn. Ladies and Gentlemen, let me introduce you to SlipKnot.

Tip ➤ Sorry Mac users, SlipKnot is for Windows only at this time, but keep your ears glued to the Internet rumor mill. I have no doubt that a Mac version of this or another product will be on the market before too long. There's too much money to be made for someone not to do it.

SlipKnot is shareware and is brought to us by the good people at MicroMind. It is available via Anonymous FTP at:

```
ftp://oak.oakland.edu/SimTel/win3/internet/slnot100.zip
```

or

```
ftp://ftp.netcom.com/pub/pbrooks/slipknot/slnot100.zip
```

It's easy to install, easy to configure, and does a decent job of bringing the WWW to the dial-up terminal user.

In order to use SlipKnot, Lynx or WWW (another text-based browser like Lynx) has to be installed on your school's computer. If typing **lynx** or **www** at your UNIX prompt does nothing for you, you're not going to be able to use SlipKnot unless you can convince someone at the computing center to install one of these programs on the server.

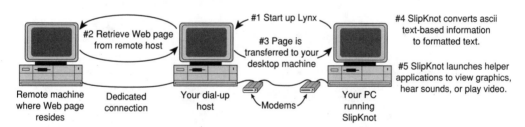

All this with a single click of the mouse.

But I digress. When you run the SlipKnot setup program, everything you need will be installed on your PC. It'll ask you to do a little bit of configuring, but much less than what you'd go through setting up a SLIP connection. Here's the config window:

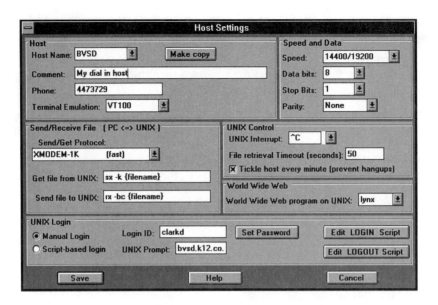

SlipKnot setup is a breeze compared to other programs, such as Trumpet Winsock.

Fill in the pertinent numbers and information, then select **Save** to return to the terminal screen. Click the Help button if you don't understand a text box.

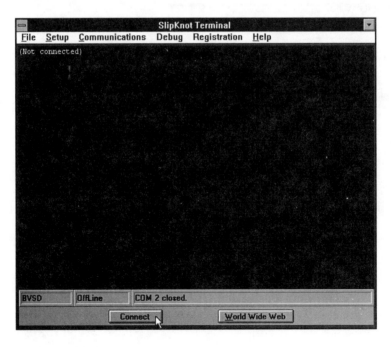

Back at the SlipKnot Terminal main screen, ready for action.

Although SlipKnot was created primarily as an interface to the World Wide Web, you can use its terminal program to do other things, too, such as getting into Pine to check your e-mail.

Ready to go? Good. Click on **Connect**. SlipKnot will connect you with your host. When you see your old familiar UNIX prompt on the screen, click on the **World Wide Web** button at the bottom of the screen.

Once inside Slipknot, it's time to connect to a site. Select **Get Document from the Internet** under the **Navigate Menu** from the main menu. Type the URL you want to connect to and hit **Enter**. Here is the same page we looked at earlier from the University of Colorado, only this time through the eyes of SlipKnot.

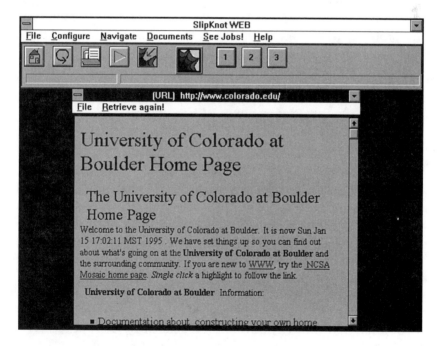

Love at first sight—finally, a graphical interface for dial-up users.

In SlipKnot, the links are highlighted and underlined, and you can click on one with your mouse to select it—no more fumbling with the arrow keys! Notice that graphics still are not displayed on the page. Displaying graphic objects is one trick that the makers of the program haven't quite figured out yet, but they've created an alternative. To view a pic, just click on its box.

SlipKnot will then download the file to your hard drive and launch a graphics viewing program to display the image in a different window. SlipKnot comes packaged with the graphics viewing software you need.

> **Tip ➤** Since the graphic files that SlipKnot views must be transferred to your hard drive, you need to make sure that you have room to store them as temporary files there. Once they're transferred, you can save them if you want, or dump them to free up room for new discoveries.

The downside to all of this wonder? SlipKnot has several limitations. The SlipKnot documentation lists the problems—these folks are very upfront about the things they need to work on. The primary limitation is that SlipKnot runs verrrrry slooooowly. If you've used only Lynx, which is also slow, you probably won't mind SlipKnot's speed, but if you're a Netscape junkie at the school lab and expect SlipKnot to measure up, forget it.

If it's quick text-based information you want, Lynx may be your best choice. However, if you aren't in a hurry, give SlipKnot a try and see for yourself what all the fuss is about over WWW graphics.

How About Netscape?

Netscape Navigator is the latest in the series of WWW browsers. You may have heard of Mosaic before; it was one of the first graphical WWW browsers. More than any other application, Mosaic brought the Web and the Internet to the attention of a lot of people. Finally, here was something that looked good. There have been several other viewers developed since Mosaic burst onto the scene, and Mosaic itself has evolved. Netscape is the latest in the series and my personal favorite. Netscape is actually a commercial product but is available for free for academic users. (In case you didn't realize it, that's you.) It comes in Mac and Windows flavors. Getting Netscape is easy—it's free. Just snag it via Anonymous FTP from:

```
ftp.mcom.com
```

Look in the netscape directory for a version to run on your operating system of choice. Turn ahead to Chapter 8 if you don't know how to FTP yet—it's fun.

Earlier in the chapter, I talked about system requirements, and if you'll recall, I said there weren't any, that you could use the Web with almost any connection. Well, that's true, but if you want to use the Web via Netscape, there are some definite minimum standards to meet:

IBM-compatible:

- An IBM-compatible computer, 386 or better
- At least 4MB of RAM
- At least 6MB of free space on your hard disk
- Windows 3.1 or higher
- VGA or Super VGA color monitor
- 9600 bps or faster modem (if you're not using a dedicated connection)

Macintosh:

- System 7.0 or higher
- At least 4MB of RAM
- At least 6MB of free space on your hard disk
- Color Mac, LC, or better
- 9600 bps or faster modem (if you're not using a dedicated connection)

Okay, technically you can use a 2400 bps modem, but you'll tear your hair out in frustration waiting for anything to happen. If your home computer doesn't measure up to these standards, find a lab on campus that has the necessary setup. This is one ride you don't want to miss.

Installing and Running Netscape

Netscape is easy to install once you have it sitting pretty on your hard drive. It is packaged as a self-extracting file, which means that all you have to do is run it. (ns16-100.exe is the name of the file to get.) The files will explode onto your hard drive. One of those files will be **set.up**. Run this program and Netscape will install itself into Windows.

The Mac version comes as a binhexed self-extracting file (netscape.sea.hqx). You will need to run StuffIt expander before you use it. (See the discussion of file compression in Chapter 8 for more information.) Once that is done, it's ready to fire up. If you're running SLIP/PPP or TIA, use your SLIP communications software (TCPMAN, Interslip, and so on) to dial into your host.

Once your connection is made, start up Netscape. The first site you'll visit when you fire up a freshly downloaded version of Netscape is the Netscape Home Page. Just start clicking away at the links, and you're off!

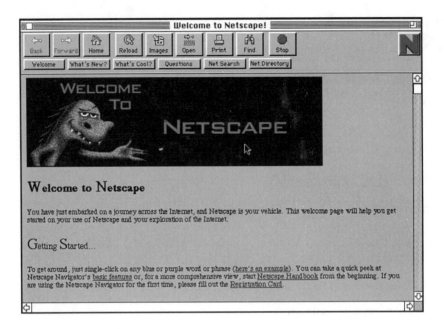

Netscape's Home Page, a jumping off place for Web surfers.

To go to a specific address (URL), click the **Open** button at the top of the window and type the address you want to go to. For example, go to the University of Colorado at **http://www.colorado.edu**.

The University of Colorado at Boulder Home Page.

> **Tip ➤**
>
> Ask around and see if your school has its own home page. Lots of schools have them, and they usually include references to useful stuff like campus telephone directories, employment opportunities, and more. Some departments even have their own pages.

Netscape Bookmarks, Newsgroups, and More

What about bookmarks, like in Lynx? Of course, a full-service program such as Netscape offers them. Just pull down the **Bookmarks** menu and select **Add Bookmark** to set one, or **View Bookmarks** to see what you have.

Want to get into Newsgroups? You can read all of your favorite newsgroups and post your own articles as well. Select **Go to Newsgroups** from the **Directory** menu.

> **Tip ➤**
>
> To be able to read newsgroups, you have to tell Netscape the name of your news server. (Get this from the system administrator if you're not sure what it is.) For the Windows version, select **Preferences** from the **Options** menu and select **Directories, Applications, and News** from the top drop-down list. Then fill in the name of the news server in the News (NNPT) Server text box.

Searching the Web with Netscape

You can wander around in the World Wide Web labyrinth for hours and find dozens of marvelous links. You can get lost easily and enjoy every minute of it. And you will, I know.

What about the times when leisurely browsing is not an option? When you have a deadline to meet and your professor is breathing down your neck, it then becomes time to search the Web. Fortunately, there are several great utilities to help you do this.

Netscape makes it very easy to search. See that button below the menu bar, the one that says Net Search? Yeah, that one right there. Click it. Go ahead, don't be shy.

Tip ➤

http://home.mcom.com/home/internet-search.html is the address to connect to if you're using a browser other than Netscape.

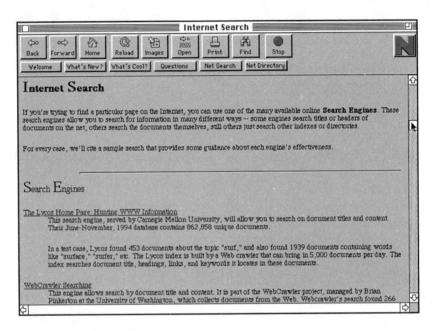

Several amazing search programs are waiting for your call.

Congratulations, you've just found a plethora of searching engines, each of them worth exploring. (Don't you just love the word plethora? I do.) All have the potential of bringing back page after page of hyperlinks on your topic. It's better than having your own research assistant! Let's look at a couple of them.

The World Wide Web Worm gives you search options of whether you want to search for documents or addresses. Click in the keywords box, and type the keyword(s) you want, then click on the **Start Search** button and let the Worm do its thing.

Chapter 7

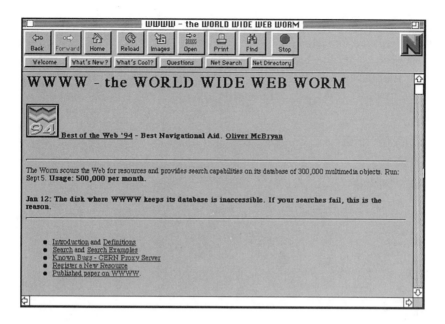

Give the Worm a try.

The WebCrawler works in a similar way. Type in the keywords, and then click on **Search**. Sit back and in a few minutes, you'll be inundated with a personalized page with links created just for you.

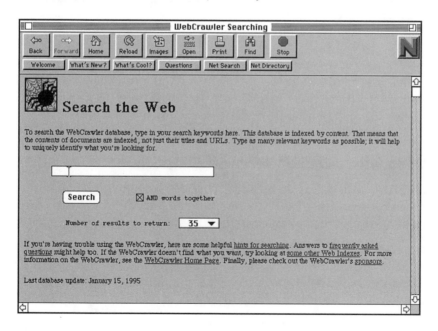

Crawl through the Web with me.

Let's do a search using the WebCrawler and see what comes back. After connecting to the Crawler, I type in my keyword; let's see what travel resources there are on the Net. (Thinking ahead here to spring break.) I will type in **travel** as my keyword. In less time than it takes for me to travel to the drinking fountain and back, the results are in.

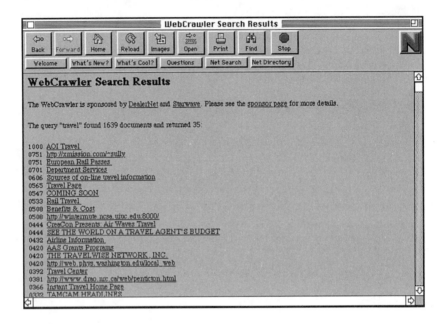

The WebCrawler Search Results window.

Each of these topics represents a link to a site containing travel information. I click on the one that looks promising and whoosh, I am there. Don't limit yourself to these two tools. Check out all of them on the page and discover which one gives you the most for your time.

Searching with a Dial-Up Terminal Connection

If you're stuck with a dial-up terminal account, you won't be able to use all of the searching utilities, even if you are using SlipKnot. You can reach what searchable indexes are available by heading to

http://www.ncsa.uiuc.edu/SDG/Software/Mosaic/MetaIndex.html

This address provides a lot more than searchable indexes; it also gives you access to Veronica, a subject listing of WWW resources, and more.

Tip ➤

If you want to connect directly to the WebCrawler or the Worm, here are the addresses to try:

World Wide Web Worm: **http//www.cs.colorado.edu/ home/mcbryan/WWWW.html**

WebCrawler: **http://webcrawler.cs.washington.edu/ WebCrawler/WebQuery.html**

Gopher and FTP on the Web

I mentioned this earlier when we were looking at Web addresses, but it's worth repeating. You can go to Gopher and FTP sites through a Web browser program just as easily as you can go to "real" Web pages. In fact, you may have used Gopher or FTP without even knowing it when you selected a link that took you to a Gopher or FTP site.

Let's say we're wanting to use FTP to pull down the latest version of Netscape. All we have to do is point our browser in the right direction.

In Netscape, pull down the **File** menu and select **Open Location**, or click on the **Open** button. In Lynx, type **g** and fill in the address at the prompt. Here's the address to use:

ftp://oak.oakland.edu/SimTel/win3

This will take us to the Windows directory at Oakland. The directories appear as folders; just click on them to navigate through them. If you've gone into this or other sites with a regular FTP connection, this is going to look somewhat familiar. With Lynx, use your arrow and Enter keys to select your directories as you would any other WWW site.

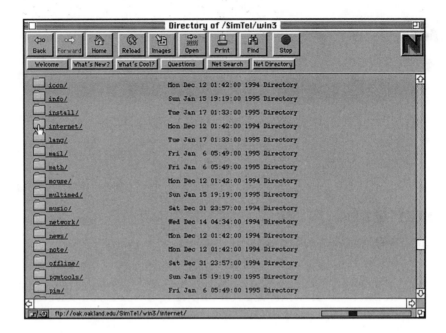

Back	Forward	Home	Reload	Images	Open	Print	Find	Stop

| Welcome | What's New? | What's Cool? | Questions | Net Search | Net Directory |

icon/	Mon Dec 12 01:42:00 1994 Directory
info/	Sun Jan 15 19:19:00 1995 Directory
install/	Tue Jan 17 01:33:00 1995 Directory
internet/	Mon Dec 12 01:42:00 1994 Directory
lang/	Tue Jan 17 01:33:00 1995 Directory
mail/	Fri Jan 6 05:49:00 1995 Directory
math/	Fri Jan 6 05:49:00 1995 Directory
mouse/	Mon Dec 12 01:42:00 1994 Directory
multimed/	Sun Jan 15 19:19:00 1995 Directory
music/	Sat Dec 31 23:57:00 1994 Directory
network/	Wed Dec 14 04:34:00 1994 Directory
news/	Mon Dec 12 01:42:00 1994 Directory
note/	Mon Dec 12 01:42:00 1994 Directory
offline/	Sat Dec 31 23:57:00 1994 Directory
pgmtools/	Sun Jan 15 19:19:00 1995 Directory
pim/	Fri Jan 6 05:49:00 1995 Directory

ftp://oak.oakland.edu/SimTel/win3/internet/

FTPing with Netscape.

If you're using Netscape, selecting a file will bring it down to your local hard drive. After selecting the file, hit **Enter**; Lynx will ask you to confirm the filename. Shorten it if you want, and hit **Enter** again. Lynx will drop it into your UNIX home directory, and you'll need to use your communications software to bring it down to your desktop machine. (Chapter 8 explains all the stuff you need to know about FTP.)

Gopher works just as easily. Fill in a Gopher address like this:

gopher://bvsd.k12.co.us

And you come to something like this:

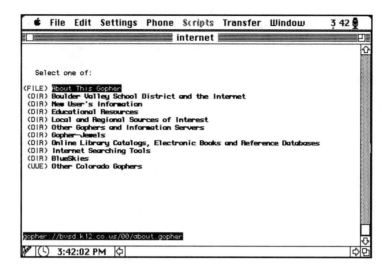

Gopher through the World Wide Web. Same information, different look.

Use Gopher the same way as you learned to in Chapter 6. Enjoy!

Creating Your Own WWW Home Page

After you've waded through a few dozen of the more bizarre and useless Web pages out there, you may come to the conclusion that any idiot can create a Web page. And you're right. It's easy, usually free, and it's a fun way to waste an afternoon. Plus, when you're done, you'll have a personal statement to make to the entire online community, or at least to any poor sucker who happens to stumble upon your page.

You can put any text you want on your Web page, plus links to graphics, sounds, video—whatever. You can also create links to your favorite other home pages, such as that remarkable Captain James T. Kirk Sing-Along Page at **http://www.ama.caltech.edu/~mrm/kirk.html**. You'll want your home page to demonstrate such creativity and cleverness that the world will be astounded and lie prostrate at your feet.

Here are a few ideas:

▮▮ Create a page that contains pointers to all of the databases on a certain academic topic. The next person who has to write a term paper on that topic will bless you for it.

■ Make a page that highlights events and news of local interest.

■ Brag about yourself; dedicate a page solely to yourself and your wonderful accomplishments. This one will be a big hit with your grandparents back home.

Are you excited yet? Good. Because I lied a little. It *is* simple, but there are a couple of things you're going to need first.

1. Information from Your System Administrator

In order for a browser to connect with your home page, there has to be some additional software installed on your host computer. Check to see if that software exists, and if not, ask "Why not?" You also need certain file permissions, and your system administrator can help with this as well. He can also give you more details about where your page should be located, and if you speak sweetly, he may also set up links to your page from the school's home page. (If your school doesn't have its own home page, you could offer to create it!)

One snag you may run into is a lack of disk space—or, to be more precise, your system administrator's unwillingness to part with disk space. Don't think of him as being selfish; he has the interests of all users at heart. Be considerate. Remember, you are sharing the disk with many other people. You may need to keep graphics to a minimum, and forego using sound and video files. Of course, this limits your creative license, but you have to work with what you can get.

A strictly text-based home page takes up very little disk space and will fit within a disk quota that has probably already been set for you. However, if you come up with something useful, something attractive and appealing, you may have a good argument for getting your quota raised a little.

2. A Basic Knowledge of HTML

HTML stands for Hyper-Text Markup Language. It's the language used in creating WWW home pages. It's not difficult, but there are precise rules you have to follow so the computer can read what you've done. (Kind of like using a number-two pencil and filling in the circle completely on those computerized test forms.) If you were able to follow the directions on your college application well enough to get accepted, you should have no problem with HTML.

HTML is as complicated as you want it to be. There are some simple, basic codes that will get you by, and many more that will create fancy stuff that hardly anyone uses. Obviously, I can't turn you into an HTML genius in a few pages, but I'll walk you through creating a home page which contains headers, basic links, and graphics. Some UNIX is required, so if you skipped Chapter 3, skip this section, too, or go back and catch up.

> **Tip ➤** You can set up your own Web server on a Mac or a PC with a direct link to the Internet, but that's a whole other story. For this example, we'll keep it simple and set up a UNIX-based home page on your school's server.

You can use any text editor to make your home page. I choose vi, because that's what's available on my system, not because I am enthralled with vi. If you have another editor, such as pico, that will work just as well. Another option is to create it using your favorite word processing program and cut and paste it into a UNIX document.

Ready! Set! Design Your Page!

Okay, it's time to start designing the page itself. When I am working on my page, I like to have two windows open at the same time, as in the following examples. The window on the left is a window opened to vi. This is where I will do my designing using Hyper-Text Markup Language (HTML). The window on the right is how my window will appear through Netscape.

How did I accomplish this? Easy, but first you have to know that I did this job in a lab with a dedicated connection. That made my job easier. You don't need a dedicated connection to design a WWW page, but it sure makes the job easier.

I used a Telnet utility to access my UNIX account on my host machine and opened up my HTML document using vi. I called the document Home.html. I put that utility into the background, opened up Netscape, and navigated to my Home page. A click is all that it takes to move between the two. Windows users can move back and forth by pressing **Alt-Tab**.

Now, I'm ready to start designing.

If the lab is really dead and you can commandeer two machines side by side, it's even easier to design your home page. Have Netscape running on one and your text editor on the other.

Here we go!

1. First, let's give my page a title. This title is what will appear as the window title, not on the page itself. I typed this:

<title>David's Home Page</title>

The <title> code at the beginning says "Begin Title," and the </title> code at the end says "End Title." Almost every HTML command will use this format: **<tag>**text**</tag>**.

You need to save any changes in your text editor before they will appear in Netscape. Save your changes and reload the page by clicking on the **Reload** button. After saving my text, my page will now look like this:

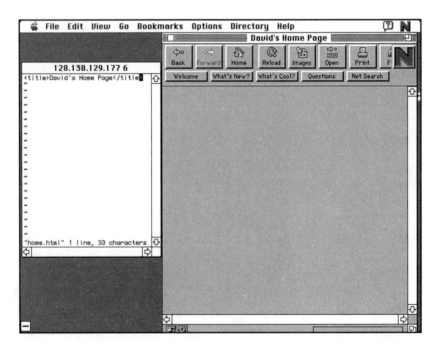

A good start.

> **Tip ➤**
>
> One of the most forgotten elements is the / in the second code. If your page doesn't work, look there first.

2. Next, I'll create my first header. There are six levels of header emphasis you can assign a piece of text. \<h1\> is the largest, \<h6\> the smallest. Since this is the top of my page, I'll choose the largest possible header to grab the attention of the reader.

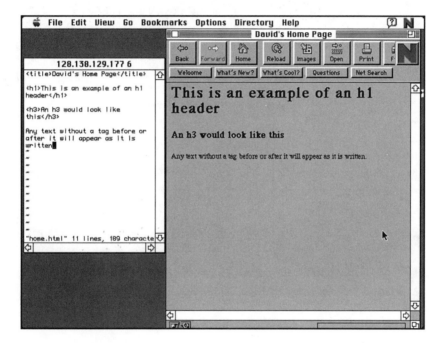

Please use more interesting headers than these.

I enter that line, save my work, and my picture magically appears.

3. Last, I create links to other sites on the Internet. This is done by using an *href*. (Don't even try to pronounce it.) The syntax looks like this:

```
<a href="128.116.1.185">This is the school where I teach </a>
```

The text This is the school where I teach will appear on the Web page and will all be clickable—that is, clicking on any of the words will make the connection to "128.116.1.185".

Contrast that with the following:

```
This is the <a href="128.116.1.185">school</a>where I teach.
```

In this example, only the word school is clickable, since it's the only word contained within the HTML codes.

Here's the page with the graphic and link:

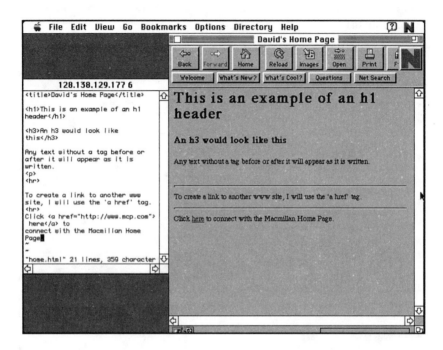

My first clickable link.

Obviously, there are a lot more HTML commands; here are a few that you may need:

\<p\>	To create a new paragraph.
\<hr\>	To create a horizontal line.
\<ul\>	To signify that an unnumbered list is about to follow.
\<li\>	Place this in front of each item in an unnumbered list to signify it is part of that list. Each item will be denoted by a dot preceding it.

Want to know more? One good place to start is Peter Kent's excellent book, *The Complete Idiot's Guide to the World Wide Web* from Alpha Books. There are also many good resources online you can check out, such as the HTML primer at:

> **http://www.ncsa.uniu.edu/General/Internet/WWW/
> HTMLPrimer.html**

Tip ➤ Netscape allows you to look at the source documents of other people's pages (that is, the text they actually typed, including the codes). This is a great way to learn new tricks on your own. Select **Source** from the **View** menu.

Great IDEAS for WWW

Where to begin? There is so much on the Web to do. Here are a few starters.

- ▥ Leave your mark on the Internet Graffiti Wall. Scribble at **http://cybersight.com/cgi-bin/cs/gw?main.**

- ▥ Search David Letterman's top-ten lists for digs at your favorite celebrity. Try out **http://bingen.cs.csbsju.edu/letterman.html.**

- ▥ Feeling guilty about sleeping in on Sunday mornings? Confess your sins at **http://anther.learning.cs.cmu.edu/priest.html.** (You can even take a look at other people's confessions.)

- ▥ Take a walk around a cleverly designed WWW home page at **http://www.cs.smu.edu:8001/afs/cs/user/phoebe/mosaic/my-house.html.** (I'm not going to tell you everything.)

- ▥ Read the job openings in higher education at **http://chronicle.merit.edu**. The home of the Chronicle of Higher Education.

- ▥ Check out your life after graduation. Get a tarot reading at **http://cad.ucla.edu/repository/useful/tarot.html.**

- ▥ Visit the first family. Say hello to Socks, the cat, at **http://www.whitehouse.gov** (the rest of the family are there, too).

- ▥ View and download marvelous fractal (and other) images at **http://akebono.stanford.edu/yahoo/Art/Computer_Generated/Fractals.**

- Meet netboy; check out **http://www.interaccess.com/netboy.html**

- Find out how the government wants access to your e-mail. Get up to date on the Clipper Chip controversy at **http://www.eff.org/pub/EFF/Policy/Crypto/**.

- Spend a somber moment at the Holocaust Museum at **http://www.ushmm.org/**.

- Can't get enough? Check out the What's New Page. This page, which is updated monthly, can be found at: **http://home.mcom.com/home/whatsnew**.

Impressing Your Friends with FTP

Internauts love acronyms. Have you noticed? FTP, SLIP, PPP, WWW, HTTP—
there are tons of them. You can lose major image points by having to ask what
any of them mean; it could make the difference between being an internaut
and an Inter-not. If you can talk FTP—and understand what you're saying to
some degree—you will be welcome in almost any Internet discussion.

> **Tip ➤** Wondering to yourself, "What do those acronyms he rattled off
> in that first paragraph mean, anyway?" Well, you'll learn about
> FTP in this chapter. SLIP and PPP were covered in Chapter 2, and
> WWW and HTTP were covered in Chapter 7.

By the way, FTP is an acronym for File Transfer Protocol.
FTP can be used as a noun as in:

"I used FTP to download my favorite game last night."

or a verb:

"I FTPed the latest DOS upgrade from Microsoft."

Both of these examples are appropriate uses of the term,
but be careful saying something like:

"I was up all night FTPing."

This may lead others to think you have a medical condition
and exclude you entirely.

Enough, Already, What Is It?

So what is this thing called FTP? How can you join the elite ranks of seasoned FTPers (pronounced "eff-tee-pee-ers") and keep up your end of the conversation? Get ready; take some notes; here we go!

FTP is one way of retrieving files. Gopher and World Wide Web are other ways, as we have seen in previous chapters. Where do the files come from? Well, lots of sites around the world have file archives on their computers and they make those files available to the rest of us, either out of the goodness of their hearts or for some other, inexplicable reason. Sounds amazing, but it's true.

You'll probably hear this process (logging onto another machine to retrieve files) referred to as "Anonymous FTP." That's because when you log onto these machines, you type in **anonymous** as your login and then fill in your e-mail address as your password. Using FTP, you can download these archived files onto the hard drive of your desktop computer.

> **Tip ➤** You can also FTP without being anonymous. Try filling in your domain name, your real username, and password. See where it takes you.

What kinds of files can you get?

- ▐▌ Shareware, freeware, and public domain software
- ▐▌ Image and video files
- ▐▌ Sound and Midi files
- ▐▌ FAQs and other text files

> **Tip ➤** FTP requires at least a basic knowledge of UNIX, so if you decided to skip over Chapter 3, now may be a good time to head back for a review session.

A word about limits. Basically, there aren't any. Unlike a BBS or an online service, there are no limits on how much time you can spend connected to a server, or how many files you can download. Your only limits are the size of your hard drive on your PC (you wouldn't want to fill it up with junk, now would you?) and, of course, the number of hours of free time you can spare. However, if you've made it this far, you're probably already hooked and what's a few more hours?

Dealing with Directories

First, a word about directories. You'll need a rudimentary understanding of the UNIX directory system to find the files you need, so turn back to Chapter 3 if you need a refresher. Once logged onto an FTP server, you'll make your way through layers of UNIX directories to find what you are looking for. So, what are you looking for? Well, for starters, look for a pub directory. (No, not a tavern. It's short for public.) Lots of servers keep the files that they're willing to share in a pub directory, to keep anonymous trespassers out of the real, working directories.

File Formats You'll Find

Most binary files (programs, image files, formatted text files) don't appear on the Internet in a usable fashion; they're usually altered in some way to make their transfer quicker or smoother. Altered how? Well, there are two basic ways a file can be altered: it can be compressed, or it can be converted to ASCII text.

With a converted file, the binary information (the 01010101s of computer talk) is converted into ASCII (the symbols you see on your keyboard—numbers, letters, symbols, and so on.) Why would someone intentionally do this to a file? To understand that, you need to understand something about sending e-mail over the Internet—unlike with an online service, you can't just attach a binary file to an e-mail message and have it delivered safe and sound. Methods of sending binary files through Internet e-mail have been developed, but they don't always work very well. Converting a binary file to ASCII text and sending that text in a message makes for a very reliable means of transporting the file. Once the file reaches its recipient, the recipient reconverts the file back to its binary form.

A compressed file, on the other hand, is still binary—it's just shrunken. The data is squeezed to create a smaller overall file to make for a quicker transfer. This is a positive feature for those who have to pay by the hour for their connection, as well as for those of us who don't want to wait around all day for a file transfer.

Either way, once a file is on your hard drive, you need to use a separate utility to expand/convert it back into a usable form. UUCODE is the most common conversion utility, and PKZip is the most common compression utility. Fortunately, these (and other) utilities are widely available on the Net.

You can usually tell which compression program was used to compress a file by the extension at the end of the file (the last few characters, usually preceded by a period). Here are some compressed formats and the utilities they take:

Table 8.1   File Types Encountered on the Internet

File extension needed	Operating system	File type	Compression utility
.hqx*	Macintosh	ASCII	Binhex
.cpt*	Macintosh	binary	Compact Pro
.sit*	Macintosh	binary	StuffIt
.zip	DOS	binary	PKUnzip
.arc	DOS	binary	ARC
.gz	DOS	binary	gzip
.tar	UNIX	binary	Tar
.Z	UNIX	binary	Compress

*StuffIt Expander will expand all these file types.

These are only some of the file types you will see on the Internet, though they're the major ones. If you own PKZip (for DOS/Windows) and StuffIt Expander (for Macs), you'll be able to handle almost everything you want to download.

An FTP Session—Step by Step

Okay, now I'm going to walk you through an FTP session where we download one of the file expansion utilities you will need. We'll go after PKZip, and we'll connect with an FTP server in Oakland, California.

Tip ➤

This transcript shows a dial-up terminal connection from the UNIX prompt. There are lots of fancy graphics-based FTP programs for those with dedicated or dial-up direct connections. If you have a choice, use one of these slick graphics apps, not this clunky old UNIX method.

This transcript will go through several steps:

1. Connecting to and logging onto the remote computer.

2. Making our way through the UNIX directories to find the file.

3. Telling the remote computer to send the file to our host machine (your school's computer).

4. Transferring the file from the host machine to your home PC.

Step 1—Logging On and Moving the File

To access an FTP site, I type **ftp** and then the address I want to connect to, in this case, **oak.oakland.edu**.

```
ftp oak.oakland.edu
```

Here's what I see:

```
Connected to oak.oakland.edu.
```

At the Name prompt, type **Anonymous** and press **Enter**. Your login name will always be anonymous when using FTP.

```
Name (oak.oakland.edu:clarkd):Anonymous
331 Guest login ok, send your complete e-mail address as password.
```

Type your complete e-mail address as your password. Your password will not show up as you type it.

```
Password: clarkd@bvsd.k12.co.us

230-                         Welcome to
230-                    THE OAK SOFTWARE REPOSITORY
230-          A service of Oakland University, Rochester Michigan

230 Guest login ok, access restrictions apply.
```

Next, we'll use the **ls** command to list the files and directories. If you paid attention in the UNIX chapter, you know the **ls** command. It asks the computer to list what is in the current directory.

```
FTP>ls

150 Opening ASCII mode data connection for file list.
lost+found
pub2
siteinfo
SimTel
Index-byname

226 Transfer complete.
118 bytes received in 0.055 seconds (2.1 Kbytes/s)
```

Let's check out what's in that SimTel directory. We'll use the **cd** (change working directory) command to change to that directory:

```
FTP>cd SimTel
```

I happen to know that SimTel is a collection of compression programs, but if you didn't know that, you could wade through the various directories till you found what you wanted.

Here's what I get when the directory is changed to SimTel:

```
250 CWD command successful.
```

Now let's use **ls** again to list the files in the SimTel directory:

```
FTP>ls
```

The computer comes back with the directories and files in that directory:

```
200 PORT command successful.
150 Opening ASCII mode data connection for file list.
msdos
.notar
README.COPYRIGHT
226 Transfer complete.
43 bytes received in 0.012 seconds (3.6 Kbytes/s)
```

Well, I know that PKZip is a DOS-based program, so let's try the msdos directory. We'll change to it:

```
FTP>cd msdos
```

and see this:

```
250-This MS-DOS collection is a mirror of SimTel, the Coast to Coast
250-Software Repository (tm).
Questions about or comments on this
250-collection should be sent to w8sdz@SimTel.Coast.NET.
```

Okay, now we'll use **ls** again to see what's in this directory. (Is all this beginning to seem familiar?)

```
FTP>ls

200 PORT command successful.
150 Opening ASCII mode data connection for file list.
zip
zoo
zmodem
textutil
uemacs
winsock

226 Transfer complete.
1956 bytes received in 1.2 seconds (1.6 Kbytes/s)
```

Hmm, it appears that the msdos directory contains still more directories. We're looking for a directory that might contain PKZip, and "zip" looks like a good choice. Let's change to it:

```
FTP> cd zip

250 CWD command successful.
```

Now the **ls** command again to see what's here:

```
FTP>ls

200 PORT command successful.
150 Opening ASCII mode data connection for file list.
00_index.txt
pkz204g.exe
unz512x3.exe
Pkzm104.exe
chkav22.zip
```

There's a bunch of files here. How do I know which is the real McCoy? Luckily, there's an index with all sorts of information in it. It's usually at the top, and, in this case, is called 00-index.txt. If you wanted to view the contents of the file, you could type the command: **get 00_index.txt ¦ more**. Since I already know from experience what I want, I dispense with the formalities and jump right in.

First, I need to set the transfer mode to binary. This lets the computer know that I'm transferring a binary file. If I were transferring a text or other ACSCII file, I wouldn't have to do this because on most servers ASCII is the default.

```
FTP> binary
200 Type set to I.
```

Now I'm ready to get the file. Here goes:

```
FTP>get pkz204g.exe

200 PORT command successful.
150 Opening BINARY mode data connection for pkz204g.exe (202574 bytes).

226 Transfer complete.
202574 bytes received in 25 seconds (7.9 Kbytes/s)
```

Success! Now let's get out of here.

```
FTP>quit

221 Goodbye.
```

Step 2—Bringing the File Home

Here is where it can get a little tricky. You've just transferred the file from the SimTel archive to your UNIX account, but it's not on your hard drive yet. You still need to download the program from the UNIX account.

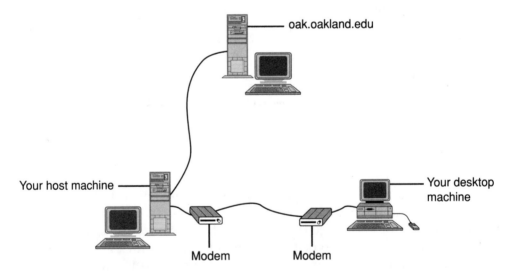

FTPing over a dial-up connection brings the file only halfway. You still need to bring the file from your host to your desktop.

There are three common downloading protocols supported by most UNIX hosts: Zmodem, Kermit, and Xmodem. You can use any of them, as long as it's one that both the UNIX host and your communications software can agree on.

> **Tip ➤** For a variety of reasons, Zmodem should be your first choice. It's fast and has a nifty recovery feature that allows you to resume a file transfer where it left off if something interrupts it.

So how do you find out which protocols are supported by your host and your software? Well, there are actually two separate issues there, so let's look at them separately. To find out what protocols your software supports, check the manual that came with it, or hunt around in the Options menu or the Help system, looking for something that might refer to file transfers.

To find out what is supported by your UNIX host you can either:

▮ Ask your system administrator.

or

▮ Try typing the commands and see what happens.

To access Zmodem, type **sz** at your prompt.

To access Kermit, type **kermit** at your prompt.

To access Xmodem, type **sx** at your prompt.

If you get a command unknown message or something to that effect, you will know that the protocol isn't supported. In that case, you will have to revert to the first means of discovery: ask your system administrator.

Assuming you have Zmodem (you lucky dog), type the following at your host's UNIX prompt to bring the file down to your hard drive:

sz -e pkz204g.exe

That's it. If it doesn't transfer correctly, the problem can frequently be found in your software settings. Look there first for a solution.

For a kermit transfer, use these commands:

Kermit
send pkz204g.exe

For an xmodem transfer, use this:

sx pkz204g.exe

Congratulations! If you followed this example step by step, you have just successfully downloaded a file via Anonymous FTP and are well on your way to becoming an Internet junkie. Depending on the size of the file and the speed of your modem, the transfer could take anywhere from a few minutes to more than an hour. A 14.4 bps modem will transfer a megabyte (a million bytes) of data in around 10 minutes. The file pkz204g.exe is about 200 kilobytes (200,000 bytes).

FTPing Via Direct Connect

FTPing on a direct connection is very neat and easy, although it doesn't provide you with a chance to show off your UNIX finesse. There are tons of graphic-based programs you can use, such as Fetch and Anarchie for the Mac, and for Windows, WS_ftp and the FTP software that comes with Chameleon.

For example, Mac users can obtain a wonderful little utility called Fetch that will pull the file down onto your hard drive, unstuff the stuffed, decode the binhexed, unzip the zipped, unpack the packed, and do just about anything else you want (short of washing your clothes). In other words, it'll bring down a file directly to your desktop machine ready for you to use.

Using Fetch, we can enter software archives by pointing and clicking where we want to go. It works like this:

1. Open Fetch.

2. Type in the address you want to connect to.

3. Fill in **anonymous** for your user ID.

4. Fill in your e-mail address for your password.

5. If you know the directory you want to go to, you can type that; otherwise, leave it blank.

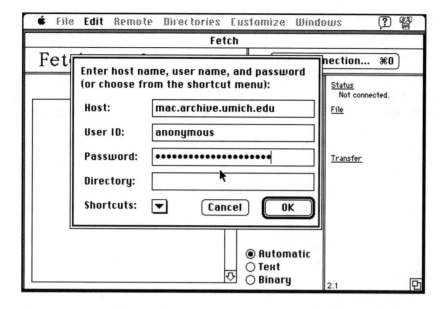

Getting Fetch up and fetching.

6. Navigate through the directories by clicking with the mouse.

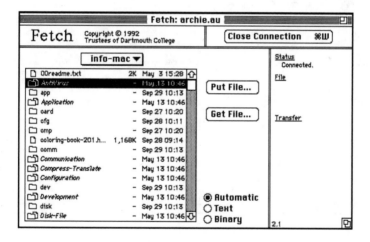

Simply click on the directories you'd like to look at.

7. Double-click on the file you want, or click once and then click on **Get File....**

8. Put your feet up and relax.

Since most dedicated connections run at a minimum of 56K, your wait will be considerably less with a dedicated connection than with a dial-up connection.

You can configure Fetch to decompress and convert your downloads automatically so that you receive your file ready to roll. Compared with what we had to go through with the UNIX-based terminal connection, this is a cinch.

Fetch isn't the only show in town, however. For Macintosh users, it has been the program of choice for quite awhile, but there's a recently released program called Anarchie (pronounced anarchy) that is growing in popularity among Mac users. The strength of Anarchie is that it includes a searching utility. Type the name of the file you want (provided you know the filename; some of them can be quite cryptic), and Anarchie searches the Net for it and tells you where it can be found. Click on the file; Anarchie makes the connection and the file is transferred. Take a look:

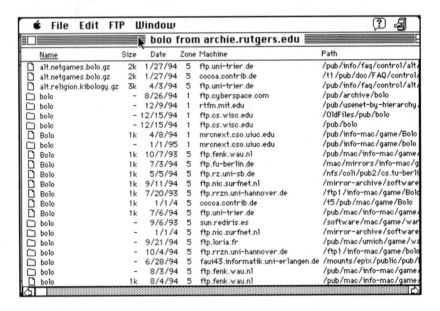

Let Anarchie do the work for you.

I asked Anarchie to do a search for the game bolo. Anarchie searched the Net using a utility called Archie and then gave me a list of several locations where I could find bolo. All I need to do is pick a site that looks good, then point and click.

Tip ➤

Anarchie is available via Anonymous FTP (how else?) from:

ftp.pht.com:/pub/mac/info-mac/comm/tcp

Windows users, don't despair; there are programs for you as well. Development in this area lags behind that of the Mac (IMHO—Don't know what IMHO stands for? Check the glossary at the back of this book. You gotta talk the talk on the Net.), but there are a couple of options. One program you may want to consider is WS_ftp. This program is available from:

hull.marcam.com:/win3/winsock

This point-and-click package makes transferring your files a cinch. Take a look:

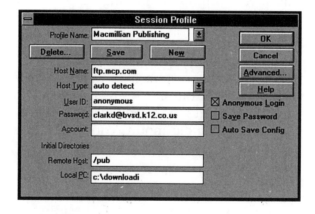

WS_ftp's Session Profile dialog box.

WS_ftp can make FTPing a pleasure instead of a pain. This dialog box lets me set my session variables, such as:

The site I want to connect to: ftp.mcp.com

My login: anonymous

My password: clarkd@bvsd.k12.co.us

Once these are set, I click **OK** and the connection is made. A second dialog box appears and shows me what is available at that site. If I see something good (I will), I can click on it to bring it down to my desktop computer.

Another program worth looking at is the FTP software that comes packaged with Chameleon. Chameleon is a full Internet access package that includes everything you need. Included in the Chameleon package is TCP/IP software, Telnet, newsreading software, and more, including an FTP utility. Chameleon is a commercial project, but a demo version is available from **ftp.netmanage.com:/pub/demos/chameleon**. Full documentation is included as well to help get you started.

Finding Which Files Are Available Using Archie

Archie is a utility that searches FTP sites. Your UNIX host may have its own Archie server (very cool) or a connection set up to one somewhere else (sort of cool), or you may have to break down and telnet to someone else's Archie server (bummer).

Try typing **archie** at your prompt. If nothing happens, it means your UNIX host doesn't have anything to offer you Archie-wise, and you'll have to telnet to a public Archie site.

Public Archie sites are like public transportation—there's a lot of it, but it's usually crowded. If the site is busy, you will be informed very politely by an automated message that varies from site to site. However, those kind people usually include a list of other sites to try. You may have to try three or four before you find one that can handle another connection. Here's a list of Archie sites you can telnet to:

Table 8.2 Archie Sites

Address	IP address	Location
archie.ans.net	147.225.1.10	(ANS server, NY (USA))
archie.au	139.130.4.6	(Australian server)
archie.doc.ic.ac.uk	146.169.11.3	(United Kingdom server)
archie.funet.fi	128.214.6.102	(Finnish server)
archie.kr	128.134.1.1	(Korean server)
archie.luth.se	130.240.18.4	(Swedish server)
archie.ncu.edu.tw	140.115.19.24	(Taiwanese server)
archie.nz	130.195.9.4	(New Zealand server)

Address	IP address	Location
archie.rediris.es	130.206.1.2	(Spanish server)
archie.rutgers.edu	128.6.18.15	(Rutgers University (USA))
archie.sogang.ac.kr	163.239.1.11	(Korean server)
archie.sura.net	128.167.254.195	(SURAnet server MD (USA))
archie.switch.ch	130.59.1.40	(Swiss server)
archie.unipi.it	131.114.21.10	(Italian server)
archie.unl.edu	129.93.1.14	(U of Nebraska Lincoln(USA))

To access any of these servers, type:

`telnet address`

The address can be either the name address or IP address. (Turn back to Chapter 2 if you've forgotten about addresses.) Log in as **archie**. If it asks for a password, type **archie** for that as well.

After scrolling through a series of introductory messages, I'll come to the Archie prompt. The following is a transcript of an Archie search. I'll be a good netizen and hook into a server close to where I live.

```
bvsd.k12.co.us~%telnet archie.unl.edu
Trying 129.93.1.14...
Connected to crcnis2.unl.edu.
Escape character is '^]'.

SunOS UNIX (crcnis2)

login: archie
Password:archie

    Welcome to the ARCHIE server at the University of Nebraska - Lincoln
    If you need further instructions, type help at the unl-archie> prompt.
# Bunyip Information Systems, 1993
# Terminal type set to 'vt100 24 80'.
# 'erase' character is '^?'.
# 'search' (type string) has the value 'sub'.
```

At the end of all this UNIX garbage is what I'm looking for: the Archie prompt. At unl, it looks like this:

```
unl-archie>
```

Prompts may vary from site to site. Most end in a >.

At this point, type:

find *<search string>*

where, of course, *search string* is the text in the filename that you're searching for. For example:

```
>find disinfectant
```

will search for the latest version of the virus protection utility, Disinfectant. You'll see a message like this:

```
Processing Case Insensitive Substring Search for 'disinfectant'
```

and within a couple of minutes the results will come in:

```
Host coombs.anu.edu.au
     Location: /pub/macintosh
     FILE -rw-rw-r-- 241606  May 20 18:20  Disinfectant35.sea.hqx

Host pippin.cc.flinders.edu.au
     Location: /pub/Mac
     DIRECTORY drwxrwxr-x 512  Apr  7 07:07  Disinfectant

Host uniwa.uwa.oz.au
     Location: /pub/Mac/antivirals
     FILE -rw-r--r-- 241605  Apr  5 09:43  disinfectant35.sea.hqx

Host brazil.cambridge.apple.com
     Location: /pub/mcl/contrib
     FILE -rw-r--r--     239303  Apr  6 1993  disinfectant-30.hqx
```

These are only a few of the entries that came back, but this is enough information to head out and pull down the file. The site at **uniwa.uwa.oz.au** looks like it has the most current version, so that's where I'll look first. To exit Archie, type:

```
>quit
```

Other commands in Archie that are useful to know include:

mail address   Mails the results of the last search to your
                          e-mail address.

lookup host   Looks up the IP address of host.

set maxhits *<number>* Sets the maximum number of responses to
                          send back.

Great Ideas for FTP

There is a ton of software, text files, and image and sound files available. Before we go on, first a word about shareware. Shareware is not freeware. If you download a piece of shareware and decide to keep it, send in your shareware fees. They are usually quite reasonable, and the authors are deserving of our support.

With that said, let's see what's out there.

- Go to **groucho.unidata.ucar.edu** to view current weather satellite images of the Earth.

- Get some great ideas of ways to confuse your roommate by FTPing to **quartz.rutgers.edu**. Look in the **pub/humor/School** directories.

- Try **seds.lpl.arizona.edu** for some stunning photographs from the Hubble Space Telescope.

- Go to **ftp.vnet.net** to check out the stats for your favorite pro football team.

- Check out the Vatican Exhibit, the Dead Sea Scrolls, and African American Art at **ftp.loc.gov**.

- The **grind.icsa.uiowa.edu** site has a great archive of gif and sound files. Create a Star Trek StartUp Screen with Captain Picard welcoming you to cyberspace.

- Head over to **quartz.rutgers.edu** and look in the **cd/pub/tv+movies** directories for info relating to your favorite couch potato pastime.

- Download the lyrics from Sting, Graham Parker, Marlene Dietrich (depending on your tastes, of course) and others from **vacs.uwp.edu**. Over 2,000 different tunes are there for the grabbing. You can also find music images and tablature here.

Top FTP Sites to Explore

These sites contain a variety of software and image and text files. Most any-thing you want can be found here. Remember to look first for a **pub** direc-tory. Next find a directory of interest to you. PC users will want to look for a directory called **pc** or **msdos**, or maybe **windows** or **win31**. For Mac folks, look for **mac** or **info-mac**.

Once in the right place, you'll be amazed and delighted by the amount of files available. Don't expect that the sites will be organized the same; they will all be a bit different. Put on your explorer persona and dive right in. If you do get lost, here are a couple of helpful commands:

cd	Changes to a directory.
ls	Lists the files in that directory.
cd /	Pops you back to the top level directory.
pwd	Stands for Print Working Directory. This command shows you the path you have taken to get where you are.

And lastly, don't get carried away, there's more to life than mining the Net. (If you discover what that is, please e-mail the answer to me.) I spend far too much time with this stuff.

grind.icsa.uiowa.edu	Mirror Sites for many Mac, DOS, and UNIX sites
wuarchive.wustl.edu	Lots of software, images, and graphics
rtfm.mit.edu	USENET FAQs in abundance
oak.oakland.edu	SimTel archive for DOS
ftp.cse.nau.edu	Graphics Galore
archive.umich.edu	Great Mac Site
ftp.ncsa.uiuc.edu	Home of Mosaic and other great software to access the Internet
quartz.rutgers.edu	Go to this large humor section for a laugh
ftp.apple.com	Apple system software
ftp.microsoft.com	Updated Windows drivers and DOS upgrades

IRC, MUDs, and Other Fun Stuff

When it's late at night and you're ready for a study break, you have a few options. You can fight the sleet and snow and head down to the local hangout to look for some friends; you can run up your telephone bill with a long distance call to your girl/boy friend back home; or you can sit and stare out the window.

But wait! Why don't you log onto the Net right at your desk and make a new friend around the world, slay evil dwarves, or check out how many Pepsis have been sold out of the Columbia University pop machine in the last day. Okay, maybe that last one isn't your idea of a rocking good time, but that and other amusements await you on the Net, as this chapter will show you.

Internet Relay Chat

Internet Relay Chat (IRC) is an electronic gathering place for folks to meet and chat in real time with one another. People gather in groups of anywhere from two on up, to help solve each other's problems, discuss common concerns, or just waste time.

Tip ➤

To chat in real time over a computer network means that the words you type on your terminal appear instantaneously (or nearly so) on the screen of the person you're chatting with and vice versa.

When you enter the IRC, you'll be faced with a seemingly endless list of discussion groups you can join. (If you're using a slow modem connection, the list will be endlessly slow to work with.) In this collection of groups, you'll find the same eclectic sampling as everywhere else on the Net—the garbage and the gems are swimming in the same pool, and it may take awhile to tell the two apart.

Here's how it works. From your UNIX prompt, type **irc** and press **Enter.** This may take you into the IRC, or it may not. Some sites restrict access to the IRC. If nothing happens, talk to your system administrator and ask about getting in. Another option is to telnet to a public IRC site. (Tel what? If you've forgotten about Telnet, flip back to Chapter 2 for a refresher.) Check out the Yanoff list (a popular list of Internet resources) for some public IRC sites. To find out how to get a copy, type **finger yanoff@alpha2.csd .uwm.edu** at your UNIX prompt.

The IRC is about as free flowing as the Internet gets. Anybody can create a real time discussion group and invite others to join. However, before you do that, spend a little time looking around. Sample some of the fare and decide whether this is really what you want to be doing late on a Saturday night. IRC isn't for everybody.

Once into the IRC, you'll see a window that looks like this:

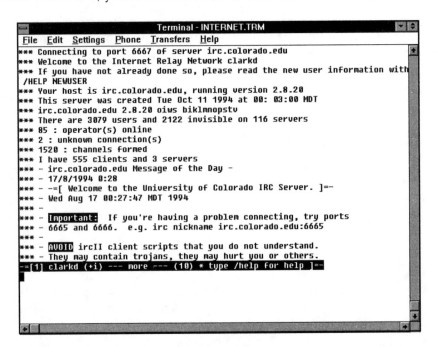

Welcome to the world of non-stop chatter in IRC.

Look like a bunch of gibberish? Well, yeah, basically it is, and it doesn't really tell you a lot. As with just about everything else on the Internet, you have to speak the language to use the tool. Fortunately, the language isn't that hard. You have to precede every command you give in IRC with a /. Notice what it says near the top of the screen:

```
/HELP NEWUSER
```

That's a command to get yourself started with IRC. Type that command, and you'll get the following information:

```
              NEW USER INFORMATION FOR IRC

This file contains some caveats for people new to IRC. It is not a guide
to commands for IRC. For a brief guide to commands for new users, see
/HELP INTRO.

See /HELP ETIQUETTE for a guide to good manners on IRC.

IRC is an international network servicing 20 or more countries. There are
over 2000 registered users, and a similar number of regular unregistered
users. Do not expect everybody to speak English.

The primary means of identification is currently by nickname. This can be
modified with /NICK, and registered with NickServ. (/MSG NickServ HELP
for information on NickServ.) Note, however that some nicknames are
duplicated, and some people will impersonate others by using their nick-
names. If you have any doubts about the identity of somebody using a given
nickname use /WHOIS NickName to find out more. This gives detailed infor-
mation on the person using the NickName. For example, if you are getting
abusive messages from "Fred", type:

/WHOIS Fred

If the information displayed is not the same as that which you would
expect for Fred, it is probably a case of impersonation.

Recently some users have been tricking others into allowing them to
control their IRC sessions or damaging their files. If somebody asks you
to type a command and you don't know what it does, use /HELP CommandName
to find out more about it first. In particular, /ON has been used to cause
trouble and is now initially disabled for new users. Additionally, /QUI is
short for /QUIT and will terminate your IRC session. If you see any
message asking you to type /QUI or /QUIT, ignore it.

Some new users have been baffled by "CTCP" messages appearing on
the IRC session. These are messages from other users, asking your
client to perform some service for them. They are generally
generated by somebody typing in a CTCP command. See /HELP CTCP.

If you have not already done so, read the HELP files INTRO and
ETIQUETTE.
```

This document gives you a good starting place to jump off. It has some pointers to other commands you may want to try, including:

/HELP ETIQUETTE

/HELP INTRO

and just plain

/HELP

and, of course, the all important

/QUIT

to get you out of this mess and back to the familiar territory of your UNIX prompt. (Isn't it scary that the UNIX prompt seems familiar to you by now? Don't worry. You're not morphing into a computer geek just yet.)

Assuming that you're feeling brave enough to explore these uncharted waters, let's head out. The command to find out what folks are talking about is:

/LIST

Type the command, hit **Enter**, and settle back while topics flash across your screen. These topics will be presented to you in no particular order. Here's some of the ones you may see:

```
*** #Dallas    5
*** #silly     7
*** #Emyrs     2
*** #Qu        1
*** #wolfden   3
*** #Desi      2
*** #asatru    7
*** #Oklahoma  2
*** #ImagiNet  1
*** #IThinkYou 3
*** #sann      3
*** #aikman    2
*** #redheads  7
*** #Twilight_ 1
*** #GoKi      3
*** #walton    2
*** #Johann    2
*** #Internet- 1    Snow??   Yes, we have snow. . .
*** #Oasis     7    ALL MY FRIENDS ARE HERE!!!!!!!!!!!
*** Prv        1
```

```
***  #3do        1
***  #emacs      1          the new power shell.
***  #washbowl   1
***  #feyzo      2
***  #bunbun     2
```

> **Tip ➤**
> Does the list scroll by too fast to read? Well, some communications programs let you set up a buffer that will hold a certain number of lines that you've already seen (like 40 or so). If you set up your comm program for this, you can scroll back and see the text that flashed across the screen at your leisure.

The *** signs on the left are just garbage. Ignore them. The next column is the name of the channel. Just as commands are always preceded by a / sign, channel names always have # in front of them. The number in the next column tells you how many people are online at that particular moment. Notice you see a lot of 1s there. Many chat channels are just left open by the channel operator and are probably inactive. Notice also that there's a subject on some of the channels. The subject is optional. It's created by the person who started that particular discussion (the channel operator) to further entice you to join in.

Joining a Channel

To join in on one of these discussions, type:

/join #*groupname*

Be sure to include the # sign in front of the name of the group. So to join the group #silly, I'd type:

/join #silly

> **Tip ➤**
> As with listservs and newsgroups, it's a good idea to watch what's going on in a chat channel for awhile before jumping in.

From this point on, whatever you type on the screen will be seen by the other people in that channel, unless you preface it with a / sign. (Remember, the / lets the machine know that you're typing a command, not a comment.) Here are a few other commands you can try:

/NAMES	Shows the nicknames of all users on each channel.
/MSG *<nick> <msg>*	Sends a private message to the specified person. Only the specified nickname will see this message.
/NICK	Changes your nickname.
/QUIT	Exits IRC.
/HELP *<topic>*	Gets help on all IRC commands.
/WHO *<channel>*	Shows who is on a given channel, including nickname, username, host name, and real name.
/WHOIS *<nick>*	Shows the "true" identity of someone.
/LEAVE *<channel>*	Use to leave a subscribed channel.

That should be enough to get you started. Plead for help if you get stuck—there are dozens of folks on the IRC who will give you advice, sometimes more than you want.

Starting Your Own Channel

Perhaps you've gone through the list of topics, and you can't find that one perfect group you've been looking for. Maybe you feel like having a conversation on the breeding practices of wild yaks, or something that no one else has thought of. You don't have to barge into the Lonely_Singles channel and start talking about yaks; you can create your own channel.

If you're a power-monger, you'll love creating a channel. It makes you the demigod of the channel, the king of the hill. As the channel operator, you can invite other people to join you, make the channel private, assign a password, and even kick obnoxious people off who want to discuss something other than yaks.

Creating the channel is a simple procedure. Just type:

/join #*groupname*

For example, to stay with the yak theme, type:

/join #yaks

If there isn't already a channel by that name, IRC will create one called yaks, and you're open for business. The next time somebody uses the /list command, yaks will be on the list.

Great Ideas for Using IRC

IRC can be a great source of fun and information. Unlike accessing a database on the Net, you interact with real people. (I assume they are people; on the Net, you never know.) That can be an advantage or a disadvantage, depending on how you look at it. In any case, here are a few ideas to get you started:

▮ Use IRC to practice reading/writing a foreign language. Somewhere in that list, you'll find every major language spoken somewhere, and many of the less common ones are represented as well.

▮ The IRC can be a place to get immediate information and advice on a variety of topics. Having trouble getting your Mac to run smoothly? Join the channel **#macintosh** for a free troubleshooting session.

▮ Paint with friends across the globe using Homer Paint. Homer Paint is a program for Macintosh that lets you telepaint over the IRC. Homer Paint only works over a connection that can support graphics, such as a dedicated or dial-up direct connection. You also need to get the software before you can do it. Use Archie to search for "homer," and then download the program with FTP. (Chapter 8 has all the details about Archie and FTP.)

▮ Join the Jeopardy channel and bone up for your local Trivia Bowl or just have fun.

▮ If you're feeling shy your first time in the IRC, try jumping into the hot tub. Typing **/join #hottub** will start you off. There is usually a conversation happening here and some friendly folks to get to know.

Want to Know More About IRC?

If you want to learn more about using the IRC, FTP on over to **cs-ftp.bu.edu** and look for the IRC Primer. (Chapter 8 tells you how to use FTP, in case you've forgotten.) The IRC Primer is a good source for info, and it comes in plain text and PostScript versions. You can find it in the /irc/support directories. Look for IRC primer1.1txt. There is also an IRC tutorial in the /irc/support/old directories with some good information. These files are listed as tutorial.1, tutorial.2, and tutorial.3.

Other sources of IRC information include:

■ **Newsgroups:**
   alt.irc
   alt.irc.questions
   alt.irc.recovery

■ **World Wide Web resources:**
   http://www.fnet.fi/~irc/
   http://www.enst.fr/~pioch/IRC/IRC.html

■ **FTP sites:**
   ftp.funet.fi /pub/unix/irc
   ftp.acsu.buffalo.edu /pub/irc
   cs-ftp.bu.edu /irc/support

■ **Gopher sites:**
   gopher.luth.se
   Look in FAQs, alt, and irc/ for the latest IRC FAQ.

These aren't the only sites with IRC information, but this should be enough to send you on your way. The best place to learn about the IRC is on the IRC itself, so don't be too afraid of making a fool of yourself—we all do that. The important thing is to have fun while you're doing it.

MUDs and MOOs

MUD stands for Multi-User Dungeon. No, it's not an electronic haven for sadomasochists. It's just a simulated environment online, kind of like those old text-based adventure games where you type a command like **GO WEST** or **OPEN DOOR**, and the computer responds with text that tells you what happens as a result. The difference with a MUD is that there are other real, live players wandering around in the game at the same time as you, and you can interact with them.

MUDs come in a variety of different flavors. There are action-oriented MUDs, where people come together to do battle over dragons, princesses, spaceships, and what-have-you. There are MUDs that are tamer, where folks join efforts to build communities. To get a sampling of MUDs (and their cousins MOOs, MUSHEs, and MUCKs), gopher to **gopher.cs.ttu.edu**. Go into the following directories:

Other Gopher and Information Servers

Interactive MOO Gophers

You'll get the following menu, and it's just a matter of pushing the right button from here on in:

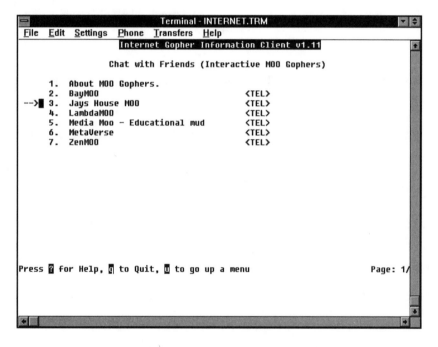

The Interactive MOO Gopher menu.

I tried:

```
3. Jays House MOO     <Tel>
```

The <TEL> is short for Telnet. It tells you that you'll be leaving gopherspace for the connection and telnetting to another site. When you make your selection, you'll see a warning message. Sometimes, there will be important information in the message, such as what you should use as a login and password to make the connection.

Here's the window that popped up for me:

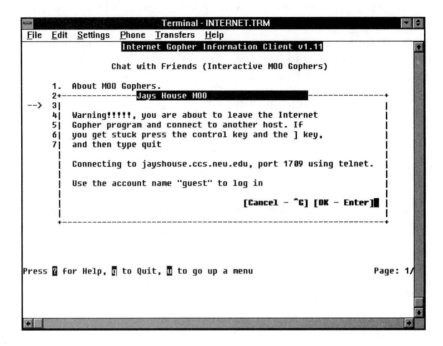

After choosing a selection, you'll get this window of warning.

The pertinent info it provides me:

▐▌ If I should get stuck, I can type ^] (control-right bracket) to get out of it.

▐▌ The address I am connecting to is **jayshouse.ccs.neu.edu 1709**. I can write this down and telnet there directly next time.

▐▌ I use the login **guest**.

I duly noted these tidbits, hit **Enter**, and was swept into the following:

```
Trying 129.10.111.77...
Connected to vesuvius.ccs.neu.edu.
Escape character is '^]'.
Welcome to JHM--coming from Dave, that's entirely phatic.

   This isn't a game.  It's a place where friends hang out and people
work on various projects.  For more information, type 'help purpose' once
you've connected.
```

```
A few useful commands:

   'connect Guest'                          to connect to a guest character.
   '@quit'                                  to disconnect, either now or later.
   'connect <character-name> <password>'    if you have a character.
   'idle'                                   to see roughly how idle jhm is.

(phat.ic \'fat-ik\ \-i-k(*-)le-\ aj [Gk phatos, verbal of phanai to speak] :
     revealing or sharing feelings or establishing an atmosphere of sociability
     rather than communicating ideas {~ communion} - phat.i.cal.ly av)
connect guest
*** Connected ***
Underground
This is a dark, cramped space.  It appears to be very crowded in here; you
keep bumping into what feels like drainage pipes, alligators, and other
people (apparently sleeping).  One useful thing that you've discovered in
your bumbling about is a manhole cover above you.

   * Welcome to JHM.
As it says above, this is not a game, and people here will take your
actions seriously.  Type:

help manners -  to learn about the standards of behavior here
@911         -  if you require emergency assistance
@tutorial    -  to learn how to use MOO.

   * Note that other users of this MOO will be able to tell where you have
connected from.

There is new news.  Type 'news' to read all news or 'news new' to read
just new news.
```

This is obviously one of the tamer ones and looks like it may be a good place to meet some interesting people. Try typing in some of the commands and let the computer lead you. If you get stuck somewhere, more than likely there will be someone nearby to give you a hand and tell you what to do next. Some MUDs even have people online just for that purpose, to help newcomers feel comfortable.

Feeling More Adventurous?

There are many different kinds of MUDs, and not all of them are as benign as that last one. Let's look at an adventure MUD. The following MUD is called PrimalMud. You access it directly by telnetting to **jeack.apana.org.ua4000**.

Before beginning, I have to create a character for myself. (The bold stuff below is what I typed.)

```
By what name do you wish to be known? Sartory
Did I get that right, Sartory (Y/N)? y
New character.
Give me a password for Sartory:
```

I typed a password, but it doesn't show up on-screen.

```
Please retype password:
```

Same thing again.

```
What is your sex (M/F)? m
```

Just out of habit, I chose male. I could be a female character if I wanted. (Don't dream it; be it.)

```
Select a Race ('?' for Race Information).
[ 1]  Ogre
[ 2]  Deva
[ 3]  Haruchai
[ 4]  Elf
[ 5]  Changling
[ 6]  Human
[ 7]  Orc
[ 8]  Kobold
[ 9]  Dwarf
[10]  Gnome
[11]  Kenda
[12]  Pixie

Race: 4
```

Let's go with Elf. I've always had a thing for elves.

```
Select a class to base your rolled statistics on:
  [C]leric     (WIS,INT,STR,DEX,CON,CHA)
  [T]hief      (DEX,STR,CON,INT,WIS,CHA)
  [M]agic User (INT,WIS,DEX,STR,CON,CHA)
  [W]arrior    (STR,DEX,CON,WIS,INT,CHA)
  [S]elect stats manually

Class: m
```

I'll be a magic user this time. It's the only one of the choices that I couldn't be in real life if I wanted. I'm now set up as a magic-wielding elf named Sartory. Now to enter the game:

```
Welcome to PrimalMUD!
0) Exit from PrimalMUD.
1) Enter the game.
2) Enter description.
3) Read the background story.
4) Change password.
5) Delete this character.

Make your choice: 1
```

Selecting **1** here takes me into the game, which is what I want. Since this is an all-text adventure, I will have to learn the commands. Once I enter the game, there's an option that I select that helps me in that department. From there, the only limitations are my imagination and my need for sleep.

> **Tip ➤**
>
> **Warning!** You'll encounter many different people here, and not all of them will be friendly. Expect to bite the dust early your first few times out; you will, sometimes when you least expect it. Learn from your mistakes—you can always log on again and start fresh with a new character or resurrect your old one and give him/her new life.

Want More Info About MUDs?

Another site worth checking out for MUD information is **gopher actlab.rtf .utexas.edu.** This site has pointers to MUDs of all kinds, and also some quite helpful information about MUDs—the different kinds, what they mean, and so on. Plus, when you choose

```
3.  Jack In (Connect directly to MUDs) /
```

you're provided with a selection of MUDs according to different topics.

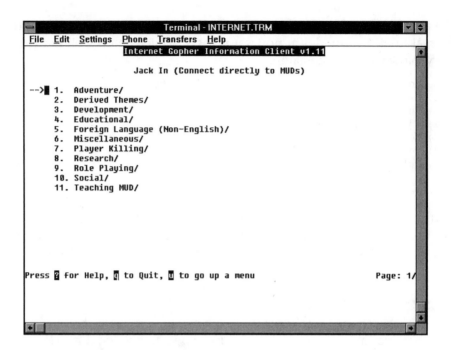

A list of different MUDs to choose from.

Still more info can be found on the **newsgroup rec.games.muds**. It's even possible to start your own MUD or interactive virtual environment with the permission of your system administrator.

Boring but Necessary Advisory Note

I feel it's necessary to add a word of caution here. I don't mean to sound like your parents, but *be careful*. MUDs and other online games can be very addictive. While they can be a wonderful way to meet people and to exercise your creative powers, they can also be a major time sink. Exercise a touch of moderation in playing these, and you'll do fine.

Many schools restrict access to MUDding because of the addictive nature and the huge amount of computing resources eaten up when hundreds of MUD-crazed students stay online for 6–8 hours at a time. It would be a good idea to check with the folks who set up your Internet account for you to find out if there are any MUD restrictions.

But Wait, There's More... Other Games on the Net

Fantasy and role-playing games aren't the only shows in town on the Internet. Not by a long shot. Chess, backgammon, Tetris, and lots more are available in online versions, where you can compete with other real, live people. Here's a World Wide Web address that can be your one-stop shopping mall for these:

http://wcl-rs.bham.ac.uk/GamesDomain

This is the World Wide Web home page of the Games Domain. This site is a repository for FAQs, games spoilers, links to other games' home pages, FTP sites, and more. As of this writing, there are a total of over 230 links, and this list is continually being added to.

If you can, get in with Netscape or another WWW browser; here is what you'll see. If you can get in with Lynx, the same information will be there. It just won't look as nice.

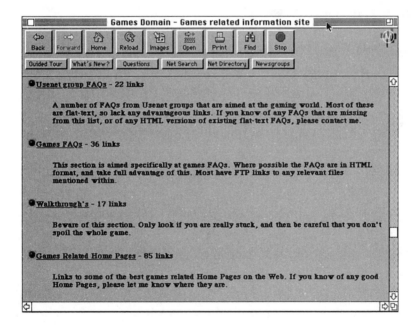

You could spend weeks wandering around in here.

Get into it, push some buttons, and see where it takes you. You may be amazed.

Great Ideas for Having Fun

Not all these have to do with IRC and MUDs, but they're all almost entirely useless and lots of fun. Don't stay up too late, now!

- If you're looking for more of a short-term relationship with your terminal some evening and would like just a quick burst of entertainment for a few hours, try **telnet astro.temple.edu 12345** or **telnet argo.temple .edu 12345**. (Just type those commands exactly as-is at your UNIX prompt.)

- Maybe you need a humorous quote to spruce up that late research paper. This address will give you a funny quote each time you log in:

  telnet astro.temple.edu 12345

- To find out how your favorite soft drink sales are faring at some major universities, try one of these:

  finger coke@cs.cmu.edu
  finger graph@drink.csh.rit.edu
  finger pepsi@columbia.edu or
  finger coke@xcf.berkeley.edu

- On a more serious note, try **finger copi@oddjob.uchicago.edu** for a daily listing of what happened on that day in the past.

- Use **finger quake@gldfs.cr.us.gov** to find out what is shaking in different parts of the world (that is, to keep up with current earthquake activity).

- Use **finger nasanews@space.mit.edu** to find out the latest from NASA.

- Check out the World Wide Web site **http://metaverse.com**. If you are into the blues, they have them here. You can download sound and image files. Warning, though: you're going to need some serious hard disk space and some time to kill to if you want to retrieve these files.

- Play Find the Spam. Point your WWW browser to **http:// sp1.berkeley.edu/findthespam.html**. I'm not going to tell you any more about this one; you'll need to check it out for yourself.

When it comes to having fun on the Net, the sky is the limit. There are an amazing number of creative people out there designing wacky and wonderful ways to pass the time. One link leads to the next; one contact will lead you to another. Get in there, push some buttons, and see where it takes you.

Getting Down to Business: Some Research Strategies

After you're tired of the games, the chat sessions, the free-wheeling exploration and discovery, it's time to get serious. Once you've learned to use the tools described in the previous chapters, fiddled with their options, and fine tuned them to suit your needs, why not put them to good use? The Internet can make researching a topic exciting.

I know *exciting* and *research* aren't two words that usually go together, but give it a chance; you'll be amazed at the amount of information you can pull down without leaving home. Amazed and maybe even excited.

In this chapter, we'll look at a couple more Internet research tools I haven't told you about yet: WAIS and Netfind. WAIS looks for information, Netfind for people. Then we'll take all the tools into consideration and plan out a research strategy.

WAIS

WAIS stands for Wide Area Information Server. (It's pronounced "ways.") It's a great tool for locating documents on the Internet that deal with a particular topic. You pick the databases you want searched, pop in your keywords, and retrieve the results. Sounds simple, huh?

To start out, let's look at a WAIS server and perform a search. As with just about everything else on the Internet, there's more than one way to get into WAIS: you can either use Gopher or Telnet. We'll look at both.

Having Your WAIS with a Gopher

One easy way to get to WAIS is with a Gopher. In Gopher, select **Other Gophers and Information Servers** and look for WAIS.

```
          Other Gophers and Information Servers

     1.  All the Gopher Servers in the World/
     2.  Search All the Gopher Servers in the World <?>
     3.  Search titles in Gopherspace using veronica/
     4.  Africa/
     5.  Asia/
     6.  Europe/
     7.  International Organizations/
     8.  Middle East/
     9.  North America/
    10.  Pacific/
    11.  Russia/
    12.  South America/
    13.  Terminal Based Information/
-->  14.  WAIS Based Information/
    15.  Gopher Server Registration.
```

Making that selection will bring you to another menu.

```
              WAIS Based Information

-->  1.  List of all WAIS Sources/
     2.  READ THIS!.
     3.  WAIS Databases sorted by Letter/
     4.  WAIS databases sorted by Subject (Experimental), UB2, Lund, Sweden/
```

Here is where you can make a selection about which database to search. Typing **1** at this point will bring up every searchable database WAIS has to offer. There were 616 as of this writing. Maybe that's more than you want to wade through. If you know the name of the database, select **3** for an alphabetical organization. If you don't know the name, and scrolling through page after page of sources is not the way you want to spend your Sunday afternoons (or any other time), type **4**. Then select

```
    2.  Subject tree (based on UDC)/
```

from the next menu. Doing so will bring you to this:

```
              Subject tree (based on UDC)

-->  1.  General, Bibliography, Library science/
     2.  Philosophy, Psychology, Ethics/
     3.  Religion, Theology/
     4.  Social sciences/
     5.  Mathematics, Natural sciences/
     6.  Applied sciences, Medicine, Technology/
```

```
 7.  Art, Architecture, Music, Sports/
 8.  Linguistics, Philology, Literature/
 9.  Geography, Biography, History/
```

Now this looks like something we can work with. Let's see if we can come up with some information on black holes. I'm referring to the ones in space, not life after graduation. We'll look in number **5**, and open up the Astronomy Databases. Here they are:

```
 1.  AAS_jobs: American Astronomical Society Job Register Listings <?>
 2.  AAS_meeting: Abstracts, current American Astronomical Society m.. <?>
 3.  AAS_meeting_Summer92: Abstracts, June 92 American Astronomical .. <?>
 4.  AAS_meeting_Summer93: Abstracts, June 93 American Astronomical .. <?>
 5.  AAS_meeting_Winter93: Abstracts, Jan 93 American Astronomical S.. <?>
 6.  ADC_documents:  <?>
 7.  ANU-Radiocarbon-Abstracts:  <?>
 8.  ANU-Urban-Research-L:  <?>
 9.  ANU-ZenBuddhism-Calendar:  <?>
10.  ASK-SISY-Software-Information: Software Information System of t.. <?>
11.  NASA-directory-of-servers:  <?>
12.  NASA_Missions: NASA mission payload information <?>
13.  NSSDC_CD-ROM: CD_ROM's avail. NASA's National Space Science Dat.. <?>
14.  SPACEWARN: NASA SPACE-WARN bulletins <?>
15.  WGAS:  <?>
16.  abstracts-aa:  <?>
17.  abstracts-aas:  <?>
18.  abstracts-apj:
```

Uh-oh, looks like a lot of gibberish. Well, yes and no. I'm sure all of these mean something to somebody, but if you look hard enough, something will make sense. What you need to know is that all of these selections represent a searchable database with information relating to astronomy. This is just the first page. There are 39 databases in all in this category.

I don't see anything particularly exciting on this page so I'll jump ahead (by hitting **Spacebar**) to the next page. There I find a couple that look promising.

```
33.  sci.astro.hubble:  <?>
34.  smithsonian-pictures:  <?>
35.  stsci-docs:  <?>
36.  stsci-old-preprint-db:  <?>
37.  stsci-preprint-db:  <?>
```

sci.astro.hubble is obviously a newsgroup. smithsonian-pictures seems to make sense to me as well, but stsci-preprint-db? Well, not everything needs to make sense. Although...

Let's do a search on black holes. Choose:

```
 5.  AAS_meeting_Winter93: Abstracts, Jan 93 American Astronomical S.. <?>
```

After selecting, you are prompted to type a keyword.

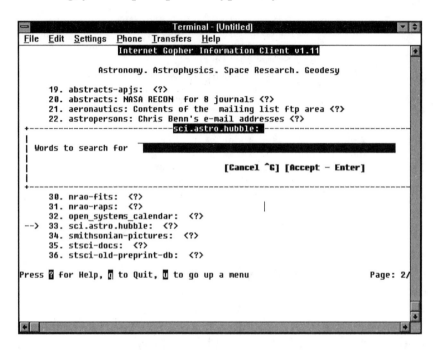

Type the word(s) you're looking for, and away you search.

Type **black holes** and in less than a minute, more than 30 responses will be sent your way, including:

```
--> 1.   2905.tex S.K. Chakrabarti and<> RE: Dynamics of Magnetic Flux Tube...
    2.   8404.tex Sandip K. Chakrabart<> RE: Binary Black Holes in Stationa...
    3.   8508.tex R.Ramaty<> RE: Compton Backscattered Annihilation Line fr...
    4.   3505.tex K.P. Rauch \& R.D. B<> RE: The Caustic Structure of the K...
    5.   6510.tex Masaru Hamabe<> RE: Central Holes in Galaxy Disks -- How ...
    6.   4908.tex Daniel Puche<> RE: Star formation and the evolution of dw...
    7.   3206.tex K.Mitsuda<> RE: Measuring Black Hole Masses from X-ray Ob...
    8.   10606.tex Michael Eracleous<> RE: Double-Peaked H$\alpha$ Emission...
    9.   2008.tex P.C.Schmidtke, A.P.C<> RE: The X-ray Eclipse of the Black...
   10.   9002.tex R.D. Blandford<> RE: Compton Gamma Ray Observatory Observ...
   11.   3803.tex J.W. Haller, M.J. Ri<> RE: Evidence for a 2$\times$$10^6$...
   12.   7301.tex C.D. Bailyn<> RE: Evidence for a Black Hole in the X-ray ...
   13.   2901.tex C. Winkler<> RE: COMPTEL Observations of Black Hole Candi...
```

To view a document, select it, and it appears on your screen. You can then mail the document back to yourself or save it in a local file, as described in the Gopher chapter (that was Chapter 6, for those of you who are keeping score).

Gopher is probably the easiest way to search the WAIS, but it doesn't give you the option of searching more than one database at a time, and this is a severe limitation. Let's look at another alternative that's more difficult to use, but more powerful.

Power-WAIS with Telnet

Instead of gophering to a WAIS site, you can telnet directly to it. If you've worked with Telnet before in previous chapters, you know that it's a less-than-graceful way of doing business. You're faced with a grim-looking prompt such as login:, and it doesn't get much friendlier from there. However, telneting directly to a WAIS site enables you to select several different databases before you start your search—and that feature alone can save you hours of grief.

To connect with a WAIS server, telnet to any of these addresses. (The **swais** or **wais** I've listed after the address is the command you type in response to the login: prompt.)

```
sunsite.unc.edu      swais

wais.wais.com        wais

quake.think.com      wais
```

Here's a sample login sequence:

```
telnet sunsite.unc.edu

Trying 198.86.40.81...
Connected to sunsite.unc.edu.
Escape character is '^]'.

**************** Welcome to SunSITE.unc.edu *****************
SunSITE offers several public services via login. These include:

For a simple World Wide Web client,            login as lynx
For a simple WAIS client (over 500 databases), login as swais
For WAIS search of political databases,        login as politics
For WAIS search of LINUX databases,            login as linux

login: swais
TERM = (unknown) vt100
```

Notice that I specified vt100 as my terminal type. That's a pretty safe bet if you're using almost any kind of personal computer to log onto a remote UNIX computer. It's sort of the standard/generic terminal type.

Once you are logged in, the listing of WAIS sources will be on your screen, like this:

```
 IS                        Source Selection            Sources: 76
   #          Server                       Source              Cost
 001:  [      sunsite.unc.edu]  alt-sys-sun                    Free
 002:  [                    ]  American-Music-Resource          Free
 003:  [                    ]  avi_files                       Free
 004:  [            calypso]  bush-speeches                     Free
 005:  [                    ]  carter-oh                       Free
 006:  [                    ]  clinton-speeches                 Free
 007:  [                    ]  clinton-speechess                Free
 008:  [            calypso]  cold-fusion                       Free
 009:  [      sunsite.unc.edu]  Community-IdeaNet               Free
 010:  [calypso-2.oit.unc.ed]  Dr-Fun                          Free
 011:  [                    ]  eisenhower-oh                   Free
 012:  [      sunSITE.unc.edu]  eric-digests                   Free
 013:  [      sunsite.unc.edu]  Fascism                        Free
 014:  [          bittyblue]  foo                              Free
 015:  [                    ]  ford-finding-aids                Free
 016:  [      sunsite.unc.edu]  fusion-digest                  Free
 017:  [            calypso]  govnii                            Free
 018:  [            calypso]  govnpr                            Free

 Keywords:

 <space> selects, w for keywords, arrows move, <return> searches, q quits, or ?
```

With this kind of search, you first select all of the sources you want searched. To do that, move from source to source using the arrow keys, and when you find a source you want included in your search, press the **Spacebar** to mark it.

Tip ➤

You can do a keyword search for sources by typing /. If you know the name or part of the name of the source you want to search, this is very handy. After typing /, fill in the name of the source or the part you know, and WAIS will take you there.

Once you have selected all of your sources, you are ready to let WAIS do the work for you. Performing a search for information on NAFTA (North American Free Trade Agreement), I found three sources that looked promising:

```
clinton-speeches
npr
nafta
```

Next, I typed **w** and was prompted for a keyword at the bottom of my screen:

```
Keywords:nafta

Enter keywords with spaces between them; <return> to search; ^C to cancel
```

Then I hit **Enter** to search. In about thirty seconds, WAIS came back with 15 items relating to NAFTA:

```
SWAIS                           Search Results                    Items: 15
 #    Score     Source                      Title                        Lines
001:  [1000]  (clinton-speeches)       ANALYSIS: Talking Points - 10/5    63
002:  [1000]  (nafta)   0anonymous.civ.utoronto.ca      0/.pub/academ
003:  [1000]  (nafta)   +INFO: 0anonymous.civ.utoronto.ca       0/.pub
004:  [ 350]  (clinton-speeches)         TRADE: Position Paper           230
005:  [ 350]  (clinton-speeches)         TRADE: Position Paper           228
006:  [223]   (nafta)  NORTH AMERICAN AGREEMENT          3006
007:  [211]   (nafta)  UNDERSTANDING BETWEEN THE          141
008:  [129]   (nafta)                                    3028
009:  [129]   (nafta)                                    3028
010:  [94]    (nafta)       NOTES                         312
011:  [84]    (clinton-speeches)     VP DEBATE ANALYSIS: Encyclopedi    697
012:  [58]    (clinton-speeches)     FOREIGN TRADE:Speech- Raleigh  915
013:  [58]    (nafta)       PART FOUR                    3144
014:  [49]    (clinton-speeches)     DEMOCRATIC PARTY PLATFORM           1066
015:  [0] (npr)    Search produced no result. Here's the Ca   169
```

Tip ➤

WAIS-based information is in a constant state of change. If you were to perform the exact same search as in this example, you'll most certainly receive different information.

Information was returned from two of my sources (`clinton-speeches` and `nafta`). The third (npr) produced nothing, but this is plenty of information to keep me busy for an afternoon. To view any of these, I select the article I would like to read using the arrow keys, and then press **Enter**. The text appears.

If, after reading the text, you decide this is something you can use, you can:

▌ Mail a copy of the speech to yourself by typing **m**.

▌ Save a copy of the file in your home UNIX directory by typing **S**.

Either of these options will call up a prompt, either for an e-mail address or a filename. Once saved or mailed, the file is easily retrievable by you at any time you need it.

Here are some other useful commands in WAIS (you can access this window in WAIS by typing ?):

j, Down Arrow, ^N	Move down one source
k, Up Arrow, ^P	Move up one source
J, ^V, ^D	Move down one screen
K, Esc v, ^U	Move up one screen
###	Position to source number ##
/sss	Search for source sss
Spacebar, period	Select current source
=	Deselect all sources
v, comma	View current source info
Enter	Perform search
s	Select new sources (refresh sources list)
w	Select new keywords
X, -	Remove current source permanently
o	Set and show swais options
h, ?	Show this help display
H	Display program history
q	Leave this program

Finding People with Netfind

Trying to find the e-mail addresses of other people on the Internet can be an exercise in frustration. There is no such thing as a complete Internet phone book—and there probably never will be. Trying to put something together would be an impossible task, considering how fast new people are coming onto the Internet and how much the services that the hosts provide vary. Even if there were such a phone book, not everyone would have access to it, because not all hosts would install the special software needed to access it.

So what am I saying here? Don't always expect to be able to find the people you're looking for on the Internet. I've failed in several attempts to locate people. That hasn't stopped me from trying, though, and it shouldn't stop you either.

So let's log into a Netfind server and search for someone I *know* we can find—me. There are several different servers you can connect to that will do your search for you. You can reach these all via a Telnet connection.

bruno.cs.colorado.edu (University of Colorado, Boulder)

dino.conicit.ve (Nat. Council for Techn. & Scien. Research, Venezuela)

ds.internic.net (InterNIC Directory and DB Services, S. Plainfield, NJ)

eis.calstate.edu (California State University, Fullerton, CA)

krnic.net (Korea Network Information Center, Taejon, Korea)

malloco.ing.puc.cl (Catholic University of Chile, Santiago)

monolith.cc.ic.ac.uk (Imperial College, London, England)

mudhoney.micro.umn.edu (University of Minnesota, Minneapolis)

netfind.ee.mcgill.ca (McGill University, Montreal, Quebec, Canada)

netfind.fnet.fr (Association FNET, Le Kremlin-Bicetre, France)

netfind.icm.edu.pl (Warsaw University, Warsaw, Poland)

netfind.if.usp.br (University of Sao Paulo, Sao Paulo, Brazil)

netfind.sjsu.edu (San Jose State University, San Jose, California)

netfind.vslib.cz (Liberec University of Technology, Czech Republic)

nic.uakom.sk (Academy of Sciences, Banska Bystrica, Slovakia)

redmont.cis.uab.edu (University of Alabama at Birmingham)

Choose a site and connect with it from your UNIX prompt, like this:

telnet *address*

For this example, I'll choose the server at California State University:

```
telnet eis.calstate.edu
Trying 130.150.102.33...
Connected to eis.calstate.edu.
Escape character is '^]'.
```

```
SunOS UNIX (eis.calstate.edu)

login: netfind


================================================================================
Welcome to the California Online Resources for Education  Netfind server.
================================================================================


I think that your terminal can display 24 lines.  If this is wrong,
please enter the "Options" menu and set the correct number of lines.

Top level choices:
        1. Help
        2. Search
        3. Seed database lookup
        4. Options
        5. Quit (exit server)
```

Note that for the login, I used **netfind**. That will be true on all of the Netfind servers. To do a search, I will choose **2**. If you need help, you can select **1** or just keep reading here. Selecting **2** brings me to this:

```
Enter person and keys (blank to exit) -->
```

Type in what you know about the person. Each word must be separated by a space. No commas, no periods. Let's do a broad search and see what happens.

```
Enter person and keys (blank to exit) -->clark colorado
```

I hit **Enter** and wait. What the machine comes back with is a lengthy list of domain names in Colorado and a request to be more specific if I can. Armed with what I know about myself, I comply:

```
Enter person and keys (blank to exit) -->clark boulder colorado
```

The machine begins to reel off all the domain names in Boulder, Colorado but still comes back with a request to be a bit more specific. Okay, I know that I'm a teacher; I also know that many school districts have k12 or edu in their addresses. I'll include those in my search.

```
Enter person and keys (blank to exit) --> clark boulder  colorado edu
Please select at most 3 of the following domains to search:
0. naropa.edu (the naropa institute, boulder, colorado)
1. ncds.edu (national corperative data share, boulder, colorado)
2. acc.colorado.edu (academic computing center, university of colorado,boulder)
3. astro.colorado.edu (astronomy department, university of colorado, boulder)
4. ba.colorado.edu (business school, university of colorado, boulder)
```

```
5. bogus.colorado.edu (unixops sysadmin group, university of colorado, boulder)
6. bvsd.co.edu (boulder valley school district, boulder, colorado)
7. casa.colorado.edu (center for astrophysics and space astronomy, university
   of colorado, boulder)
8. cats.colorado.edu (computing and technology services, university of
   colorado, boulder)

Enter selection (e.g., 2 0 1) -->
```

Including the **edu** did the trick for me. I'm given a list of domains I can work with. The search actually came back with 24 domains in Boulder that match the search criteria. Netfind asks me to select a maximum of 3 of these sources to find. I only need one: **6.**

I'm then presented a list of all the Clarks with accounts on the bvsd machine, and I find myself among them.

```
Login name: clarkd       (messages off)  In real life: David Clark
Office: Columbine/P, 443-0792            Home phone: 828-3185
Directory: /users/teacher/clarkd         Shell: /usr/local/etc/CNSlogin
On since Dec 11 13:54:40 on ttyp6 from tco15.Colorado.E
No Plan.
```

Notice that this is the same information that you would get if you used the **finger** command to locate someone on your own server. Finger is one of the tools that Netfind used to perform its search. Once it knows the domain, it can just send a **finger** command and the results come pouring in.

Searching the Internet White Pages

I told you that there wasn't a phone book, but there *is* an attempt to create an Internet White Pages for colleges and universities. Accessing this will give you a listing of the schools that are hooked up. You can then choose which institution you want to do a search in. To get into this service, gopher to **ucunix.san.uc.edu** and select

```
-->  15. E-Mail White Pages (Ph, Whois, and X.500)/
```

and you'll receive the following options:

```
            E-Mail White Pages (Ph, Whois, and X.500)

-->  1.  About Phone Directory.
     2.  All the directory servers in the world/
     3.  North America/
     4.  Asia Pacific/
     5.  Europe/
     6.  Africa/
```

This service is organized geographically. I'll do a search for an old college buddy at the University of Nebraska in Lincoln. His name is David Billesbach. Choose **3. North America.**

```
                              North America

        235.  University of Maryland at Baltimore <CSO>
        236.  University of Maryland, Baltimore County <CSO>
        237.  University of Massachusetts at Amherst <CSO>
        238.  University of Memphis <CSO>
        239.  University of Miami, Rosentiel School of Marine and Atmospheric <?>
        240.  University of Michigan (X.500 service) <?>
        241.  University of Minnesota <CSO>
        242.  University of Mississippi <?>
        243.  University of Missouri - Rolla Faculty/Staff <CSO>
   -->  244.  University of Nebraska at Lincoln <?>
        245.  University of Nebraska at Omaha <CSO>
        246.  University of Nebraska-Lincoln <CSO>
        247.  University of Nevada at Reno <?>
        248.  University of New Brunswick, Canada <CSO>
        249.  University of New Brunswick, Canada <CSO>
        250.  University of New Brunswick, Canada <?>
        251.  University of North Carolina at Greensboro/
        252.  University of North Texas <CSO>
```

Tip ➤ The <CSO> at the end of many of these stands for Computing Services Office. This is a searching utility used at many colleges and universities.

Since the University of Nebraska has a couple of options, I'll look at `244. University of Nebraska at Lincoln <?>`. Selecting this brings up a prompt to type in his name; his last name is enough as it is unusual. In less time than it takes to say "Billesbach," I have my results.

```
        -200:1:          alias: DBILLESBACH
        -200:1:           name: BILLESBACH DAVID

        -200:1:          email: dpb@unlinfo.unl.edu
        -200:1:          phone:
        -200:1:        address:
        -200:1:              :
        -200:1:     department: NRI ENGR RES
        -200:1:          title: RESEARCH ASST PROF
```

So when would you use Netfind? To look up the addresses of relatives or friends who you suspect may be on the Net? To re-establish old friendships or start new ones? To look up the address of professors or other experts in your

Chapter 10

196

field of study and send them carefully composed queries or notes of introduction? Who knows, you may get lucky.

Use it to look up domain names or institution addresses you may have forgotten. (Remember, Netfind will come back with domain names of almost anywhere in the world.) See how many people have the same name as you at Harvard University. :-)

Here are some great ideas for research:

▪ Need facts quick? Connect to the CIA World Fact Book. This collection of informational tidbits on countries around the world can be found at: **http://www.ic.gov/94fact/fb94toc/fb94toc.html.**

▪ Dictionaries abound on the Internet. Here is one to try: **gopher:// gopher.princeton.edu:5003/7.**

▪ Can't remember your high school chemistry? Left your book at your boyfriend's? Access the periodic table of elements at: **gopher:// ucsbuxa.ucsb.edu:3001/11/.Sciences/.Chemistry/.periodic.**

▪ Roget's Thesaurus can be found at: **gopher://joeboy.micro.umn.edu/ 11/Ebooks/By%20Title/roget.**

▪ Britannica Encyclopedia is available for searching online; however, you have to subscribe to this service. For more information, browse to: **http://www.eb.com:180/eb.html.**

▪ For people in the school of education, ERIC is indispensable. ERIC provides a searchable index of a wide variety of topics in the field of education at: **gopher://ericir.syr.edu/1.**

▪ The online writing lab (owl) at Purdue University provides services to help undergraduates writing research papers. Here's their spiel:

```
The Purdue University Writing Lab serves the entire Purdue community and
offers outreach services to other Internet users as well. Our goal in the
lab is to provide one-to-one interaction with writers who make appoint-
ments or drop in to see us. In tutorials, we talk with writers planning
their papers or in the midst of writing them. We hear a lot of questions
such as "Does this fit the assignment?" or "How should I start this
paper?" Don't be surprised if we ask a question in response. That gets the
conversation going and helps the writer think.
```

This interactive service takes place through e-mail. For information, send a message to **owl@sage.cc.purdue.** Type the words **owl-request** in the subject line.

Their World Wide Web site is also a great jumping off place for research with pointers to several other reference sites. **http://owl.trc.purdue.edu** is the address.

Speaking of jumping off sites:

▌▌ The Virtual Reference Desk located at the University of California/Irvine is another good place to find reference materials. The address is: **gopher://peg.cwis.uci.edu:7000/11/gopher.welcome/peg/uci.**

▌▌ Once there was the Reader's Guide to Periodical Literature for researching information contained in periodicals. Now there is UNCOVER. UNCOVER keeps track of nearly 17,000 different periodicals and has a database containing over five million articles. Sound too good to be free? It is. Searching the database is free; however, to retrieve an article, you will have to shell out $8.50, plus a copyright fee ($3–$5). The article (including graphics and any charts included) will be faxed to you within 24 hours. Kind of pricey if you ask me, but knowing it's there may save your rear end in a pinch. Telnet to: **database.carl.org** to see what it is all about.

Brushing Up on Your Research Skills— The Internet Hunt

Do you like a challenge? Would you like to improve your Internet research skills? Would you like to win fabulous prizes while doing it? Then the Internet Hunt is for you.

Well, all right, I hyped up the prizes thing a bit, but you can win free magazine subscriptions and signed copies of Internet Guides by being the first one to come up with the right answers.

Here's how it works. At the beginning of each month, the questions are posted to a variety of sources. The questions are submitted by many seasoned nettrekkers to Rick Gates at the University of Arizona in Tucson. (Apparently Rick has some spare time on his hands.) The questions are given a point value as to their difficulty. Then it's off to the races to see who can come up with the answers first. The winners take home the prizes mentioned above.

Even if you aren't into the competitive thing, the hunt can be a great way to sharpen your skills and make you aware of resources you didn't know existed. Archives from past hunts are available. Questions, answers, and additional information regarding the hunt are available from:

Gopher Sites

```
gopher.cic.net
gopher.cni.org
```

FTP Sites

```
ftp.cni.org pub/net-guides/i-hunt/
ftp.cic.net pub/internet-hunt
```

Mailing Lists

```
libref-l@kentvm
edtech@msu.edu
nettrain@ubvm
net-happenings@is.internic.net
```

USENET Groups

```
alt.bbs.internet
alt.internet.services
```

Putting Together a Research Strategy

We've covered a lot of tools and a lot of searching utilities. After the silliness and initial excitement is over, you'll want to put them to work to get something useful done, preferably something that will help lead you to that four-year degree at the end of the tunnel.

Let's look at a scenario. Mary, a senior in the School of Education at the University of Smartville has a paper due. Her assigned topic is "Constructivism: Theory and Practice."

Don't worry, I'm not going to make you read her paper. We're just going to set up an organizational framework for Mary to find the sources using the tools we've discussed thus far. You don't even need to know what constructivism is. Just fill in your own keywords in the searches that follow.

Mary weighs her options. She can:

▮▮ Hike across campus to the library.

▮▮ Make up something on her own.

▮▮ Look for some electronic sources of information on the Internet.

Right up front, I need to tell you, the Internet isn't going to replace a trip to the library—at least not yet. There are still times when you'll have to put on your walking shoes and hunt through the stacks. However, you can learn how to do that in another book. For the purposes of this book, Mary wants to stay home tonight. (There goes option 1.) She considers option 2 for only the slightest time, and then powers up her PC and proceeds to option 3.

First, she considers the tools at her command that she thinks may help her:

- e-mail

- Gopher

- USENET Groups

- World Wide Web

- WAIS

Mary starts with e-mail, knowing that a listserv search could take a few minutes after she sends it off. She composes a message to

```
listserv@listserv.net
```

with the message:

```
list global /education
list global /educational philosophy
list global /educational psychology
list global /constructivism
```

and sends it off. One of these searches should bring back something (a starting place anyway). Then she gets to work searching Gopher while waiting for the response.

She tries a Veronica search, fills in the word **Constructivism**, and gets this:

```
Veronica at PSInet is busy.
```

Grrrr...

```
Veronica at SUNET is busy.
```

Grrrr again.

Finally Veronica at NYSERnet has an opening, and what an opening. Fifty-five items on Constructivism are returned, including:

```
1.  Social Constructivism/
2.  Re: Constructivism--What is it?.
3.  Re: Constructivism--What is it?.
```

```
4.  Re: Constructivism--What is it?.
5.  Constructivism - what is it?.
6.  Constructivism, technology, and at-risk students.
7.  Constructivism.
8.  Re: Constructivism--What is it?.
9.  RE: Opinion on Constructivism Approach to Teaching.
```

Mary spends all night pouring through these articles. There's a wide range of materials from e-mail messages from other students looking for examples of the theory in classrooms, to responses to these questions and papers written that discuss the theory. Mary reads the ones that look interesting and e-mails copies of the sources she thinks she can use back to herself. She also writes down the e-mail addresses of some of the authors. These can be some valuable resources for her as well. A good start, Mary.

Next time Mary logs on, she checks her e-mail. The searches for constructivism and educational philosophy returned nothing. The search for education psychology came back with one list. The search for education brought back nearly two hundred different lists where she can get information. There is a wide variety of educational topics represented in the list, including:

```
JESSE          JESSE@ARIZVM1.BITNET
               Open Lib/Info Sci Education Forum
LSE            LSE@WAYNEST1.BITNET
               Legal Studies Education
NAEB-L         NAEB-L@RITVM.BITNET
               National Association of Educational Buyers
```

While she is sure that these lists have relevance to the people who frequent them, they're not for her. She looks for some that may include input from classroom teachers and professors of education. Three lists will probably give her all the e-mail she could ever want, and she finally subscribes to:

```
L-EDUC         L-EDUC@PSUVM.BITNET
               College of Education List
NICE           NICE@MIAMIU.BITNET
               Network for Innovative Colleges of Education
               (NICE)
PHILOSED       PHILOSED@SUVM.BITNET
               Students and Teachers Discussing Philosophy of Education
```

She saves the e-mail message that lists the listservs in a folder in Pine, in case she wants to look at it again. Then she starts to subscribe to the lists above.

Mary knows that it wouldn't be a great idea to post her questions right away and reads the posts for a couple of days to determine which may be the best list to post her query. When finally the time comes, she creates a carefully worded message to post to the group.

```
Hello,

My name is Mary and I am a senior in the School of Education. I am writing
a paper entitled "Constructivism in Public Education, Theory and Practice"
and would like some help. I would appreciate your thoughts on the follow-
ing questions:
What does constructivism mean to you as a practicing educator?
Do you employ constructivist thinking in the preparation of
your lessons or teaching environment.

Also, can you point me to any good resources, electronic or otherwise,
that might help me with my report?

I promise to give full credit in my bibliography citations for any infor-
mation you might provide me.

Thanks in advance,

Mary
```

While waiting for the replies to roll in, Mary turns her attention to the World
Wide Web. Since she's at home, she uses Lynx to enter the Web, remember-
ing to stop in at the lab on campus and do a more thorough search using
Netscape tomorrow. But for tonight, Lynx will do the trick.

She connects up with the Internet MetaIndex at:

```
http://www.ncsa.uiuc.edu/SDG/Software/Mosaic/MetaIndex.html
```

This is a good place to start. From this site, she can use searching utilities,
such as the World Wide Web Worm. She can also search through some of the
subject indexes housed there.

She uses the Worm and nothing comes back on Constructivism. She then
moves down the page to the subject listings and finds education as one of the
choices in the Subject tree list at Rice University.

```
Select one of:
(FILE)  About the RiceInfo collection of "Information by Subject Area"
 (DIR)  More about "Information by Subject Area"
 (DIR)  Clearinghouse of Subject-Oriented Internet Resource Guides (UMich)
  (?)   Search all of Gopherspace by title: Jughead (from WLU)
 (DIR)  Search all of Gopherspace by title: Veronica
 (DIR)  Search all of RiceInfo by title: Jughead
 (DIR) Aerospace
 (DIR) Agriculture and Forestry
 (DIR) Anthropology and Culture
 (DIR) Architecture
 (DIR) Arts
 (DIR) Astronomy and Astrophysics
 (DIR) Biology
 (DIR) Census
```

```
(DIR) Chemistry
(DIR) Computer Networks and Internet Resource Guides
(DIR) Computing
(DIR) Economics and Business
(DIR) Education
```

Selecting education brings her to a large listing of educational sites available on the Web. She looks for a searchable database. She'll know when she finds one because the name will be preceded by a (?). She doesn't have to go far until she runs into ERIC.

```
 (DIR) EDUCOM Gopher Server
 (DIR) EDUPAGE: back issues
(FILE) EDUPAGE: current issue
 (DIR) EE-Link, the Environmental Education Gopher
 (DIR) EE-Link, the Environmental Education Gopher
   (?) ERIC (Educational Resources Information Center) Digests
   (?) ERIC (Educational Resources Information Center) Digests
 (DIR) ERIC Clearinghouse on Assessment and Evaluation
 (TEL) ERIC Database (1983 to current)
(FILE) Ednet Educator's Guide to Email Lists
 (DIR) Education Policy Analysis Archives
 (DIR) Educational Testing Service (NJ)
 (DIR) Educom Gopher
(FILE) Electronic Tools in an actual classroom (Sheldon Annis)
 (DIR) Empire Internet Schoolhouse (NY)
 (DIR) Empire Internet Schoolhouse (from NYSERNet)
 (TEL) Federal Information Exchange
 (TEL) Federal Information Exchange (FEDIX)
 (DIR) Federal Information Exchange (FEDIX) Gopher
 (DIR) Food & Agricultural Education Information System (FAEIS)
 (DIR) Free Education Mail Foundation (FrEdMail) (Bonita, CA)
(FILE) Global Systems Analysis and Simulation Association
```

She chooses ERIC, is prompted for her keyword, types **constructivism**, and waits. In nothing flat, she receives three citations back.

```
    Select one of:

(FILE) Title: Trends in Educational Technology 1991. ERIC Digest
(FILE) Title: Thinking in Outdoor Inquiry. ERIC Digest
(FILE) Title: Whole Language in an Elementary School Library Media Center.
       ERIC Digest
```

Mary mails the files back to herself so she can read them later or print them out if she needs a hard copy.

Knowing there is much more to find in the Web, she returns to the MetaIndex and continues her search. Mary searches her .newsrc for newsgroups relating to education. First she opens the file using the vi editor.

```
vi .newsrc
```

Next she types / to search the list of newsgroups. When prompted for a keyword, she types **k12**. Mary is playing it smart here. She knows the syntax of newsgroup naming and knows that typing **constructivism** or even **education** will bring back nothing. She knows there is a set of newsgroups for k12 (kindergarten–12th grade) teachers and looks there first.

```
k12.chat.elementary: 1-18602
k12.chat.junior! 1-31470
k12.chat.senior! 1-60531
k12.chat.teacher: 1-21682,21762-21763,21790
k12.ed.life-skills! 1-503
k12.ed.math! 1-5112
k12.ed.music! 1-3249
k12.ed.science! 1-6353
k12.ed.soc-studies! 1-1972
k12.ed.special! 1-1587
k12.ed.tag! 1-1851
misc.education! 1-16694
```

She chooses a couple that look good for her inquiry: `k12.chat.teacher` and `misc.education`. Now she spends some time reading the postings that are already there before deciding that these are the appropriate places to place her query. The she types **nnpost k12.chat.teacher** at her prompt. She drops the message in the newsgroup and has a cup of coffee.

The time it took Mary to perform these searches (excluding time reading the articles) was less than an hour. She'll check her e-mail and newsgroups regularly over the next couple of days for replies to her queries and can expect several back from each of the letters she posted. As she becomes more and more familiar with the listservs and newsgroups, she will know exactly which groups are appropriate for what questions and what kinds of responses she should get back.

Next on Mary's platter will be a WAIS search. I won't walk you through that (I just did earlier in this chapter), but that search, too, should return a good deal of information for Mary to use.

One More Time, from the Top

Hard to remember all of this? Here is the capsulation of all Mary went through.

E-mail

Search for mailing lists on your topic and post a request for information.

Gopher

Use Veronica to do a keyword search.

Access a Gopher subject tree heading, such as Gopher-Jewels, and search for your topic.

USENET

Search for a newsgroup that discusses your topic and post a request for information.

WWW

Use one of the many searching utilities, such as the WWWW or the Web Crawler, to do a search on your topic, or access a Web Subject Tree Heading, such as those found in the Internet MetaIndex, and search for your topic.

WAIS

Perform a WAIS search.

There, that wasn't so bad, was it? It sure is better than going through microfiche in the library or dusting off huge volumes of old journals. Don't forget: Research is only the beginning. The real work of assembling your paper begins when the research has been assembled.

Separating the Treasure from the Trash

The greatest strength of the Internet is the free flow of information.

The greatest *weakness* of the Internet is also the free flow of information.

Do you see what I'm getting at? Anybody and their dog (with some help) can put any kind of garbage out on the Internet, providing they have access to the equipment. If you pick up a book at the school library, you can be assured that several people evaluated that book before it was published, and even so, a lot of mistakes made it to press. Raw information on the Internet has not gone through even the slightest of this.

So what does that mean for information you receive on the Internet? That means, be careful. Discriminate and read carefully. Check sources and ask for collaboration on fine points.

This fact-checking can actually be a very positive thing. Going through the filtering process yourself is empowering, in that you are not relying on anyone else to tell you what is important and what you should be reading. It's also a lot of work, but nobody said this was supposed to be easy. I certainly didn't.

Realize, too, that there is going to be a fair amount of trash jumbled in with the jewels. That's why the Delete key was invented. Don't be afraid to use it.

When sending out a request for information to a listserv or newsgroup, make your request concise. If you receive information from a source that seems potentially useful, but somewhat muddled, send them a reply and ask for clarification. Be polite, but find out some information about who you will be quoting in your report.

Citing Electronic Sources

When citing an electronic source in a bibliography, here is the form you should use:

> Author. (date). _Title [Online]_. Available: (FTP, Telnet, Gopher) Location: location Directory: directory File: file.

Here are a couple of examples:

> Smith, Mary. (1990). _My Life [Online]_. Available: FTP
> Location: host.com Directory: /pub/another_dir/ File: my_life.txt

A citation of a World Wide Web cite will look a bit different:

> Smith, Mary. (1990). _My Life [Online]_. Available:
> http://www.host.net/pub/another_dir/my_life.txt

List of Resources by Academic Subject Area

This is not a comprehensive list by any means. Such a list would take more time than I have to write and more time than you have to read. These are some good jumping off places to get you started.

> **Tip ➤** Lots of these resources are in the form of mailing lists. Remember them from Chapter 4. In case you've forgotten, use the address **listserv@listserv.net** to subscribe to any of the mailing lists. In the body of the message, type **subscribe** and then your first and last name.

General Collections of Goodies

These sites are categorized by subject and contain hyperlinks and pointers to a variety of other resources.

Galaxy

World Wide Web: **http://www.einet.net/**

Gopher Jewels

Gopher: **cwis.usc.edu**

Go through **Other Gophers and Information Resources** and **Gophers by Subject** to **Gopher Jewels.**

Internet Express Gopher

Gopher: **usa.net**

Listserv Home Page

World Wide Web: **http://www.clark.net/pub/listserv/listserv.html**

Majordomo List of Lists

World Wide Web: **http://www.cc.utexas.edu/psycgrad/majordomo.html**

University of Michigan Subject-Oriented Guides

World Wide Web: **http://http2.sils.umich.edu/~lou/chhome.html**

YAHOO Hierarchical Hotlist

World Wide Web: **http://akebono.stanford.edu/yahoo**

Yanoff's Special Internet Connection List

World Wide Web: **http://www.uwm.edu/Mirror/inet.services.html**

Agriculture

Agriculture Almanac Mail Servers

Almanac mail servers contain information on a variety of information, including USDA market news and articles of interest on a variety of agricultural subjects. Send e-mail to one of these:

almanac@acenet.auburn.edu
almanac@empire.cce.cornell.edu
almanac@esusda.gov
almanac@oes.orst.edu
almanac@silo.ucdavis.edu

In the body of your message, type one or more of the following:

> **send guide**
> **send catalog**
> **send help**

Agriculture Mailing Lists

AGRIC-L   Agriculture Discussion

AGRIS-L   The Food and Agriculture Organization Library Bulletin Service

CSANR-L   Center for Sustainable Agriculture and Natural Resources

FAOLIST   Food and Agriculture Organization Open Discussion List

SANTC-L   Sustainable Agriculture & Natural Resource Management

SUSTAG-L   Discussions about Sustainable Agriculture

Agriculture Newsgroups

misc.rural

alt.agriculture.misc

alt.sustainable.agriculture

sci.agriculture

sci.agriculture.beekeeping

Agricultural Guide

A guide to agriculture-related resources to be found on the Net.

FTP: **ftp.sura.net pub/nic/agricultural.list**

CENET (Cornell Extension NETwork)

Gopher: **cesgopher.ag.uiuc.edu** and log in as **guest**.

CUFAN (Clemson University Forestry & Agriculture Network)

Telnet: **empire.cce.cornell.edu** and log in as **Public**.

CYFER-net USDA Extension Service

Gopher: **esusda.gov**

Master Gardener

Gopher: **leviathan.tamu.edu** and look in **Gardening tips**.

PenPages

Telnet or Gopher: **psupen.psu.edu** and log in using your two-letter state abbreviation.

Sustainable Agriculture

Gopher: **calypso.oit.unc.edu** and go through **Worlds of SunSITE -- by Subject** to **Sustainable Agriculture**.

Anthropology

Anthropology Mailing Lists

ANTHRO-L   General Anthropology Bulletin Board

ANTHRO-L   Anthropology Graduate Students' List Server

JWA   The Journal of World Anthropology

Anthropology Newsgroup

sci.anthropology

Anthropology Gopher Sites

Gopher: **riceinfo.rice.edu** and go through **Information by subject area** to **Anthropology and Culture**.

Gopher: **marvel.loc.gov** and go through **global** and **socsci** to **anthro**.

Gopher: **gopher.tamu.edu** and go through **Browse Information by subject** to **Anthropology**.

Virtual Library for Anthropology

World Wide Web: http://elab-server.usc.edu/anthropology.html

Archaeology

Archaeology Mailing Lists

ARCH-L   Archaeology List

ARCHSTUD   Resources and Jobs for Historical Archaeology Students

HISTARCH   Historical Archaeology

ArchNet—University of Connecticut Anthropology Department

World Wide Web: http://spirit.lib.uconn.edu/HTML/archnet.html

National Archaeology Database Information Management System

Telnet: cast.uark.edu

Robotic Tele-Excavation at USC (Mercury Project)

World Wide Web: http://www.usc.edu/dept/raiders/

Art

Art Mailing Lists

ARTCRIT   Art Criticism Discussion Forum

ARTIST-L   Student Artist Discussions

DESIGN-L   Basic and Applied Design (Art and Architecture)

FINE-ART   (Peered) Fine-Art Forum

INSEA-L   International Society for Education Through Art

LAS-L   Liberal Arts and Sciences Discussion Group

UAARTED   Art Education Issues

Digital Picture Archive

Gopher: olt.et.tudelft.nl 1251

Fine Art Forum Home Page

World Wide Web: http://www.msstate.edu/Fineart_Online/home.html

Index—World Arts Resources

World Wide Web: http://www.cgrg.ohio-state.edu/Newark/artsres.html

Louvre Museum in Paris

World Wide Web: http://mistral.enst.fr/~pioch/louvre/

New York Art Line Collection of Art and Art Resources

Gopher: gopher.panix.com

The FineArt Forum WWW Resource List

World Wide Web: http://www.msstate.edu/Fineart_Online/
art-resources.html

Astronomy

Astronomy Mailing Lists

ASTRO   Astronomy Discussion List

HASTRO-L   History of Astronomy Discussion Group

Astronomy Newsgroups

sci.space

sci.space.news

sci.astro

sci.astro.hubble

AstroWeb

World Wide Web: http://marvel.stsci.edu/net-resources.html

Center for Advanced Space Studies

Gopher: cass.jsc.nasa.gov

Guide to Stars and Galaxies

World Wide Web: http://www.eia.brad.ac.uk/btl/sg.html

NASA Extragalactic Database

Telnet: ned.ipac.caltech.edu and log in as ned.

NASA Headline News

Finger: nasanews@space.mit.edu

NASA SpaceLink

Gopher: spacelink.msfc.nasa.gov

SEDS Gopher

Gopher: seds.lpl.arizona.edu

SETI (Search for Extra-Terrestrial Intelligence)

World Wide Web: http://www.metrolink.com/seti/SETI.html

Space Environment Effects Branch

World Wide Web: http://satori2.lerc.nasa.gov/

SpaceNews

Finger: magliaco@pilot.njin.net

STInfo

Telnet: **stinfo.hq.eso.org**

Gopher: **stsci.edu**

Strasbourg Astronomical Data Center and Databases

World Wide Web: **http://cdsweb.u-strasbg.fr/CDS.html**

WebStars

World Wide Web: **http://guinan.gsfc.nasa.gov/**

Biology

Biology Mailing Lists

BIOCIS-L   Biology Curriculum Innovation Study

BIODIDAC   Electronic Discussion Group for Biology Teachers

CELLWALL   Plant Cell Wall Biology

MAMMAL-L   Mammalian Biology

MOLBIO-L   Molecular Biology Discussion

Biology Genetics Banks

e-mail: **gene-server@bchs.uh.edu**

e-mail: **retrieve@ncbi.nlm.nih.gov**

e-mail: **genmark@ford.gatech.edu**

e-mail: **blocks@howard.fhcrc.org**

Biology Newsgroups

sci.bio.technology

sci.bio

American Type Culture Collection

Telnet: **atcc.nih.gov** and log in as **search**. Use **common** as the password.

Biodiversity and Biology

Gopher: **muse.bio.cornell.edu**

Bio-Informatics Page

World Wide Web: **http://www.gdb.org/hopkins.html**

Computational Biology

Gopher: **gopher.gdb.org**

Molecular Biology Server

World Wide Web: **http://expasy.hcuge.ch/**

Museum of Natural History Gopher

Gopher: **gopher.peabody.yale.edu**

Smithsonian Institution

Gopher: **smithson.si.edu**

Botany

Botany Mailing Lists

ALGAE-L   Digest Information on Botany

Australian National Botanic Gardens

Gopher: **155.187.10.12**

Botany Databases

Gopher: **nmnhgopher.si.edu** and look in **Botany**.

Gopher: **kaos.erin.gov.au** and look in **Biodiversity**.

Missouri Botanical Garden

Gopher: **gopher.mobot.org**

World Wide Web: **http://indri.cns.udel.edu/udgarden.html**

Department of Botany at the Smithsonian Institution

Gopher: **nmnhgoph.si.edu**

Business

Business Mailing Lists

AUBER-L   Association of University Business and Economic Research

BATECH-L   Technologies in Business Education

BETS-L   Business Ethics Teaching Society

BIZLAW-L   Law Regarding Business Associations and Securities

BIZNEWS   News Service Business News Releases

BSN-D   Business Sources on the Net-Distribution List

BTECH94   Business Technology

BUSED-L   A Forum for Discussion of Business Education Teaching Practices

BUSETH-L   Business Ethics Computer Network

FINANCE   Finance Journal

LABOR   Labor Economics

MARKET-L   Marketing Information

CORRYFEE   Economics and Management

Business Newsgroups

Look for newsgroups beginning with **biz.**

misc.entrepreneurs

Commercial Business Daily

Gopher: **english-server.hss.cmu.edu**

Economic BBS

Telnet: **ebb.stat-usa.gov**

Economics Gophers

Gopher: **gopher.lib.umich.edu**

Gopher: **niord.shsu.edu**

Gopher: **ecix.doc.gov**

Gopher: **wuecon.wustl.edu 671**

Gopher: **gopher.nijenrode.nl**

Gopher: **refmac.kent.edu**

Entrepreneurs WWW

World Wide Web: **http://sashimi.wwa.com/~notime/eotw/EOTW.html**

Federal Budget

Gopher: **gopher.esa.doc.gov**

Harvard Business School Press

e-mail: **josborn@cchbspub.harvard.edu**

Internal Revenues Service

World Wide Web: **http://www.ustreas.gov/treasury/bureaus/irs/irs.html**

Mutual Funds

World Wide Web: **http://www.ai.mit.edu/stocks/mf.html**

Patent Searches

World Wide Web: **http://sunsite.unc.edu/patents/intropat.html**

Stock Market Reports

Telnet: **a2i.rahul.net** or **192.160.13.1** and log in as **guest**.

Stock Market Simulation

Telnet: **castor.tat.physik.uni-tuebingen.de** and log in as **games**.

World Bank

Gopher: **gopher.worldbank.org**

Chemistry

Chemistry Mailing Lists

CHEMCHAT   Student & Professional Chemistry Discussions

CHEMCLUB   Chemistry Club

CHEMCOM   Chemistry in the Community Discussion List

CHEMCONF   Conferences on Chemistry Research and Education

CHEMED-L   Chemistry Education Discussion List

Chemistry Newsgroups

sci.chem

sci.chem.organomet

sci.engr.chem

American Chemical Society

Gopher: **acsinfo.acs.org**

Chemistry at UCLA, Home Page

World Wide Web: http://www.chem.ucla.edu/dept/Chemistry.html

OSU Chemistry Department

Gopher: jgelder.chem.okstate.edu

Penn Chemistry Department Home Page

World Wide Web: http://www.chem.upenn.edu/chem.html

Periodic Table of Elements

Telnet: camms2.caos.kun.nl 2034

Virtual Library of Chemistry

World Wide Web: http://www.chem.ucla.edu/chempointers.html

Computer Science

Computer Science Mailing Lists

ORCS-L   Operations Research/Computer Science Interface

THEORYNT   Computer Science Theory Net

TIP   List of Theoretical Computer Science Tip

Computer Science Newsgroups

Look for newsgroups beginning with comp.

Argonne National Laboratory Mathematics and Computer Science Division Home Page

World Wide Web: http://www.mcs.anl.gov/

Computer Science Technical Reports Archive Sites

World Wide Web: http://www.rdt.monash.edu.au/tr/siteslist.html

Searchable Information Sources

World Wide Web: **http://itdsrv1.ul.ie/CSIS/computer-science-info.html**

UNIX Reference Desk

World Wide Web: **http://www.eecs.nwu.edu/unix.html**

Economics

Economics Mailing Lists

CSEMLIST   List of the Society of Computational Economics

I3ECON   Innovation in Instruction of Economics

MEMSNET   Mineral Economics and Management Society

SCE-LIST   List of the Society of Computational Economics

Economics Newsgroup

sci.econ

Economic Bulletin Board

World Wide Web (or Gopher): **gopher://una.hh.lib.umich.edu/11/ebb**

Economics Working Paper Archive

World Wide Web: **http://econwpa.wustl.edu/Welcome.html**

National Bureau of Economic Research

Gopher: **nber.harvard.edu/**

Sam Houston State University Economics Gopher

Gopher: **niord.shsu.edu**

Education

Education Mailing Lists

AEELIST   Association for Experiential Education

ASHE-L   Association for the Study of Higher Education Discussion

DEOS-L   The Distance Education Online Symposium

DEOSNEWS   The Distance Education Online Symposium

ECENET-L   Early Childhood Education/Young Children (0–8)

ECEOL-L   Early Childhood Education On-Line Mailing List

EDRES-DB   Educational Resources on the Internet-Database

EDRES-L   Educational Resources on the Internet

EDTECH   Educational Technology

GEM-L   Graduate Education for Minorities

IMSE-L   Institute for Math and Science Education

INT-ED   Education, International Students

INTDEV-L   International Development and Global Education

INTER-ED   Forum for People with Interest in International Education

JEI-L   Technology in Education Mailing List

K12ADMIN   K–12 Educators Interested in Educational Administration

L-EDUC   College of Education List

PHED-L   Planning Ph.D. in Education

PHILOSED   Students and Teachers Discussing Philosophy of Education

TAG-L   Talented and Gifted Education

Education Newsgroups

Look for newsgroups beginning with **k12.**

misc.education

Canada's SchoolNet

Gopher: **schoolnet.carleton.ca**

Dewey School of Education

World Wide Web: http://ics.soe.umich.edu/

Distance Ed. Dbase

Telnet: ndlc.occ.uky.edu or 128.163.38.10 and log in as ndlc.

U.S. Dept. of Education

Gopher: gopher.ed.gov

Chronicle of Higher Education

Gopher: chronicle.merit.edu

Deaf Education Resources

Gopher: shiva.educ.kent.edu and go to Empire Schoolhouse

Gopher: nysernet.org

Educational Sources

World Wide Web: http://home.eos.brown.edu/eos1

High School Science Instruction Development

Gopher: ids.cwis.uci.edu 7029

International Education BBS

Telnet: nis.calstate.edu

K-12 Outpost

Gopher: k12.cnidr.org

K–12 Resources

World Wide Web: http://edu-153.sfsu.edu/k12/k12.html

K–12 Schools on the Internet

World Wide Web: **http://toons.cc.ndsu.nodak.edu/~sackmann/k12.html**

KidLink Gopher

Telnet: **kids.ccit.duq.edu**

Learning Link

Telnet: **sierra.fwl.edu** and log in as **newuser**. Use **newuser** as the password.

National Education BBS

Telnet: **nebbs.nersc.gov**

Newton

Telnet: **newton.dep.anl.gov**

Science and Math Initiative

World Wide Web: **http://www.c3.lanl.gov:6060/SAMI-home**

Web 66

World Wide Web: **http://web66.coled.umn.edu/**

Engineering

Engineering Mailing Lists

ASEE-L   American Society of Engineering Education Students

CAEDS-L   Computer Aided Engineering Design (CAEDS) Interest Group

CASE-L   Computer Aided Software Engineering

CIVIL-L   Civil Engineering Research and Education

ECMA-L   Engineering College Magazines Associated

ENGRNEWS   Engineering Undergraduate News

ENVENG-L   Environmental Engineering Discussion

Engineering Newsgroups

Look for newsgroups beginning with **sci.engr**.

Engineering Web Servers and Administrators

World Wide Web: **http://epims1.gsfc.nasa.gov/engineering/administrators.html**

Cornell Engineering Library Gopher

Gopher: **gopher2.englib.cornell.edu**

Environmental Studies

Environmental Studies Mailing List

ENVST-L   Environmental Studies Discussion List

Environmental Studies Newsgroup

sci.environment

Environmental Gophers

Gopher: **gopher.econet.apc.org**

Gopher: **nceet.snre.umich.edu**

Envirolink

Gopher: **envirolink.org**

World Wide Web: **http://envirolink.org/**

Environmental Protection Agency

World Wide Web: **http://nearnet.gnn.com/wic/govt.36.html**

1994 National Environmental Scorecard

World Wide Web: **http://nearnet.gnn.com/wic/polact.06.html**

World Bank Gopher—Environmental Data Statements

FTP: **ftp.worldbank.org** and look in **/PIC/eds.**

Virtual Library of Environmental Information

World Wide Web: **http://ecosys.drdr.virginia.edu/Environment.html**

Forestry

Forestry Mailing List

GP-BCFOR   GRNSD B.C. Forests and Forestry Project

Finnish Forest Research Institute

World Wide Web: **http://www.metla.fi/**

Social Sciences in Forestry Bibliography

Gopher: **Minerva.forestry.umn.edu**

Oxford Forestry Institute

World Wide Web: **http://www.metla.fi/kotisivu.html**

Geography

Geography Mailing Lists

GEOGED   Geography Education List

GEOGFEM   Discussion List for Feminism in Geography

GEOGRAPH   Geography

GEOPOL   Discussion List for Political Geography

Geography Resources

World Wide Web: **http://zia.geog.buffalo.edu/GIAL/netgeog.html**

Geographic Server

Telnet: **martini.eecs.umich.edu 3000**

University of California—Santa Barbara Library

Gopher: **ucsbuxa.ucsb.edu** and look in **Sciences/.Geography.**

Geology

Geology Mailing Lists

GEOED-L   Geology and Earth Science Education Discussion Forum

GEOLOGY   Geology Discussion List

Geology Newsgroup

sci.geo.geology

Ask-a-Geologist

e-mail: **ask-a-geologist@octopus.wr.usgs.gov**

Earthquake Info

Finger: **spyder@dmc.iris.washington.edu** (worldwide info)

Finger: **quake@gldfs.cr.usgs.gov** (United States info)

Oklahoma Geological Survey Observatory

Gopher: **wealaka.okgeosurvey1.gov**

World Earth Science Resources on the Internet Index

World Wide Web: **http://ageninfo.tamu.edu/geoscience.html**

U.S. Geological Survey Gopher

Gopher: **info.er.usgs.gov**

Government

Government Mailing Lists
SGANET   Student Government Global Mail Network
USGA-L   Student Government Net

American Civil Liberties Union
Gopher: **aclu.org 6601**

American Politics
Gopher: **toby.scott.nwu.edu**

Bureau of Labor Statistics
Gopher: **stats.bls.gov**

Census Information
Gopher: **gopher.census.gov**

Clinton Watch
Gopher: **dolphin.gulf.net 3000**

Congress
e-mail: **congress@hr.house.gov**
FTP: **ftp.senate.gov**
Gopher: **gopher.house.gov**

C-SPAN Gopher
Gopher: **c-span.org**

Consumer Product Safety Commission
Gopher: **cpsc.gov**

Department of Justice

Gopher: gopher.usdoj.gov

Environmental Protection Agency

Gopher: gopher.epa.gov

Federal Communications Commission

Gopher: gopher.fcc.gov

Federal GPO BBS

Telnet: federal.bbs.gpo.gov 3001

FedWorld Gateway

Telnet: fedworld.doc.gov

FDA BBS

Telnet: fdabbs.fda.gov or 150.148.8.48

Health & Human Services

Gopher: gopher.os.dhhs.gov

Housing and Urban Development

Gopher: gopher.hud.gov

LEGI-SLATE

Gopher: mudhoney.micro.umn.edu 7000

Library of Congress

Telnet: locis.loc.gov

National Archives & Records

Gopher: gopher.nara.gov

Project Vote Smart
Gopher: **gopher.neu.edu 1112**

History

History Mailing Lists
AMWEST-H   American West History Forum

ANCIEN-L   History of the Ancient Mediterranean

AZTLAN   Pre-Columbian History

EMHIST-L   Early Modern History Forum

H-GRAD H-Net   History Graduate Students' Discussion List

H-IDEAS H-Net   Intellectual History List

H-POL H-Net   Political History Discussion List

H-WOMEN   Women's History Discussion List

H-WORLD H-Net   List for World History

HN-ASK-L   History Network Forum

HN-ORG-L   The History Network

HOLOCAUS H-Net   History of the Holocaust List

MEDIEV-L Medieval History

MILHST-L   Military History

OHA-L   Oral History Association Discussion List

RENAIS-L   Early Modern History–Renaissance

History Newsgroup
soc.history

Historical News Archive
FTP: **byrd.mu.wvnet.edu** and look in **pub/history/internet/hist_news/**

History Databases

Telnet: **ukanaix.cc.ukans.edu** and log in as **history**.

History FTP Server

FTP: **byrd.mu.wvnet.edu** and look in **/pub/history**.

Texas A&M History Gopher

Gopher: **gopher.tamu.edu** and look in **history.dir**.

Law

Law Mailing Lists

EASMNT-L   An Electronic Forum Discussing Issues of Property Law and Trust

EDLAW   Law and Education

LAWAID   Law School Finanacial Aid Discussion

LAWSCH-L   Law School Discussion List

LGUILD-L   The National Lawyers Guild Electronic Mailing List

PSYLAW-L   Psychology and Law, International Discussion

SPORTLAW   Sport Law

Law Newsgroup

misc.legal

American Association of Law Libraries Info System

Telnet: **lawlib.wuacc.edu** and log in as **aallnet**.

Law Library

Telnet: **liberty.uc.wlu.edu**

Law Library Reference Desk
Telnet: **law.wuacc.edu**

Law Resources List
FTP: **ftp.midnight.com** and get **/pub/LegalList/legallist.txt**.

LawNet
Telnet: **lawnet.law.columbia.edu**

Legal Directory
Gopher: **163.231.231.3**

Legal Resource Network
World Wide Web: **http://virgo.gem.valpo.edu/~medic/law.html**

Supreme Court Rulings
FTP: **ftp.cwru.edu**

WWW Law Servers
Telnet: **www.LAW.indiana.edu**

Telnet: **fatty.LAW.cornell** and log in as **www**.

Literature

Literature Mailing Lists
AMLIT-L   American Literature Discussion Group

CHICLE   Chicano Literature Discussion List

CHILDLIT   Children's Literature: Criticism and Theory

IAFA-L   Scholarly Discussion of Fantastic Literature

KIDLIT-L Children and Youth Literature List

LITERARY Discussions About Literature

MODBRITS Modern British and Irish Literature: 1895-1955

T-AMLIT Teaching the American Literatures

Literature Newsgroups

rec.arts.books

rec.arts.prose

rec.arts.poems

Dartmouth Library

Telnet: **library.dartmouth.edu**

Poetry Archives

World Wide Web: **http://sunsite.unc.edu/dykki/poetry/home.html**

World Wide Web: **http://english-server.hss.cmu.edu/Poetry.html**

World Wide Web: **http://www.cs.brown.edu:80/fun/bawp/**

Project Gutenberg

FTP: **mrcnext.cso.uiuc.edu**

World Wide Web: **http://med.amsa.bu.edu/Gutenbert/Welcome.html**

Speculative Fiction Clearinghouse

World Wide Web: **http://thule.mt.cs.cmu.edu:8001/sf-clearing-house/**

Mathematics

Mathematics Mailing Lists

CRYPTO-L Forum on Cryptology and Related Mathematics

HEC-L Higher Education Consortium for Mathematics and Science

NYJM-ALG   Extracts of Algebra Papers in the New York Journal of Mathematics

TECHMATH   Technion Mathematics Net

WVMS-L   NASA Classroom of the Future: WV Mathematics and Science List

Mathematics Newsgroups

sci.logic

sci.math

sci.math.symbolic

E-Math

Telnet: **e-math.ams.com** and log in as **e-math**. Use **e-math** as the password.

Mathematics Archives Gopher

Gopher: **archives.math.utk.edu**

Math Association of America

Gopher: **gopher.maa.org**

Math WWW Servers

World Wide Web: **http://www.csc.fi/math_topics/General.html**

NIST Guide to Available Mathematical Software

Telnet: **gams.nist.gov** and log in as **gams**.

Medicine

Medicine Mailing Lists

CCM-L   Critical Care Medicine

COMPMED   Comparative Medicine List

FAMILY-L   Academic Family Medicine Discussion

LASMED-L   Laser Medicine

PED-EM-L   Pediatric Emergency Medicine Discussion List

Cancer Information

e-mail: **cancernet@icicb.nci.nih.gov** and type **help** in the body of the message.

Medicine Newsgroups

sci.med

sci.med.aids

sci.med.physics

AIDS Information

Gopher: **odie.niaid.nih.gov**

Gopher: **gopher.hivnet.org**

AIDS Patent Project

World Wide Web: **http://patents.cnidr.org/**

Anesthesiology

Gopher: **eja.anes.hscsyr.edu**

Gopher: **gasnet.med.nyu.edu**

Breast Cancer Clearinghouse

Gopher: **nysernet.org**

Child Health Policy

Gopher: **Mchnet.ichp.ufl.edu**

DentalNet

World Wide Web: **http://www.dentalnet.com/dentalnet/**

Disability Gopher

Gopher: **trace.waisman.wisc.edu**

Drug Index (GenRx)

Telnet: **genrx.icsi.ne** and log in as **genrx**. Use **genrx** as the password.

Health Newsletter

World Wide Web: **http://cancer.med.upenn.edu:3000/**

InfoLink

World Wide Web: **http://www.biostat.wisc.edu/homepage.html**

Medical Gophers

Gopher: **gopher.med.harvard.edu**

Gopher: **caldmed.med.miami.edu**

Medical Education Information Center

World Wide Web: **http://hyrax.med.uth.tmc.edu/**

National Library of Medicine

World Wide Web: **http://www.nlm.nih.gov**

Nursing Gophers

Gopher: **nightingale.con.utk.edu**

Gopher: **gopher.csv.warwick.ac.uk 10001**

Oncology Resources

Gopher: **cancer.med.upenn.edu**

PharmWeb

World Wide Web: **http://157.142.72.77/pharmacy/pharmint.html**

Radiology

World Wide Web: **http://www.rad.washington.edu/**

Rethinking AIDS Journal Archives Online

World Wide Web: **http://enuxsa.eas.asu.edu/~jvagner/rethinking-aids**

University of Iowa College of Medicine Home Page

World Wide Web: **http://indy.radiology.uiowa.edu/ColOfMedHP.html**

Music

Music Mailing Lists

ALLMUSIC   Discussions on All Forms of Music

BLUES-L   Blues Music List

CLASSM-L   Classical Music List

EARLYM-L   Early Music List

ETHMUS-L   EthnoFORUM, a Global Ethnomusicology Forum

GUM   Grupo de Usuarios MUSIC do Brasil (GUM)

IRTRAD-L   Irish Traditional Music List

MUSIC-ED   Music Education

MUSPRF-L   Music Performance and Pedagogy

RMUSIC-L   Music Discussion List

ROCKLIST   Academic Discussion of Popular Music

SOCO-L   Southern Rock Music List

Music Newsgroups

comp.music

k12.ed.music

rec.arts.theatre.musicals

rec.music

Ethnomusicology Research Digest

Gopher: **gopher.cic.net** and look in **Electronic Serials/Alphabetic List/E/ Ethnomusicology.**

Guitar Chords/TAB

FTP: **ftp.nevada.edu**

Indiana University Music Library

World Wide Web: **http://www.music.indiana.edu/misc/ music_resources.html**

Lyric / Music Server

FTP: **ftp.uwp.edu** or **ftp.sunet.se**

World Wide Web: **http://vivarin.pc.cc.cmu.edu/lyrics.html**

Music & Brain D-base

Telnet: **mila.ps.uci.edu**

Music Library

World Wide Web: **http://www.music.indiana.edu/**

Music on the Web

World Wide Web: **http://www.art.net/Links/musicref.html**

WWW of Music

World Wide Web: **http://www.galcit.caltech.edu/~ta/music/index.html**

Oceanography

Bedford Institute Of Oceanography (Canada)

Gopher: **biome.bio.dfo.ca**

Index to Oceanography WWW Servers

World Wide Web: **http://www.whoi.edu/html/www-servers/ oceanography.html**

National Oceanic and Atmospheric Administration

Gopher: **gopher.esdim.noaa.gov**

OCEANIC Information Center

Gopher: **gopher.cms.udel.edu**

Tropical Storm Forecast

Finger: **forecast@typhoon.atmos.colostate.edu**

Paleontology

Paleontology Mailing List

VRTPALEO   The Vertebrate Paleontology Community Discussion List

Paleontology Newsgroup

sci.archaeology

Berkeley Paleontology Gopher

World Wide Web: **http://nearnet.gnn.com/wic/palaeon.02.html**

Honolulu Community College Dinosaur Exhibit

World Wide Web: **http://www.hcc.hawaii.edu/dinos/dinos.1.html**

Paleontology Server

World Wide Web: **http://nearnet.gnn.com/wic/palaeon.03.html**

Philosophy

Philosophy Mailing Lists

AYN-RAND   Moderated Discussion of Objectivist Philosophy

MDVLPHIL   Medieval Philosophy and Political Thought List

PHILCOMM   Philosophy of Communication

PHTECH-L   Philosophy and Technology

SWIP-L   Society for Women in Philosophy Information and Discussion

Philosophy Newsgroup

sci.philosophy.tech

American Philosophical Association

Gopher: **apa.oxy.edu**

Gopher via World Wide Web: **gopher://apa.oxy.edu**

Philosophy Gopher at Stanford

Gopher: **kanpai.stanford.edu**

Physics

Physics Mailing Lists

PHYS-STU   Physics Student Discussion List

PHYSHARE   Sharing Resources for High School Physics Teachers

PHYSIC-L   Physics List

PHYSICS   (Peered) Physics Discussion

PHYSJOB   Physics Jobs Discussion List

PHYSLRNR   Physics Learning Research List

Physics Newsgroups

sci.physics

sci.physics.fusion

Center for Particle Astrophysics

World Wide Web: **http://physics7.berkeley.edu/home.html**

High Energy Physics Center

Gopher: **gopher.hep.net**

Nuclear Data Center

Telnet: **bnlnd2.dne.bnl.gov** and log in as **nndc.**

Particle Information

World Wide Web: **http://pdg.lbl.gov/**

Physics News

World Wide Web: **http://www.het.brown.edu/news/index.html**

Plasma Physics Laboratory

World Wide Web: **http://www.pppl.gov/**

Political Science

Political Science Mailing Lists

POLI-SCI   Political Science Digest

POSCIM   Political Science Mailing List

PSRT-L   Political Science Research and Teaching List

Political Science Newsgroups

talk.politics.guns

talk.politics.mideast

talk.politics.misc

talk.politics.soviet

talk.politics.theory

Psychology

Psychology Mailing Lists

COMPSY-L   Midwest Forum for Community/Ecological Psychology

COUNPSY   Counseling Psychology Practice and Science

PSY-CLUB   Psychology Club (Psi Chi)

PSYCGRAD   Psychology Graduate Students' Discussion Group List

PSYGRAD   Psychology Graduate Students

PSYGRD-J   The Psychology Graduate-Student Journal: The PSYCGRAD Journal

PSYMEA-L   Developmental Psychology

PSYSTS-L   Psychology Statistics Discussion

Psychology Newsgroup

sci.psychology

Psychology Index

Gopher: **panda1.uottawa.ca 4010**

World Wide Web: **http://matia.stanford.edu/cogsci/**

The PSYCGRAD Project

Gopher via World Wide Web: **gopher://www.cc.utexas.edu:80/hGET%20/psycgrad/psycgrad.html**

Psychology Resources

World Wide Web: **http://galaxy.einet.net/galaxy/Social-Sciences/Psychology.html**

Religion

Religion Mailing Lists

ARIL-L   Association for Religion and Intellectual Life

INTERREL   Interreligion Discussion

SSREL-L   Scientific Study of Religion

WMSPRT-L   Women's Spirituality and Feminist-Oriented Religions

Religion Newsgroups

talk.religion.misc

talk.religion.newage

soc.religion.christian

soc.culture.jewish

Atheism Web

World Wide Web: **http://www.mantis.co.uk:80/atheism/**

Baha'i Faith

World Wide Web: **http://oneworld.wa.com/bahai/**

Christian Resource List

World Wide Web: **http://saturn.colorado.edu:8080/Christian/list.html**

Gabriel's Horn

Telnet: **twinbrook.cis.uab.edu 7777**

Jerusalem One Gopher

Gopher: **jerusalem1.datasrv.co.il**

JewishNets

Telnet: **www.huji.ac.il**

Gopher: **shamash.nysernet.org**

World Wide Web: **http://sleepless.acm.uiuc.edu/signet/JHSI/judaism.html** and log in as **JEWISHNET.**

NY-Israel Gopher

Gopher: **israel.nysernet.org 71**

Religion on the Web

World Wide Web: **http://www.einet.net/galaxy/Community/ Religion.html**

Religion-Specific Resources

Gopher: **marvel.loc.gov** and look in **global/phil/religions.**

Sociology

Sociology Mailing List

SOC-MSU@MSU.EDU   Sociology Mailing List

Sociology Newsgroups

Look for newsgroups beginning with **soc.** and **soc.culture.**

Veterinary Medicine

Veterinary Medicine Mailing Lists

VETCAI   Veterinary Medicine Computer Assisted Instruction

VETMED   Veterinary Medicine

NetVet

Gopher: **netvet.wustl.edu**

World Wide Web: **http://netvet.wustl.edu/**

No Access Through Your School?

If you're reading this chapter, you've probably just found out that you can't get Internet access through your school, and you're searching for options. Maybe your school connection works just fine, but you're wanting to set your parents up with an Internet account. Whatever.

Finding a service provider is becoming ridiculously simple—they're springing up all over. You shouldn't have any trouble locating an organization that will gladly take your money and give you an account. However, prices and services vary widely from place to place, so you'll want to do a little research before you jump at an offer, to avoid getting screwed.

Knowing the constraints of a student's budget, I've organized the options from cheapest to most expensive. Keep reading until your wallet starts hurting, then take a break.

Local Bulletin Boards

More and more local bulletin board services (BBSs) are setting up gateways into the Internet. The money you'll have to spend will vary, as will the degree of Internet accessibility.

On these private systems, the going rate is whatever the sysop (system operator) feels like charging. Some of these are one-person operations run out of a basement. They can be funky and charming, as well as buggy and frustrating. Even so, it's worth a couple of hours and a few phone calls to check out the BBSs in your area that offer Internet connectivity.

E-mail and USENET are the two most common functions you'll run into on a local board. Big-time features, such as FTP, Telnet, World Wide Web, and Gopher, will only be found on large, well-established boards, because these features cost more money and require more equipment to maintain. Many of the smaller BBSs run as part-time hobbies, not real businesses.

> **Tip ➤** Even if it turns out that the bulletin boards in your area don't offer any Internet services, it's very likely that you'll meet people on them who are knowledgeable about the Internet. One of these folks may be able to point you in the right direction and tell you where to look.

Freenets

You're going to be hearing more about Freenets. A Freenet is a community-based bulletin board system that offers electronic access to the masses. By the people, for the people—great concept, huh?

A Freenet is a great place to look for Internet access, and also a great place to volunteer some time. Freenets work similarly to public broadcast stations and depend upon the people involved to make it work. There are Freenets operating in 10 different countries and in 42 states.

> **Tip ➤** Can't find a Freenet? Start one of your own. Doing so would be a great project for a student group looking to make a difference. Maybe you could even wrangle some credit for an independent study.

Here's a partial list of the known Freenets. The complete list is available via Anonymous FTP from nptn.org. Look in the /pub directory. You can also find some documents there on how to start a Freenet in your area.

UNITED STATES

Alabama

Mobile Free-Net - Mobile
Voice: 205-344-7243
e-mail: geoffp@netcom.com

Tuscaloosa Free-Net - Tuscaloosa
Voice: 205-348-2398
e-mail: rdoctor@ua1vm.ua.edu

Alaska

AnchorNet - Anchorage
Voice: 907-261-2891
e-mail: pegt@muskox.alaska.edu

FairNet - Fairbanks
Voice: 907-474-5089
e-mail: ffmob@aurora.alaska.edu

Arizona

AzTeC - Tempe
Voice: 602-965-5985
e-mail: joe.askins@asu.edu
Modem: 602-965-4151
Telnet:129.219.13.60
Visitor login: guest (password: visitor)

Arkansas

Greater Pulaski County Free-Net - Little Rock
Voice: 501-666-2222
e-mail: john.eichler@grapevine.lrk.ar.us

California

Los Angeles Free-Net - Los Angeles
e-mail: aa101@lafn.org
Voice Info: 818-954-0080
Modem: 818-776-5000
Telnet: lafn.org
Visitor login: Select #2 at first menu

Davis Community Network - Davis
Voice: 916-752-7764
e-mail: acmansker@ucdavis.edu

Orange County Free-Net - Orange County
Voice:714-762-8551
e-mail: palmer@world.std.com

Sacramento Free-Net - Sacramento
Voice: 916-484-6789
e-mail: sndview@netcom.com

Silicon Valley Public Access Link - San Jose
Voice: 415-968-2598
e-mail: msiegel@svpal.org

Santa Barbara RAIN - Santa Barbara
Voice: 805-967-7246
e-mail: rain@rain.org

Colorado

Denver Free-Net - Denver
Voice: 303-270-4300
e-mail: drew@freenet.hsc.colorado.edu
Modem: 303-270-4865
Telnet: freenet.hsc.colorado.edu
Visitor login: guest

Connecticut

Danbury Area Free-Net - Danbury
Voice: 203-797-4512
e-mail: waldgreen@bix.com

CPBI - Free-Net - Hartford
Voice: 203-278-5310 ext 1230
e-mail: steela@csusys.ctstateu.edu

Florida

SEFLIN Free-Net - Broward County
Voice: 305-357-7318
e-mail: currye@mail.seflin.lib.fl.us
Modem: 305-765-4332
Telnet: bcfreenet.seflin.lib.fl.us
Visitor login: visitor

Alachua Free-Net - Gainesville
Voice: 904-372-8401
e-mail: 76314.352@compuserve.com
Modem: 904-334-0200
Telnet: freenet.ufl.edu
Visitor login: visitor

Tallahassee Free-Net - Tallahassee
Voice: 904-644-1796
e-mail: levitz@cs.fsu.edu
Modem: 904-488-5056
Telnet: freenet.fsu.edu
Visitor login: visitor

Miami Free-Net - Miami
Elizabeth Curry
Voice: 305-357-7318
e-mail: currye@mail.seflin.lib.fl.us

Orlando Free-Net - Orlando
Voice: 407-833-9777
e-mail: bruce@goliath.pbac.edu

Georgia

Worth County-Sylvester Ga. Free-Net - Sylvester
Voice: 912-776-8625
e-mail: guske@freenet.fsu.edu
Modem: 912-776-1255

Hawaii

Maui Free-Net - Maui
Voice: 808-572-0510
e-mail: don.regal@tdp.org

Idaho

Panhandle Free-Net - Sandpoint
Voice: 208-265-2955
e-mail: solutions@ins.infonet.net

Illinois

Prairienet - Champaign-Urbana
Voice: 217-244-3299
e-mail: abishop@uiuc.edu
Modem: 217-255-9000
Telnet: prairienet.org   (192.17.3.3)
Visitor login: visitor

Shawnee Free-Net - Carbondale
Voice: 618-549-1139
e-mail: ad592@freenet.hsc.colorado.edu

Indiana

Michiana Free-Net Society - Granger
Voice: 219-282-1574
e-mail: dmclaugh@darwin.cc.nd.edu

Iowa

CedarNet - Cedar Falls
Voice: 319-273-6282
e-mail: muffoletto@uni.edu

Iowa Knowledge Exchange - Des Moines
Voice: 515-242-3556
e-mail: garyb@ins.infonet.net

Kentucky

Pennyrile Area Free-Net - Hopkinsville
Voice: 502-886-2913
e-mail: mroseberry@delphi.com

Owensboro Free-Net - Owensboro
Voice: 502-686-4530
e-mail: donna@ndlc.occ.uky.edu

Louisiana

Baton Rouge Area Interactive Network - Baton Rouge
Voice: 504-346-0707
e-mail: anniemac@acm.org

Greater New Orleans Free-Net - New Orleans
Voice: 504-286-7187
e-mail: nrrmc@uno.edu

Maine

Maine Community Access Network- Freeport
Voice: 207-287-6615
e-mail: efrey@mmp.org

Maryland

Free State Free-Net - Baltimore
Voice: 410-313-9259
e-mail: aduggan@well.sf.ca.us

Community Service Network - Easton
Voice: 410-822-4132
e-mail: david_boan@martha.washcoll.edu

Massachusetts

UMASSK12 - Amherst
Morton Sternheim
Voice: 413-545-1908
e-mail: mms@k12.ucs.umass.edu
Modem: 413-572-5583 or 413-572-5268
Telnet: k12.ucs.umass.edu
Visitor login: guest

Michigan

Greater Detroit Free-Net - Detroit
Voice: 810-574-8549
e-mail: info@detroit.freenet.org
Modem: < service not available >
Telnet: detroit.freenet.org
Visitor login: visitor

Great Lakes Free-Net - Battle Creek
Voice: 616-961-4166
e-mail: merritt_tumanis@fc1.glfn.org
Modem: 616-969-4536
Visitor login: visitor

Huron Valley Free-Net - Ann Arbor
Michael Todd Glazier
Voice: 313-662-8374
e-mail: michael.todd.glazier@umich.edu

Minnesota

Twin Cities Free-Net - Minneapolis
Voice: 507-646-3407
e-mail: fritchie@stolaf.edu

Northfield Free-Net - Northfield
Voice: 507-645-9301
e-mail: andreacris@aol.com

Mississippi

Magnolia Free-Net - Jackson
Voice: 601-354-1027
e-mail: tlowe@ccaix.jsums.edu

Meridian Area Free-Net - Meridian
Voice: 601-482-2000
e-mail: ric4aardvark@delphi.com

Missouri

Columbia Online Information Network (COIN) - Columbia
Voice: 314-443-3161 (ext. 350 for Voice mail)
e-mail: ebarrett@bigcat.missouri.edu
Modem: 314-884-7000
Telnet: bigcat.missouri.edu
Visitor login: guest

ORION - Springfield
Voice: 417-837-5050 ext. 15
e-mail: annie@ozarks.sgcl.lib.mo.us
Modem: 417-864-6100
Telnet: ozarks.sgcl.lib.mo.us
Visitor login: guest

KC Free-Net - Kansas City
Voice: 816-340-4228
e-mail: josbourn@tyrell.net

Montana

Big Sky Telegraph - Dillon
Voice: 406-683-7338
e-mail: franko@bigsky.dillon.mt.us
Modem: 406-683-7680
Telnet: 192.231.192.1
Visitor login: bbs

Nebraska

Omaha Free-Net - Omaha
Voice: 402-554-2516
e-mail: lowe@unomaha.edu

Nevada

> Las Vegas International Free-Net - Las Vegas
> Voice: 702-795-7267
> e-mail: scott@gate.vegas.com

New Hampshire

> The Granite State Oracle - Manchester
> Quentin Lewis
> Voice: 508-442-0279

New Mexico

> New Mexico Free-Net - Albuquerque
> Voice: 505-277-8148
> e-mail: lnewby@unm.edu

> Santa Fe Metaverse - Santa Fe
> Voice: 505-989-7117
> e-mail: grizz@lanl.gov

New York

> Buffalo Free-Net - Buffalo
> Voice: 716-877-8800 ext 451
> e-mail: finamore@ubvms.cc.buffalo.edu
> Modem: 716-645-3085
> Telnet: freenet.buffalo.edu
> Visitor login: freeport

> CASSYnet - Corning
> Voice: 607-936-3713
> e-mail: freenet@scccvb.corning-cc.edu
> Southern Tier Free-Net - Endicott
> Voice: 607-752-1201
> e-mail: cubicsr@vnet.ibm.com

> Rochester Free-Net - Rochester
> Voice: 716-594-0943
> e-mail: jerry@rochgte.fidonet.org

North Carolina

> Mountain Area Information Network - Asheville
> Voice: 704-255-5207
> e-mail: a6plnet@uncecs.edu

Triangle Free-Net - Chapel Hill
Voice: 919-968-4292
e-mail: hutch@tfnet.ils.unc.edu

Forsyth County Free-Net - Winston-Salem
Voice: 919-727-2597 ext 3023
e-mail: annen@ledger.mis.co.forsyth.nc.us

North Dakota

SENDIT - Fargo
Voice: 701-237-8109
e-mail: sackman@sendit.nodak.edu
Modem: 701-237-3283
Telnet: sendit.nodak.edu
Visitor login: bbs (password: sendit2me)

Ohio

Cleveland Free-Net - Cleveland
Voice: 216-368-2982
e-mail: jag@po.cwru.edu
Modem: 216-368-3888
Telnet: freenet-in-a.cwru.edu
Visitor login: Select #2 at first menu

Greater Columbus Free-Net - Columbus
Voice: 614-292-4132
e-mail: sgordon@freenet.columbus.oh.us
Modem: 614-292-7501
Telnet: freenet.columbus.oh.us
Visitor login: guest

Dayton Free-Net - Dayton
Voice: 513-873-4035
e-mail: pvendt@desire.wright.edu
Modem: 513-229-4373
Telnet: 130.108.128.174
Visitor login: visitor

Youngstown Free-Net - Youngstown
Voice: 216-742-3075
e-mail: lou@yfn.ysu.edu
Modem: 216-742-3072
Telnet: yfn2.ysu.edu
Visitor login: visitor

Akron Regional Free-Net - Akron
Voice: 216-972-6352
e-mail: r1asm@vm1.cc.uakron.edu

Oklahoma

Ponca City/Pioneer Free-Net - Ponca City
Voice: 405-767-3461
e-mail: philber106@aol.com

Pennsylvania

Lehigh Valley Free-Net - Bethlehem
Voice: 610-758-4998
e-mail: tpl2@lehigh.edu

Pittsburgh Free-Net - Pittsburgh
Voice: 412-622-6502
e-mail: iddings@clp2.clpgh.org

Rhode Island

Ocean State Free-Net - Providence
Voice: 401-277-2726
e-mail: howardbm@dsl.rhilinet.gov
Modem: 401-831-4640

South Carolina

MidNet - Columbia
Voice: 803-777-4825
e-mail: bajjaly@univscvm.csd.scarolina.edu

Greenet - Greenville
Voice: 803-242-5000 ext 231
e-mail: sgr002@sol1.solinet.net

GreenCo-NET - Greenwood
Voice: 803-223-8431
e-mail: oukmddn@cluster1.clemson.edu

Tennessee

Jackson Area Free-Net - Jackson
Voice: 901-425-2640
e-mail: dlewis@jscc.cc.tn.us
Telnet: 198.146.108.99
Modem: 901-427-4435
Visitor login: guest

Texas

Rio Grande Free-Net - El Paso
Voice: 915-775-6077
e-mail: donf@laguna.epcc.edu
Modem: 915-775-5600
Telnet: rgfn.epcc.edu
Visitor login: visitor

Austin Free-Net - Austin
Voice: 512-462-0625
e-mail: jevans@versa.com

North Texas Free-Net - Dallas
Voice: 214-320-8915
e-mail: ntfnadm@ntfn.dcccd.edu

Tarrant County Free-Net - Fort Worth
Voice: 817-763-8437
e-mail: jcoles@pubcon.com

Houston Civnet - Houston
Voice: 713-869-0521
e-mail: paul@sugar.neosoft.com

San Antonio Free-Net - San Antonio
Voice: 210-561-9815
e-mail: mlotas@espsun.space.swri.edu

Vermont

Lamoille Net - Morrisville
Balu Raman
Voice: 802-888-2606
e-mail: braman@world.std.com

Virginia

    Central Virginia's Free-Net - Richmond
    Voice: 804-828-6650
    e-mail: kguyre@cabell.vcu.edu
    Telnet: freenet.vcu.edu
    Visitor login: visitor

    VaPEN - Richmond
    Voice: 804-225-2921
    e-mail: hcothern@vdoe386.vak12ed.edu
    Telnet: vdoe386.vak12ed.edu

    Blue Ridge Free-Net - Roanoke
    Voice: 703-981-1424
    e-mail: obrist@leo.vsla.edu

Washington

    Seattle Community Network - Seattle
    Randy Groves
    Voice: 206-865-3424
    e-mail: randy@cpsr.org
    Modem: 206-386-4140
    Telnet: scn.org
    Visitor login: visitor

    Tri-Cities Free-Net - Tri-Cities
    Voice: 509-586-6481
    e-mail: tcfn@delphi.com
    Modem: 509-375-1111

Wisconsin

    Chippewa Valley Free-Net - Eau Claire
    Voice: 715-836-3715
    e-mail: smarquar@uwec.edu

AUSTRALIA

    Melbourne Free-Net - Melbourne
    Voice: +61 3-652-0656
    e-mail: pbancroft@ozonline.com.au

CANADA

Alberta

> Calgary Free-Net - Calgary
> Voice: 403-264-9535
> e-mail: delton@acs.ucalgary.ca

> Edmonton Free-Net - Edmonton
> Voice: 403-423-2331
> e-mail: adavis2@vm.ucs.ualberta.ca

British Columbia

> Voice: 604-368-2233
> e-mail: kmcclean@ciao.trail.bc.ca
> Modem: 604-368-5764
> Telnet: 142.231.5.1
> Visitor login: guest

> Victoria Free-Net - Victoria
> Voice: 604-385-4302
> e-mail: shearman@freenet.victoria.bc.ca
> Telnet: freenet.victoria.bc.ca
> Visitor login: guest

Manitoba

> SEARDEN Free-Net - Sprague
> Voice: 204-437-2016
> e-mail: larry_geller@mbnet.mb.ca

> Blue Sky Free-Net Of Manitoba - Winnipeg
> Voice: 204-945-1413
> e-mail: bdearth@gateway.eitc.mb.ca

New Brunswick

> York Sunbury Community Server - Fredericton
> Voice: 506-453-4566
> e-mail: mikemac@unb.ca

Newfoundland

> St. John's Free-Net - St. John's
> e-mail: randy@kean.ucs.mun.ca

Nova Scotia

 Cape Breton Free-Net - Cape Breton
 Voice: 902-862-6432
 e-mail: dmacmull@fox.nstn.ns.ca

 Chebucto Free-Net - Halifax
 Voice: 902-425-2061
 e-mail: els@cs.dal.ca

Ontario

 National Capital Free-Net - Ottawa
 Voice: 613-788-2600 ext 3701
 e-mail: aa001@freenet.carleton.ca
 Modem: 613-564-3600
 Telnet: freenet.carleton.ca
 Visitor login: guest

 Toronto Free-Net - Toronto
 Voice: 416-978-5365
 e-mail: laine@vm.utcc.utoronto.ca

Quebec

 Free-Net du Montreal Metropolitain - Montreal
 Voice: 514-278-9173
 e-mail: ssacks@cam.org

Saskatchewan

 Moose Jaw Free-Net - Moose Jaw
 Voice: 306-694-2510
 e-mail: locke@gdilib.unibase.sk.ca

 Great Plains Free-Net - Regina
 Voice: 306-584-9615
 e-mail: rhg@unibase.unibase.sk.ca

 Saskatoon Free-Net - Saskatoon
 Voice: 306-966-5920
 e-mail: scottp@herald.usask.ca

Don't despair if you don't see one listed in your area. New Freenets are popping up all the time. For current information, contact:

National Public Telecomputing Network
Box 1987
Cleveland, OH 44106
Voice: 216-247-5800
e-mail: tmg@nptn.org

Local Service Providers

Before 1992, you couldn't just buy your way onto the Internet—you had to know the right people or belong to the right organization. In 1992, with the reorganization of the Net, some very smart individuals discovered that they could make money by selling Internet access. (Must have been college graduates.)

Today, more than a few people are getting very, very rich from selling Internet connections, and one of your options is to locate one of these people and put a few more dollars into his pocket.

Competition among service providers is getting stiff—there are some great deals out there now. Most providers offer SLIP/PPP dial-up connections, 1-800 access, and technical support. Most of them offer full Internet capabilities (all the bells and whistles, including World Wide Web, FTP, and so on), but be sure to ask about the services you want before signing on the dotted line.

You should ask a service provider the same set of questions that you asked in Chapter 2 regarding setting up an account, plus a few more:

- Is there a startup fee?
- What is the pricing structure?
- Is there a different charge for a prime time connection vs. off hours?
- Is there a monthly fee?
- Is there phone support available?
- Do you have 1-800 service? Is there an extra charge for using this?
- Can you supply me with TCP and client software?
- What is the size and speed of your modem pool?
- How many users do you currently serve?

This last one is important. If you are signing on with a company that has 25 modem lines available and 500 users, plan on long evenings listening to busy signals.

So how do you go about locating these providers? There is a list of public service providers available via e-mail on the Internet that you can request.

Yes I can hear the groans all the way from your house to mine. If you don't have access, how can you get the list? Well, you can't. At least, not the whole list. I've included an abbreviated version at the end of this chapter. If you want the whole thing, ask a friend who has an account to retrieve the information for you, or perhaps you who has a free account can download a copy and share the information with the less fortunate. Here's the scoop:

Send an e-mail message to **info-deli-server@netcom.com**. In the body of the message, write **send PDIAL**. Mail the message. In a short time, you will receive a rather long list organized by area codes. Everything you need to know will be there. Prices, what you can and cannot do with the system, how to contact them, and more.

Two other useful commands you can send to the same address:

subscribe pdial This will get you on a list to receive updated copies of the list.

subscribe Info-Deli-News Use this to get additions and change notifications.

Another online source of information is the NixPub listing. This is a list of PublicAccess UNIX sites and is available via Anonymous FTP from vfl.paramax.com. Look in the pub/NixPub directories. Here is an example of what you'll find there:

```
Legend:    $   - Fee                  -$  - No Fee
           24  - 24 Hours/Day         -24 - Not 24 Hours/Day
           H   - Courier HST          A   - Anonymous UUCP
           P   - Telebit PEP          F   - Anonymous FTP
           V   - V.32[bis]            I   - Live Internet Connection
           W   - Worldblazer TurboPEP M   - Electronic Mail
                                      N   - USENET News
                                      S   - UNIX Shell
                                      T   - Multiple Telephone Lines
```

```
================================================================

Updated                 System                      Speed
Last    Telephone #     Name      Location           Range    Legend
.....   ................  .........  ..................  .........

03/93 201-759-8450^  tronsbox  Belleville      NJ 300-FAST  24 -$ MNPST
03/93 203-661-1279   admiral   Greenwich       CT 300-FAST  24 -$ AHMNPTV
03/93 206-328-4944^  polari    Seattle         WA 300-FAST  24  $ MNPST
03/93 206-367-3837^  eskimo    Seattle         WA 300-FAST  24  $ MNSTVW
03/93 206-382-6245^  halcyon   Seattle         WA 300-FAST  24  $ IMNPST
03/93 206-747-6397^  seanews   Redmond         WA 1200-FAST 24 -$ MNV
03/93 212-420-0527^  magpie    NYC             NY 300-FAST  24 -$ APTWV
03/93 212-675-7059^  marob     NYC             NY 300-FAST  24 -$ APT
07/93 212-787-3100^  panix     New York City   NY 1200-FAST 24  $ IMNPSTV
03/93 214-436-3281^  sdf       Dallas          TX 300-FAST  24 -$ AMNPSTV
03/93 214-705-2901^  metronet  Dallas          TX 300-FAST  24  $ IMNSTV
07/93 215-348-9727   jabber    Doylestown      PA 300-FAST  24 -$ AMNPTV
07/93 215-539-3043^  cellar    Trooper/Oaks    PA 300-FAST  24  $ HMNTV
03/93 216-481-9445   wariat    Cleveland       OH 300-FAST  24  $ AMNSV
03/93 216-582-2460^  ncoast    Cleveland       OH 1200-FAST 24  $ MNPST
03/93 217-789-7888   pallas    Springfield     IL 300-FAST  24  $ HMNSTV
06/93 301-220-0462^  digex     Greenbelt       MD 300-2400  24  $ IMNST
03/93 301-924-5998   highlite  Laurel          MD 1200-FAST 24  $ MNSTV
03/93 303-871-3324^  nyx       Denver          CO 300-FAST  24 -$ MNST
03/93 309-676-0409   hcs       Peoria          IL 300-FAST  24 -$ MNT
```

Enough of online alternatives already. If you had access, you wouldn't be reading this chapter. Okay, I hear you. The rest of the chapter is for those of you with a connection disadvantage.

Here are a few numbers you can try:

ALABAMA

Name	Nuance Network Services
Modem	Contact for number
e-mail	staff@nuance.com
Voice	205-533-4296 Voice/recording

ARIZONA

Name	Evergreen Communications
Modem	602-955-8444
e-mail	evergreen@libre.com
Voice	602-955-8315

Name	Internet Direct, Inc.
Modem	602-274-9600 (Phoenix);
	602-321-9600 (Tucson); login: guest
e-mail	info@indirect.com (automated)
Voice	602-274-0100 (Phoenix), 602-324-0100 (Tucson)

ALASKA

Name	University Of Alaska Southeast, Tundra Services
Modem	907-789-1314
Voice	907-465-6453

CALIFORNIA

Name	a2i communications
Modem	408-293-9010(San Jose)
	415-364-5652(Redwood City); login: guest
e-mail	info@rahul.net
Voice	408-293-8078

Name	The Cyberspace Station
Modem	619-634-1376 login: guest
e-mail	help@cyber.net

Name	Institute for Global Communications/IGC Networks (PeaceNet, EcoNet, ConflictNet, LaborNet, HomeoNet)
Modem	415-322-0284 (N-8-1), login: new
e-mail	support@igc.apc.org
Voice	415-442-0220

Name	The Whole Earth 'Lectronic Link
Modem	415-332-6106 login: newuser
e-mail	info@well.sf.ca.us
Voice	415-332-4335

COLORADO

Name	Colorado Supernet
Modem	Call for number
e-mail	info@csn.org
Voice	303-273-3471

Name	Community News Service
Modem	719-520-1700 ID: new, Passwd: newuser
e-mail	service@cscns.com or usa.net
Voice	719-592-1240

Name	Nyx, the Spirit of the Night; Free public Internet access provided by the University of Denver's Math and Computer Science Department
Modem	303-871-3324
e-mail	aburt@nyx.cs.du.edu
Voice	Login to find current list of volunteer "Voice" helpers

DELAWARE

Name	Systems Solutions
Modem	Contact for info
e-mail	sharris@marlin.ssnet.com
Voice	302 378-1386, 800 331-1386

DISTRICT OF COLUMBIA

Name	The Meta Network
Modem	Contact for numbers
e-mail	info@tmn.com
Voice	703-243-6622

Name	International Internet Association
Voice	202-387-5445

(Check this one out if you live in the DC area; it's free!!)

FLORIDA

Name	CyberGate, Inc
Modem	305-425-0200
e-mail	info@gate.net
Voice	305-428-GATE

ILLINOIS

Name	InterAccess
Modem	708-671-0237
e-mail	info@interaccess.com
Voice	800-967-1580

Name	MCSNet
Modem	312-248-0900 prompts
e-mail	info@genesis.mcs.com
Voice	312-248-UNIX

Name	XNet Information Systems
Modem	708-983-6435 V.32bis and TurboPEP
e-mail	info@xnet.com
Voice	708-983-6064

MARYLAND

Name	Clark Internet Services, Inc. (ClarkNet)
Modem	410-730-9786, 410-995-0271, 301-596-1626, 301-854-0446, 301-621-5216 login: guest
e-mail	info@clark.net
Voice	Call 800-735-2258 then give 410-730-9764 (MD Relay Svc)

MASSACHUSETTS

Name	Nearnet
Modem	Contact for numbers
e-mail	nearnet-join@nic.near.net
Voice	617-873-8730

Name	The World
Modem	617-739-9753 Login: new
e-mail	office@world.std.com
Voice	617-739-0202

Name	North Shore Access
Modem	617-593-4557 (v.32bis, v.32, PEP) Login: new
e-mail	info@northshore.ecosoft.com
Voice	617-593-3110 Voicemail

Name	NovaLink
Modem	800-937-7644 'new' or 'info', 508-754-4009 2400, 14400
e-mail	info@novalink.com
Voice	800-274-2814

MICHIGAN

Name	Merit Network, Inc.—MichNet project
Modem	Contact for number
e-mail	info@merit.edu
Voice	313-764-9430

Name	MSen
Modem	Contact for number
e-mail	info@msen.com
Voice	313-998-4562

NEBRASKA

Name	Network Information Center
e-mail	nic@mid.net
Voice	402-472-7600

NEVADA

Name	Nevadanet
e-mail	info@nevada.edu
Voice	702-895-4580

NEW HAMPSHIRE

Name	MV Communications, Inc.
Modem	603-424-7428; Login: info
e-mail	info@mv.com
Voice	603-429-2223

NEW YORK

Name	Echo Communications
Modem	(212) 989-8411 (v.32, v.32 bis); Login: newuser
e-mail	horn@echonyc.com
Voice	212-255-3839

Name	Maestro
Modem	(212) 240-9700; Login: newuser
e-mail	info@maestro.com
Voice	212-240-9600

Name	MindVOX
Modem	212-989-4141; Login: mindvox guest
e-mail	info@phantom.com
Voice	212-989-2418

Name	PANIX Public Access Unix
Modem	212-787-3100; Login: newuser
e-mail	alexis@panix.com, jsb@panix.com
Voice	212-877-4854

NORTH CAROLINA

Name	CONCERT-CONNECT
Modem	Contact for number
e-mail	info@concert.net
Voice	919-248-1999

Name	Vnet Internet Access, Inc.
Modem	704-347-8839, 919-406-1544, 919-851-1526; Login: new
e-mail	info@char.vnet.net
Voice	704-374-0779

OHIO

Name	Freelance Systems Programming
Modem	513-258-7745 to 14.4 Kbps
e-mail	fsp@dayton.fsp.com
Voice	513-254-7246

Name	APK- Public Access UNI* Site
Modem	216-481-9436
e-mail	zbig@wariat.org
Voice	216-481-9428

OREGON

Name	RainDrop Laboratories
Modem	503-293-1772 (2400), 503-293-2059 (v.32, v.32 bis)
e-mail	info@agora.rain.com

PENNSYLVANIA

Name	Telerama Public Access Internet
Modem	412-481-5302 Login: new (2400)
e-mail	info@telerama.pgh.pa.us
Voice	412-481-3505

Name	Teleport
Modem	503-220-0636 (2400), 503-220-1016 (v.32, v.32 bis); Login: new
e-mail	info@teleport.com
Voice	503-223-4245

RHODE ISLAND

Name	Anomaly
Modem	401-331-3706
e-mail	info@anomaly.sbs.risc.net
Voice	401-273-4669

Name	The IDS World Network
Modem	401-884-9002, 401-785-1067
Fees	$10/month or $50/half year or $100/year
e-mail	sysadmin@ids.net
Voice	401-884-7856

TEXAS

Name	The Black Box
Modem	713-480-2686 (V32bis/V42bis)
Fees	$21.65 per month or $108.25 for 6 months
e-mail	info@blkbox.com
Voice	713-480-2684

Name	Texas Metronet
Modem	214-705-2901/817-261-1127 (V.32bis), 214-705-2929(PEP); Login: info, or 214-705-2917/817-261-7687 (2400); Login: signup
e-mail	info@metronet.com
Voice	214-705-2900, 817-543-8756

Name	South Coast Computing Services, Inc.
Modem	713-661-8593 (v.32), 713-661-8595 (v.32bis)
e-mail	info@sccsi.com
Voice	713-661-3301

Name	RealTime Communications (wixer)
Modem	512-459-4391 Login: new
e-mail	hosts@wixer.bga.com
Voice	512-451-0046 (11 a.m.–6 p.m. Central Time, weekdays)

VIRGINIA

Name	Wyvern Technologies, Inc.
Modem	804-627-1828 Norfolk, 804-886-0662 Peninsula
e-mail	system@wyvern.com
Voice	804-622-4289

WASHINGTON

Name	Eskimo North
Modem	206-367-3837
e-mail	nanook@eskimo.com
Voice	206-367-7457

Name	Halcyon
Modem	206-382-6245 Login: new, 8N1
e-mail	info@halcyon.com
Voice	206-955-1050

Name	Northwest Nexus Inc.
Modem	Contact for numbers
e-mail	info@nwnexus.wa.com
Voice	206-455-3505

Name	Olympus—The Olympic Peninsula's Gateway to the Internet
Modem	Call for number
e-mail	info@pt.olympus.net
Voice	206-385-0464

WEST VIRGINIA

Name	WVNET
e-mail	cc011041@wvnvms.wvnet.edu
Voice	304-293-5192

CANADA

ALBERTA

Name	PUCnet Computer Connections
Modem	403-484-5640 (v.32 bis); Login: guest
e-mail	info@PUCnet.com
Voice	403-448-1901

BRITISH COLUMBIA

Name	BCnet
e-mail	Mick@BC.net
Voice	604-291-5029

MANITOBA

Name	MBnet
e-mail	Gerry_Miller@MBnet.MB.CA
Voice	204-4747-8230

NEWFOUNDLAND

Name	NLnet
e-mail	wilf@kean.ucs.mun.ca
Voice	709-737-8329

NOVA SCOTIA

Name	NSTN Inc.
e-mail	dow@nsts.ns.ca
Voice	902-486-6786

ONTARIO

Name	HookUp Communication Corporation
Modem	Contact for number
e-mail	info@hookup.net
Voice	519-747-4110

QUEBEC

Name	Communications Accessibles Montreal
Modem	514-931-7178 (v.32 bis), 514-931-2333 (2400bps)
e-mail	info@CAM.ORG
Voice	514-931-0749

ONTARIO

Name	UUnorth
Modem	Contact for numbers
e-mail	uunorth@uunorth.north.net
Voice	416-225-8649

PRINCE EDWARD ISLAND

Name	PEINet
e-mail	admin@peinet.ca
Voice	902-892-7346

SASKATCHEWAN

Name	SASK#net
e-mail	dean.jones@usask.ca
Voice	306-966-4860

Remember, this is only a partial list; there are a lot more providers out there and more on the way. If you don't see one in your geographical area, check out one in a different part of the country as many offer 1-800 service. Generally, 800 services cost more, so if you can dial in with a local number, you will be better off and have more money to spend on the important things, such as concert tickets and weekends at the beach.

Tip ➤ If you see an e-mail address that begins **info@**, that means that you usually will receive an automated reply from a computer, so don't bother writing long request messages.

In addition, there are at least four national periodicals you can pick up at your local newsstand that can give you current pointers to service providers or bulletin boards in your area. *Internet World, Online Access, Connect,* and *BoardWatch* magazines all will have clues about where to pick up an Internet account. Pull one off the shelf and browse through the ads.

Commercial Online Services

Commercial online services, such as America Online, CompuServe, and PRODIGY have been around for quite awhile, although they've only recently started offering Internet services. Each offers quite a bit more than just Internet connectivity; they generally have their own graphical software, and provide e-mail, discussion groups, games, and files to download.

If you're a beginner to computers, an online service may be perfect for you. They tend to be much easier and friendlier to use than a UNIX prompt (what isn't?), and help is only a mouse click or two away.

> **Tip ➤** Most online services have introductory offers that give you your first 5–10 hours free. Ask about these when you sign up. Don't start shelling out the bucks until you have to.

When you initially sign on, a major credit card number will be required. (Nothing's free.)

Here they are listed in alphabetical order with all of the pertinent information:

America Online

1-800-827-6364

If you on't already have a dozen disks from AOL sitting on your desk, you have been living on a different planet. Take a trip to your local newsstand and look for the 'zine wrapped in plastic with the Free Disk Included label on the outside. Odds are 10–1 it is a disk from America Online offering five free hours. Pick it up, plop it in your computer, double-click the icon, and the software does the rest.

America Online offers easy access to the Internet. Internet Connection is one of the choices on the main menu of the latest release of its access software. In addition to the features listed below, AOL will be offering FTP and World Wide Web in the near future.

Fees: $9.95 basic monthly service charge. That includes five hours of connect time. Additional connect charges are $2.95 per hour.

Internet Accessibility: USENET, Gopher, WAIS, e-mail.

CompuServe

1-800-848-8990

CompuServe has been around for a long time. Subsequently, it is one of the larger services. CompuServe offers the CompuServe Information Manager (affectionately known as CIM) that makes navigation around the service a simple matter.

Fees: $8.95 basic monthly service charge gives you unlimited access to basic service. e-mail is included in the basic services. To access other Internet utilities, you will have to pay an additional $4.80/hour if you are connecting at 2400 bps or lower and $9.60/hour at higher speeds.

Internet Accessibility: USENET, Telnet, FTP, e-mail, Web, and Gopher servers are being developed.

Delphi

1-800-695-4005

Delphi was the first major online service to offer full Internet access. When the other services saw the interest this created, following suit seemed natural, and they are rushing to catch up. Delphi is working on a new graphical interface called Cityscape; look for it in the middle of 1995. When signing up, ask about the Phoenix Internet Express, which includes a program called InterNav that will allow users to make faster connections to the Internet. Delphi also offers a good collection of online help files and other resources to help you get started.

Fees: You have two options:

- $10 basic monthly service charge. That includes 4 hours of nonprime time connect time. $9/hour for prime time.

- 20/20 plan. One time $19 enrollment fee gives you 20 hours of nonprime connect time. $9/hour for prime time.

Both plans also charge $3/month for Internet use at any time.

> **Tip ➤** What are the prime time and nonprime hours for your service provider? This varies slightly from service to service. Generally think 8 a.m.–6 p.m, M–F for prime time, but don't get caught; waiting that extra hour can save you in connect time charges.

Internet Accessibility: e-mail, USENET, FTP, Gopher, WAIS, IRC, Telnet, and WWW.

eworld

1-800-775-4556

eworld is Apple's attempt to break into the world of mainstream online services. It is the new kid on the block and entered the digital marketplace in June, 1994. This one is for Macintosh users only. Their Internet access is very limited at this time. A Windows version is in the making and greater Internet access is on the horizon.

Fees: $8.95 basic monthly service charge. That includes two hours of non-prime-time connection.

Internet Accessibility: e-mail. That's it. Look for more Internet offerings soon.

GEnie

1-800-638-6936

GEnie is in the process of developing full Internet access and may be in place by the time this book reaches you. They have just developed a graphical interface for Windows that makes sending and receiving e-mail a snap.

Fees: $8.95 basic monthly service charge. That includes four hours of non-prime time connection. Prime time use is $12.50/hour, non-prime time is $3/hour.

Internet Accessibility: e-mail.

PRODIGY

1-800-PRODIGY

PRODIGY was one of the last major services to offer an Internet gateway for e-mail. They have since seen the error of their ways and are moving to catch up with the rest of the big boys and will be offering a greater degree of Internet access soon. They have a new interface, code named P2, that is scheduled to appear early in 1995. This interface will be a windows-like application and should make the interface easy to use.

Fees: $14.95 basic monthly service charge, and $0.10 for every e-mail to or from the Internet.

Internet Accessibility: e-mail and USENET.

Is an Online Service in Your Future?

Online services have their advantages. They generally offer graphical interfaces to their own archives and databases, which are usually quite large. They are easy to navigate and (compared to the Internet) well organized. If you get into one of these, you may find that you don't really need some of the Internet utilities like FTP, as the service will have a large software archive of its own, but not the vast variety of the Internet. Many of these have their own bulletin board systems, called forums, where you can find information about the Internet (and other topics).

Let's get serious for a moment. If your school doesn't have Internet access by now, something is wrong. Find out why. Talk to the folks at your computing center and ask when your school is coming online. Most universities are, or will be, connected. Many of the larger school districts are putting in lines, and grant money is available for rural districts that want to connect. If you are not connected, all it takes is a motivated person who thinks that this is something worth having. Maybe that person is you, but if not, consider transferring next semester.

FAQs for Students

FAQ stands for Frequently Asked Questions. (You'll quickly grow tired of the "just the FAQs, ma'am" jokes, so get them out of your system as soon as possible.) A FAQ is a document created to answer questions around a topic. These topics can be very specific or broad depending on who is writing them. There's no set format for FAQs, and the job of producing them is assigned to nobody in particular, so you won't find any consistency in them. There are FAQs for most of the USENET and listserv discussion groups in existence.

FAQs evolved for a very simple reason. Consider having to answer the same set of questions over and over from every newbie who joins a newsgroup. That's a waste of time and a waste of bandwidth. It's much easier to send off a simple message to answer naive questions, such as this:

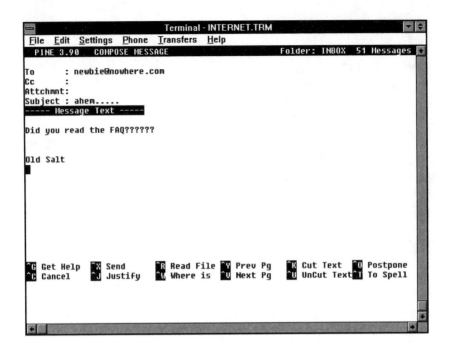

```
━                    Terminal - INTERNET.TRM              ▼ ◆
 File  Edit  Settings  Phone  Transfers  Help
   PINE 3.90   COMPOSE MESSAGE                Folder: INBOX   51 Messages ◆

 To      : newbie@nowhere.com
 Cc      :
 Attchmnt:
 Subject : ahem.....
 ----- Message Text -----

 Did you read the FAQ??????


 Old Salt
 █




 ^G Get Help  ^X Send      ^R Read File ^Y Prev Pg  ^K Cut Text   ^O Postpone
 ^C Cancel    ^J Justify   ^W Where is  ^V Next Pg  ^U UnCut Text ^T To Spell
```

Time to hang your head in shame.

If you ever receive such a piece of e-mail, you'll know that you've been branded a digital newbie and it's time to lay low for awhile as anything you say will not be taken seriously. Always read the FAQ for a newsgroup or listserv before posting, and you can save yourself some embarrassment.

> **Tip ➤** FAQs have begun to evolve for more than USENET and listserv topics. FAQs exist for specific Internet software and utilities, for artificial intelligence and many popular computer games.

So, to keep you from asking stupid questions and making a complete fool of yourself, I've tried to anticipate your questions and put together this FAQ list for students on the Internet. If you have more questions that I don't address here, send them to me at **clarkd@mcp.com** for inclusion in future editions. (To ensure future editions, tell your friends to buy this book!)

How Can I Get Politically Active on the Internet?

First, begin by reading the pc (politically correct) primer at:

http://www.umd.umich.edu/~nhughes/htmldocs/pc.html

for the answers to such questions as, "Can I still be politically correct if I'm a white male?" The answer is yes, but to find out the particulars, look it up for yourself.

Second, let's get serious. One way to make your voice heard is to send a letter to the President. **president@whitehouse.gov** is the address. Tell him what you think about the job he's doing and why you think he should/ should not get another four years. Then sit back and wait. In a few moments, you'll receive a reply.

This is exciting: e-mail from the White House! Keep your fingers steady as you hit those keys to read it. Contain your excitement, and then register your disappointment at the polls in November when you read:

```
Thank you for writing to President Clinton via electronic
mail.  Since June 1993, whitehouse.gov has received over 300,000
messages from people all over the world.

    Although the volume of mail prevents the President from
personally reviewing each message, the mail is read by White House staff.
Your concerns, ideas, and suggestions are carefully recorded ....
```

The VP does the same for you at **vice.president@whitehouse.gov**. Al has been an advocate of the development of a National Information Infrastructure. Let him know to keep up the good work.

Next, take a trip to the White House at **http://www.whitehouse.com**. Sign the guest book and listen to a speech by the President. Okay, I know this isn't real political involvement, but you have to get it out of your system and do it at least once.

Information about contacting your representatives in the Senate or House of Representatives can be found at:

gopher://gopher.eff.org/00/CAF/civics/gov.contact

The Senate has developed its own FTP server at **ftp.senate.gov**. Find documents, press releases, and more here pertaining to the Senate and its members. They also have a Gopher server at (where else?) **gopher.senate.gov**. The House also has a Gopher. Can you guess the address? **gopher.house.gov**.

Very good; this is all starting to make sense, isn't it? And if that's not enough, more information on the House and Senate can be found at:

```
gopher gopher.inform.umd.edu and follow the links:
Educational Resources
Academic Resources by Topic
United States and the World
United States
National Agencies
Legislative Branch
Congress
```

Here's what you'll get:

```
    Select one of:

 (FILE) 103rd congress firsts
  (DIR) Congressional Quarterly (CQ) Gopher
  (DIR) Congressional Voting Records (1993 LCV Environmental Scorecard)
  (DIR) High-Performance Computing
  (DIR) House Committee on Banking, Finance and Urban Affairs
  (DIR) House of Representatives Email and Internet Connections
  (DIR) Legi-Slate Gopher (Bill & Federal Register Info - 103rd Congress)
  (DIR) Making Government Work Office of Technology Assessment
  (DIR) United States House of Representatives Gopher
  (DIR) United States Senate Gopher
  (DIR) Women In Congress Biographies
 (FILE) congressional reform briefing listserv
 (FILE) dem-net is a discussion list on electorial politics & democratic party
 (FILE) democratic biographies
 (FILE) house phone numbers
 (FILE) members not returning to the house
 (FILE) senate phone numbers
 (FILE) women in the house (election 92)
 (FILE) women in the senate (election 92)
```

Check out your representative's report card according to the Voters' Telecom Watch at **gopher://gopher.panix.com/11/vtw**. (A lot of other good links are here, too.) Democrats can join the listserv **DEM-NET@NETCOM.COM** to discuss democratic ideals and topics, and republicans can check out **REPUB-L@MARIST.BITNET** for the other side of the coin. Libertarian? Go to **http://www.lp.org/lp/lp.html**.

That's enough of the main-line information stuff. If underground and radical appeal to you (you know, the stuff the government won't tell you), start with **http://www.eff.org**. Co-founded by John Gilmore and John Perry Barlow (Grateful Dead lyricist; you know it's gotta be cool), the Electronic Frontier Foundation describes themselves as:

A nonprofit civil liberties public interest organization working to protect freedom of expression, privacy, and access to online resources and information.

Next, spend some time with *Mother Jones* magazine at:

http://www.mojones.com/motherjones.html

For the hard core cyberrebels among you, check out Vince Cate's Crypto-rebel and Cypherpunk page. You can find link after link here on what the government would like to do to you. Look for this at:

ftp://furmint.nectar.cs.cmu.edu/security/README.html

For those with a more conservative side to your personalities, you are not forgotten. Right Side of the Web can be found at:

http://www.clark.net/pub/jeffd/index.html

This site contains links for those living to the right of center. Rush Limbaugh will give you an earful at:

http://eskinews.eskimo.com/~jeremyps/limbaugh-info.html

Of course, the best place to get politically active is on the local scene. Here are some ideas:

■ Use your connection to disseminate information on local issues or raise local issues.

■ Create a Web home page that publishes what's going on in your city council or student government.

■ Get involved in the Freenet movement and bring connectivity to people and places that may otherwise miss out on the information age.

If You're Driving at the Speed of Light in Your Car and You Turn On Your Headlights, What Happens?

Ask your physics professor.

What Environmental/Social Action Groups Are on the Net, and How Can I Contact Them?

A wonderful collection of group links is available at:

http://www.ai.mit.edu/projects/ppp/polact.html#Activism

Here is a tasting of the alphabet soup you'll find there:

```
Public Interest Groups
        + APT: Alliance for Public Technology
        + America Responds to AIDS
        + ACLU: American Civil Liberties Union
        + Amnesty International
        + CARAL: California Abortion and Reproductive Rights Action
          League-North
        + Cannabis Action Network
        + Center to Prevent Handgun Violence
        + Communications for a Sustainable Future
        + CPSR: Computer Professionals for Social Responsibility
        + EFF: Electronic Frontier Foundation
        + Families Against Mandatory Minimums
        + Foundation for National Progress - (Mother Jones magazine)
        + The Freedom Forum
        + Friends of the Earth
        + Greenpeace
        + The Milarepa Fund
        + National Center for Missing and Exploited Children
        + The National Child Rights Alliance
        + NRA: National Rifle Association
        + NSS: National Space Society
          (ARInternet interactive public policy forum on "Should we
          return to the moon?")
        + SEAC: Student Environmental Action Coalition

     Organizational Networks
     + EarthWeb
     + HungerWeb
     + EnviroLink
     + Institute for Global Communications (IGC)
     + EcoWeb
```

This collection is part of the Political Participation Project. They have set up a wonderful page with a lot more information and links. You can access their main home page at:

http://www.ai.mit.edu/projects/ppp/polact.html

If the desire to make the world a better place burns in you, this is a site not to miss. Another great jumping off place is The Progressive Directory at:

http://www.igc.apc.org/

This site holds (among other things) a subject-oriented menu for social action groups:

```
     * Animal Rights
     * Differently Abled
     * Environment
```

```
* Health
* Human Rights
* Indigenous Peoples
* Labor
* Lesbian, Bisexual, Gay & Queer
* Media Issues
* Nonviolence
* Peace
* Race & Ethnicity
* Women
* Other Progressive Sites
```

That's just the start of what you will find there. Between these two sites, you'll find plenty of opportunities to get involved. Good for you.

Have You Ever Imagined a World with No Hypothetical Situations?

All the time.

How Can I Go About Looking for a College on the Internet?

Most every college or university has a Gopher server, and that is probably the best place to look for information. Just look at **Other gopher and information servers**, and then go geographically to the school of your heart's desire.

Many are putting up Web pages as well. The following site has some great links to over 600 Web pages housed at universities all over the world:

http://www.mit.edu:8001/people/cdemello/univ.html

What kind of information can you expect to find at either of these sites? That depends entirely on the site. No uniform information to be found here among the institutions. Some will tell you absolutely nothing. Don't go to those schools. With others, you'll be able to get community information, housing options, look through course offerings, and get financial aid information.

Did You Say Financial Aid?

Yes, one-stop shopping for financial aid information on the Internet can be found at:

http://nearnet.gnn.com/wic/ed.16.html

This site houses a collection of links to provide you with information on financial aid for graduate and undergraduate students. Here's the menu you'll get:

```
[IMAGE] Scholarships, Fellowships, and Grants
[IMAGE] Other Information Sources
[IMAGE] Contests
[IMAGE] University Financial Aid Offices
[IMAGE] Free Documents
```

Purdue University has a Student Loan counseling office available. Although the information was written with Purdue in mind, much of the information is valid for students at other schools. **gopher:// oasis.cc.purdue.edu:2525/11/cnslr** is the place to look. Here's what you'll see:

```
                    STUDENT LOAN COUNSELOR
              YOU HAVE REACHED THE INFORMATION PAGE


        Select one of:

     (FILE) About Loan Counselor
      (DIR) Rights and Responsibilities
      (DIR) Facts About Student Loans
     (FILE) Managing Loan Indebtedness
     (FILE) List of Lenders Who Participate in Higher Education Loans
     (FILE) Alternative Financing
       (?)  Search "Loan Counselor"
      (DIR) SSINFO Gopher's Root Menu
```

You Know That Little Indestructible Black Box That's Used on Planes? Why Can't They Make the Whole Plane out of the Same Substance?

I don't know.

How Can I Use the Internet to Find a Job?

The first thing to do, of course, is get yourself out there. Talk to people via mailing lists and newsgroups. You may not realize it, but the fact that you have networking skills is a big plus in looking for a job. Information technology is hot, hot, hot! Work it into your résumé somehow.

Speaking of résumés, *publish your résumé*. There are two ways to do it. First, put it on your own home page. Won't your prospective employer be impressed when you tell him that he can get the latest scoop on you at **http://myschool/mypage/myresume.html**. Either that or he'll be too embarrassed to tell you he doesn't have a clue what you're talking about and will hire you on the spot.

The other option is to publish it at:

http://garnet.msen.com:70/0/occ/resume01.txt

Calling up this URL brings down this message:

```
Make your resume available to thousands of employers across
the country through OCC on Internet.  The OCC online keyword
searchable database is available to all employers who have
Internet access.  There are no charges for employers to access
your resume, and no charge to you if you enter your own resume
online.
```

You can either enter your résumé yourself online or ship them ten bucks, and they'll do it for you.

What Is the Monsterboard and Why Should I Care?

The Monsterboard is a compilation of links relating to job information. With it, you can do a search using the following criteria to look for opportunities:

▌▌ Limit search to specified job industries

▌▌ Limit search to specified job locations

▌▌ Limit search to specified job disciplines

▌▌ Limit search to specified job titles

You can browse through their list of potential employers if you know the name of a company you'd like to work for, or just want to see who's offering what. Look for it at **http://www.monster.com/**. Need an internship? Go to the cyberfair. Check out the employers listed there. All this and more can be found at **http://www.monster.com/**.

Am I going too fast for you? Maybe you're not ready to approach potential employers. You need a little information. Some time to let the last four years sink in. Baloney, you're just scared, but here's a source to get some advice before taking the dive, er, I mean the plunge. Go to:

gopher://sun.cc.WestGa.edu/00/coop/tips/About

to see this:

```
(FILE) About Tips, Trends and Statistics
 (DIR) WGC Career Resource Manual [sun.cc.westga.edu]
 (DIR) Employment Statistics [una.hh.lib.umich.edu]
 (DIR) Job Descriptions [umslvma.umsl.edu]
 (DIR) Job Hunting Strategies (Leads, resumes, interviews...)
 (DIR) Reference Lists (On and Offline)
```

Look good? That'll keep you busy for a few days. You'll find information about federal jobs as well as jobs in the private sector.

Not ready for the private sector? How about a job at a university? Here's how to locate some listings at major universities. You can find the Academic Positions Network at **gopher://wcni.cis.umn.edu:11111/1**.

The Chronicle of Higher Education lets you search geographically for a position. Head to **http://chronicle.merit.edu/.ads/.links.html**. Another place to look is **http://ageninfo.tamu.edu/jobs.html**. This site has a long listing of in-house vacancies at a variety of universities.

Had enough? No luck with those? Try **gopher://garnet.msen.com/11/occ** to pull up this baby:

```
(FILE) Questions and Comments to: occ@mail.msen.com
 (DIR) About Online Career Center
 (DIR) Company Sponsors and Profiles
 (DIR) Employment Events
 (DIR) Career Assistance
 (DIR) FAQ - Frequently Asked Questions about OCC
 (DIR) '94 College & University Resume Books/Diskettes
 (DIR) * Search Jobs
 (DIR) * Search Resumes
 (DIR) * Other Employment Databases/
 (DIR) Recruitment Advertising Agencies
 (DIR) "Online Career Center" On Campus
 (DIR) Help Files: Keyword Search/Enter Resume/Print
(FILE) How To Enter A Resume
(FILE) Online Career Center Liability Policy
```

Now that's got to be enough to at least get you started. All of these sources have links that take you to other links: addresses to write to, questions to ask, and so on. If you can't find a good beginning here, maybe you better look into grad school.

How Can I Find Romance on the Net?

Ahem, I've tried to stay away from this one for as long as I could, but I knew you'd ask. Consider this. Relationships are complicated enough when you can see the other person's eyes. What's going to happen when the only clue you get is whether they can spell or not?

If you're really serious about wanting to give this a try, this site has links to several services on the Internet in the boy-meets-girl (or whatever) business:

http://akebono.stanford.edu/yahoo/Business/ Products_and_Services/Personals

Here you can read personal ads left by others, write an ad of your own, or do a search for the person of your dreams based on their religion, body type, education, and so on. I'm not going to go into a lot of detail about this; you'll need to check it out for yourself to see if it's for you.

Wouldn't you really rather call up a friend and go to a movie or something?

If I Don't Get out of Town for Spring Break, I'm Going to Explode from Stress. How Can the Net Help?

To begin with, if you really want to get out of town, you'll have to leave your computer terminal. If you can't bear to be away from it and don't have a laptop to take with you, don't even bother reading the rest of this. It will just depress you. Maybe consider taking a "virtual vacation." (Hey, the Internet is great, but everybody needs to get away.)

Nevertheless, you can find plenty of travel information on the Net. If you know where you would like to go, gopher to the city, state, or country. Look for a Gopher menu that has some recreational info you can use. Many of these sites will contain information about the area including good restaurants, entertainment, and tourist attractions. Often you can find these details at a local college in the community selection of their Gopher menu.

Here are some other resources:

▐ Airline Toll-Free Numbers

gopher://cs4sun.cs.ttu.edu/00/Reference%20Shelf/Airline

▐ Amtrak Schedules

gopher://gwis.circ.gwu.edu/11/General%20Information/Train

▐ Round the World Traveler's Guide

http://yahoo.ncsa.uiuc.edu/davet/travel/rtw.guide

▐ Tourist Information Sources, by location

http://www.mbnet.mb.ca/lucas/travel/

Use this service to do a search for information on a specific location.

■ Tourism Offices Worldwide Directory

http://www.mbnet.mb.ca/lucas/travel/

■ Also check out the travel links to be found at:

http://galaxy.einet.net/

http://akebono.stanford.edu

How Can I Avoid Looking Like a Dweeb Online?

Let's assume that you are not a dweeb; that'll make my job easier.

1. Read the FAQs for any newsgroups or mailing lists that you're interested in. Don't ask questions that are answered in those documents. (Does it sound like I'm harping on this? I am.)

2. Follow the rules of netiquette. Not sure what they are? Read Arlene Rinaldi's Netiquette paper at: **http://rs6000.adm.fau.edu/faahr/ netiquette.html**

3. Lurk before you leap. Find out what's happening before you put your two cents in. This goes for news, mailing lists, and IRC.

What's the Proper Etiquette for E-Mailing a Professor?

Respectfully.

Where Can I Post Notices for Items I Want to Sell?

Newsgroups are the keys here. Look for a local newsgroup (one with your college or city name in it). Do a **grep .newsrc ads** at your UNIX prompt to find out if there's one just for such postings. (Don't know what grep .newsrc ads means? It means you skipped the chapter on newsgroups; go back and review.)

Can I Take Classes Online, So I Don't Have to Leave My Computer to Go to Class?

Yes, Distance Learning is hot. Look for more schools to start offering online classes. Here is a listing of schools that presently offer classes online. Listings of classes vary from school to school, as does the tuition. I'll leave it up to you to get the particulars:

Boise State University
208-336-7120

California Institute of Integral Studies
800-225-3276
DrSteveE@aol.com
JohnQ@ciis.com

Edgewood College
1-800-225-3276

Heriot-Watt University
1-800-225-3276

Michigan State University
800-225-3276

(The three above are both administered by EUN: the Electronic University)

New Jersey Institute of Technology
210-596-3177

The New School
212-229-5880

New York Institute of Technology
800-222-NYIT

New York University
212-998-7190

Rochester Institute of Technology
716-475-5089

Rogers State College
800-225-3276

Salve Regina
800-225-3276

The Union Institute
800-486-3116

University of Phoenix
800-388-5463

What Kind of Goodies Are Best for Bribing Sysops?

I'm not sure; send me 10 pounds of chocolate, and I'll see if I can come up with an answer.

Software Resource List

As you're reading along in this book, you may find yourself thinking, "Yeah, that sounds like great software, but where do I get it?" Well, this appendix tells you.

First, a note about addresses. All the addresses listed are FTP addresses. You can get to them through FTP, as you learned in Chapter 8, or through World Wide Web, as you learned in Chapter 7. If you go through WWW, instead of **http://** at the beginning of the address, you'd type **ftp://**. (If that doesn't make any sense to you, go back and reread Chapter 7.)

Next, a note about shareware, freeware, and copyrights. Most of the software that's free for the downloading on the Internet isn't really free; it's shareware. The authors make their programs available to you to try on a no-obligation basis. If you find out that you use the program regularly, you're honor-bound to register it and pay the small fee that the author asks for. Each program you download will include some sort of registration information and a statement about how you can and can't use and distribute it. Pay attention; this stuff is important.

Finally, a word about file compression. Most programs you download will come to you in some compressed state; there will be one tidy little compressed file that contains all the files you need to run the program. For Macintosh, the files will usually have the extension .SEA or .SIT. SEA files are self-extracting archives, while IBM-compatibles will usually be .ZIP, or .EXE.

The .SEA and .EXE files are self-extracting. You just copy them to your hard disk and run them like programs, and the files contained inside will automatically be decompressed. With all those other formats (plus others I didn't mention), you'll need a special decompression program, such as StuffIt for the Mac or PKUnzip (pkware) for IBM-compatibles. See Compression Tools in the listing that follows for the locations of some of these tools.

Software for Dial-Up Terminal Connections

If you want to connect to an Internet server (such as a school's computer) through a dial-up terminal connection, you'll need a basic communications program. Here's a list of some basic comm programs available on the Net, plus some extra programs (such as SlipKnot) that make your dial-up terminal connection more graphical.

For Windows

Telemate
Communications program
ftp.utas.edu.au
File name: tm400-1.zip
                tm400-2.zip
                tm400-3.zip
                tm400-4.zip

Telix
DOS communications program
oak.oakland.edu:/SimTel/msdos/telix
File name: tlx322-1.zip
                tlx322-2.zip
                tlx322-3.zip
                tlx322-4.zip

SlipKnot
Graphical World Wide Web browser for dial-up user
oak.oakland.edu/SimTel/win3/internet
File name: slnot100.zip

Appendix

For Macintosh

Zterm
Solid communications program
ftp.pht.com:/pub/mac/info-mac/comm/term
File name: zterm-10b3.hqx

Inter Slip
Required for SLIP connections
ftp.pht.com:/pub/mac/info-mac/comm/term
File name: inter-slip-installer-101.hqx

MacTCP
Note: This is built into System 7.5. Otherwise, you'll need to get this from Apple.

Software for Direct Connections

Dial-up direct connections and dedicated connections can take advantage of the ever-growing pool of Internet graphical software out there. Here's a brief sampling—there are lots more.

For Windows

Cello
World Wide Web browser
hull.marcam.com:/win3/winsock
File name: cello.zip

Eudora
e-mail interface
lorien.Qualcomm.com:/quest/windows/eudora/1.4
File name: eudor144.exe

IRC for Windows
IRC client for windows
hull.marcam.com:/win3/winsock
File name: irc4win.zip

Netscape
Graphical interface to access the World Wide Web
ftp2.mcom.com:/netscape/windows
File name: ns16-100.exe

Remsock
Pseudo-SLIP software for PCs
oslonett.no/Shareware/Windows/Comm/
File name: remsock.zip

Trumpet Winsock
TCP Stack for Windows, also includes a variety of software to access the Internet.
Note: TCP support will be built into Windows 95 when released.
hull.marcam.com:/win3/winsock
File name: twsk20b.zip
(The home for Winsock software is winftp.cica.indiana.edu. They're very busy; good luck trying to get it.)

Telnet
Telnet utility
ftp.ncsa.uiuc.edu:/Telnet/DOS
File name: tel2308b.zip

WinGopher
Gopher interface
ftp://ftp.cuhk.hk/pub/gopher/PC
File name: wgopher.zip

For Macintosh

CU-see-me
Video conferencing utility
ftp.pht.com:/pub/mac/info-mac/comm/tcp
File name: cu-see-me-070b1.hqx

Eudora
e-mail interface
lorien.Qualcomm.com:/quest/mac/eudora/2.1
File name: eudora211.hqx

Anarchie
Search and FTP all in a single bound!
ftp.pht.com:/pub/mac/info-mac/comm/tcp
File name: anarchie-14.hqx

Fetch
File transfer utility
ftp.pht.com:/pub/mac/info-mac/comm/tcp
File name: fetch-212.hqx

Homer
Software to access the IRC
ftp.pht.com:/pub/mac/info-mac/comm/tcp
File name: homer-0934.hqx

Maven
Audio conferencing tool
ftp.pht.com:/pub/mac/info-mac/comm/tcp
File name: maven-20d23.hqx

NCSA Telnet
Telnet utility
ftp.ncsa.uiuc.edu:/Telnet/Mac
File name: Telnet2.6/

Mosaic Netscape
Graphical interface to the World Wide Web
ftp2.mcom.com:/netscape/mac
File name: netscape.sea.hqx

NewsWatcher
USENET reading program
ftp.pht.com:/pub/mac/info-mac/comm/tcp
File name:newswatcher-20b22.hqx

Turbo Gopher
Click and point your way into gopherspace.
ftp.pht.com:/pub/mac/info-mac/comm/tcp
File name: turbo-gopher-20b2.hqx

Media Tools

Media Tools are programs that support the images, sounds, video, and what-
not that you snag on the Internet.

For Windows

Lview 3.1
gif/jpeg viewer
ftp.ncsa.uiuc.edu:/Web/Mosaic/Windows/viewers
File name: lview31.zip

MPEG Player 3.2
MPEG movie viewer
ftp.ncsa.uiuc.edu
File name: mpegw32h.zip

Wham
Sound utility
ftp.ncsa.uiuc.edu:/Web/Mosaic/Windows/viewers
File name: wham131.zip

For Macintosh

Jpeg View
Image viewer
ftp.ncsa.uiuc.edu:/Web/Mosaic/Mac/Helpers
File name: jpeg-view-33.hqx

Sparkle
MPEG movie player
ftp.ncsa.uiuc.edu:/Web/Mosaic/Mac/Helpers
File name: sparkle-223.hqx

Sound Machine 2.1
Sound player
ftp.ncsa.uiuc.edu:/Web/Mosaic/Mac/Helpers
File name: sound-machine-21.hqx

Compression Tools

As I said earlier, most of the programs you'll get are compressed. You need a compression tool to restore them to normal size and capability. Here are a few common tools.

For Windows

PKUnzip
oak.oakland.edu:/pub/pc-blue/utility
File name: pkunzip.exe

For Macintosh

StuffIt Expander
ftp.ncsa.uiuc.edu:/Web/Mosaic/Mac/Helpers
File name: stuffit-expander-352.hqx

The Internet Adapter (Mac or Windows)

The Internet Adapter, or TIA, as I call it through most of this book, is in a class all by itself.

marketplace.com:/tia
Send e-mail to info@marketplace.com for information about how to install and receive software license.

Words You Should Know

alias A simple name that is substituted for a command name to make it easier to remember. For example, **alias oakland ftp oak.oakland.edu** creates an alias so you need only type **oakland** to make an FTP connection to oak.oakland.edu.

America Online An online information service that provides e-mail, discussion groups, file downloading, and partial Internet access for a monthly fee.

Anonymous FTP A system where you, as a member of the Internet, can download files from certain sites without needing a login name and password. You use anonymous as your login name and your e-mail address as your password.

Archie An Internet utility for searching FTP sites around the world.

ASCII Stands for American Standard Code for Information Interchange. A standard for computer-generated characters, such as numbers, letters, and symbols.

article A posting in a USENET newsgroup.

bandwidth A measurement of the amount of data that can be transferred by a line at a time. The wider the bandwidth, the more data that can move at once.

baud The speed at which a modem can physically transfer data. The maximum baud rate for most modems and PCs is 14400 baud. Contrast this to bps.

bps Stands for bits per second. A measurement of the number of bits that can be transferred per second over a line. Up to 9600, baud and bps are the same. For bps rates higher than 9600, the transfer is happening at 9600 baud, but the data is being compressed so that the number of bits transferred per second increases.

BBS Stands for Bulletin Board System. A computer system, often local, where users can dial in with their modems to share information, play games, download files, and so forth. These systems are often located in your neighbor's basements.

BFN Stands for "Bye, For Now."

BinHex A method by which Macintosh binary files (programs, graphics, formatted text) are converted into ASCII text. This enables the file to be transferred via e-mail. It has to be "debinhexed" on the other end before it can be used.

BITNET Stands for "Because It's Time NETwork." BITNET is a large network of computers that's been around for a long time. Many of the LISTSERV discussion groups had their beginnings through BITNET.

BTW Stands for "By The Way."

Cello A graphical World Wide Web Browser for Windows users who have some type of direct connection (dedicated or dial-up). Cello allows the user to view graphics, watch video, and hear sound files.

chat To talk... er, write, interactively online with another user. When you chat with someone, your typed words appear on his screen (nearly) simultaneously with your own.

client A piece of software used to access the Internet that acts on your behalf. Gopher is client software that retrieves information from the Internet for you. Can also be a computer system that uses the resources of another computer on the network.

CompuServe An online information service that offers e-mail, forums, file downloading, news, and more—all the usual stuff. CompuServe is known for being more business-oriented than other online services. CompuServe offers Internet e-mail and USENET newsgroups and may be offering more Internet features in the near future.

compressed file A file that is shrunken to take up less disk space or to transfer faster. You must decompress the file with a decompression utility before you can use it.

cyberspace   When is a space not a space? When it's the "space" that you enter when you log onto an online service or connect to the Internet. Cyberspace is the virtual arena where computer mediated communication takes place.

dedicated connection   A cable connection between your computer and the host computer. It's "on" all the time, even when you're not using it, and the line (cable) is "dedicated" for that use—it has no other purpose. Direct connections are very fast, making them ideal for graphical software use. Contrast this to dial-up terminal and dial-up direct connections.

dedicated line   A high-speed telephone line that is permanently wired into the Internet. This line moves information directly from your computer to the rest of the Internet.

dial-up   To connect to a host computer using your modem and some phone lines. Contrast this to a dedicated connection.

dial-up direct   A connection type that connects your computer directly to the Internet, passing through the host computer. From the computer's point of view, it's the same as a dedicated connection, which means you can use all the cool graphical software. Contrast this to dial-up terminal.

dial-up terminal   A connection type that connects your computer to the host computer as a "dumb terminal." In other words, your keyboard and monitor become your means of accessing the host computer, and your own computer's brain sits dumbly by and watches. Dial-up terminal is a rather limited way of connecting to the Internet, since it doesn't let you use graphics.

domain name   A name given to a host computer on the Internet. The domain name of your host computer will be part of your e-mail address. My address is **clarkd@bvsd.k12.co.us**. The **bvsd** is the name of the machine, **k12** is my network combined with **co** (for Colorado) and **us** (for United States) Collectively, **bvsd.k12.co.us** forms my domain name.

download   To transfer files from one computer to another. When the file is coming to your computer, you're downloading it. When it's moving from your computer to someone else's, you're uploading it.

Elm   A UNIX program used for reading e-mail. Elm is an older program and has limited functionality. Many people prefer Pine, a newer program.

e-mail   Stands for electronic mail. A system by which people send and receive messages using their computers over a network (such as the Internet!).

emoticon   See *smiley*.

Ethernet   A common networking scheme used to link computers together so they can share data.

Eudora   An e-mail program for Mac/Windows that can be used with a direct Internet connection (dedicated or SLIP/PPP). Eudora has a graphical interface that allows the user point-and-click accessibility.

FAQ   Stands for Frequently Asked Questions. A document about a given topic in a question/answer form.

finger   A UNIX program used to find information about other users.

flame   An offensive newsgroup posting or piece of e-mail.

follow-up   A response in a newsgroup to a posted article.

Freenet   A community-based network providing various electronic services to local users, such as Internet access.

freeware   Software that is distributed free of charge by the author (bless his or her heart), who retains the copyright.

FTP   Stands for File Transfer Protocol. A method by which files are transferred over the Internet.

FWIW   Stands for "For What It's Worth."

FYI   Stands for "For Your Information."

Gateway   A computer system that transfers data between computers that are running different operating systems.

GEnie   An online Information Service that offers all the usual online service stuff, plus some Internet access.

Gopher   A piece of UNIX software that allows you to tunnel through the Internet and retrieve information. When entering Gopher, you encounter a menu that helps you navigate the Internet.

gopherspace   The arena you are playing in when you fire up your Gopher program.

host   A computer connected directly into a network, such as the Internet. When dialing into the Internet, you connect into your host computer and manipulate this machine to surf the Net.

HTML   Stands for "Hyper-Text Media Language." It's a simple programming language used in creating World Wide Web Home Pages.

hypertext   A system by which users can jump from site to site around the Internet by means of hyperlinks. Using these links, a user can hop around the

Internet connecting to a variety of sites around a topic of interest. The World Wide Web is the Internet's best example of a hypertext based system.

IMHO   Stands for "In My Humble Opinion."

Internet Relay Chat   Also known as IRC. A UNIX program that lets people join together on the Internet to chat. When entering the IRC, you can join discussions centering around specific topics or hop in the hot tub and just see what's happening.

IP   Internet Protocol. The standard set of rules by which information zips over the network and lands in the right place (most of the time).

IRC   See *Internet Relay Chat.*

ISDN   Stands for Integrated Services Digital Network. ISDN is a digital telephone service—the phone lines of the future. Most standard phone lines can't carry digital information (they carry sounds), so digital info from your computer has to pass through a modem on both ends to be translated. An ISDN line eliminates the need for a modem, which in turn speeds up the data transfer.

Jughead   An internet searching utility that searches Gopher menus based on a keyword provided by you. Jughead is similar to Veronica, but does not perform as detailed of a search, but that's Jughead for you.

Kermit   A popular frog on Sesame Street; also a popular downloading protocol used to move files between computers via modems and phone lines.

LISTSERV   It's not an acronym, but rather an abbreviation for List Server. LISTSERV is a set of discussion groups that meet through e-mail on the Internet. LISTSERV also refers to the UNIX software that manages the discussions.

login   The procedure of making a connection with your host computer. This procedure includes filling in your name and password. Login also refers to the name you use when accessing your host computer.

.login   A file that exists invisibly in your home UNIX directory. You can alter this file to make changes to your UNIX account, such as changing the look of your prompt from the boring **csh>** to something more exciting, such as **I exist for you only>**.

Lynx   A text-based browser for the World Wide Web.

Majordomo   UNIX software used to manage discussions via e-mail.

MIME   Stands for Multipurpose Internet Mail Extensions. It's a system that uses e-mail to send computer files, such as graphics and video. MIME works similarly to BinHex and UUENCODE in that it changes the binary information into a subset of ASCII.

Mirror Site   An FTP site that duplicates the holdings of another site. It can be useful if the original site is extremely busy.

modem   A device that enables a computer to send and receive data over regular phone lines. A modem converts analog (sound) signals to digital (computer) information, and vice versa. Modems can be built into your computer or sit as another box on your desk connected to your computer by a cable. (Just what we needed, more cables.)

netiquette   The rules of etiquette governing communication over the Internet. NEVER USING CAPITALS WHEN SENDING E-MAIL UNLESS YOU WANT TO BE PERCEIVED AS SHOUTING is an example of a netiquette rule.

Netscape   A World Wide Web browser that supports graphics, sounds, and video files. It requires a direct connection (dedicated or SLIP/PPP) to work. It's very popular, and with good reason—check this one out.

newsgroup   One of over 6,000 discussion groups happening on the Internet around most any known subject.

newsreader   A program used to read newsgroups.

online mail reader   Just the opposite of offline mail reader. You are connected every moment you are reading and composing. Pine is an online mail reader.

online   When you have a connection to another computer, you are said to be online. Offline is the rest of your life.

offline mail reader   This is a nifty type of mail software that allows you to compose and read your mail without being connected. To do this, the program downloads your mail onto your hard drive. You can then read and reply at your leisure. This is especially good news for those who have to pay through the nose for every minute of connect time. Eudora is an offline mail reader.

OTOH   Stands for "On The Other Hand."

packet switching   A system by which information is broken down into smaller pieces, called packets, and transferred independently over the Internet. When received by another computer, these packets are put together; and bingo, you have something that makes sense. (Usually.)

permanent connection   A connection to the Internet using a dedicated, high-speed phone line. Your school's host computer probably has a permanent connection, and if you're using a computer that's directly hooked to it, such as in a computer lab, then you have a permanent connection, too, by association. If you use a modem to dial into the host computer, you don't have a permanent connection.

Pine   A UNIX e-mail program. Stands for "Pine Is Not Elm." (Elm is an older e-mail program.) Pine is rapidly becoming the UNIX e-mail program of choice because of ease of use. (Notice I used ease of use and UNIX in the same definition. Not many people can do that!)

PPP   Stands for Point to Point Protocol. A set of rules for managing a dial-up direct connection. There are several sets of rules, any one of which will work; PPP is one, and SLIP is another.

public domain software   Software that is not owned by anyone. This software may be freely copied, altered, and distributed. Contrast with freeware and shareware.

Remote login   The act of connecting with another computer at another location. See *Telnet*.

RTFM   Stands for "Read The (insert favorite F word here) Manual."

Server   A computer or program that offers a service to another computer or program. For example, I use my Gopher client software (the software on my hard drive) to access the Gopher server software to retrieve my information. The computer containing the information I want "serves" it up to me, so it's the server. My computer takes what is offered, so it's the client.

Service Provider   An organization that offers Internet access to people. These providers charge for their access, and some get very rich.

shareware   Software posted in a try-before-you-buy mode. This software is frequently free for the downloading, but if you continue to use it, you are honor-bound to compensate the author.

shell   UNIX software that processes the commands you give at your UNIX prompt. There are various shell versions available including the C Shell, Bourne Shell, and Korn Shell. Depending on which shell you use (or was set up for you), the commands you type at your UNIX prompt may vary.

signature   A series of lines at the end of an e-mail or news posting giving information about the author. These lines are usually automatically attached to the posting and frequently include pithy sayings or words of wisdom.

SLIP Stands for Serial Line Internet Protocol. A set of rules for managing a dial-up direct connection. There are several sets of rules, any one of which will work; SLIP is one, and PPP is another.

smiley A text version of a smile, such as :) (turn your head to the side). These are used to express emotion in e-mail and USENET postings. Also called emoticons.

TCP/IP Stands for Transmission Control Protocol/Internet Protocol. It's an agreed-upon system of transferring data over the Internet. To use a dedicated or dial-up direct connection, you must run a TCP/IP program, unless TCP/IP support is built into your operating system.

Telnet A means of logging into other computers on the Internet, as if you were a local user on that system. When telnetting to another computer, you frequently will be asked to provide a login name and password.

The Internet Adapter A UNIX program that sits in your home and works with your communications software to provide a "pseudo-SLIP" connection. Using TIA, you can use Internet client software (Netscape, Cello, Mosaic, and so on) over a phone line.

TIA See *The Internet Adapter*.

token ring A networking scheme used to create a local area network—that is, to connect computers at a single site together. This network can then be piped out to the Internet.

UNIX A popular computer operating system widely used on the Internet. Many hosts use UNIX as their operating system and require basic knowledge of UNIX commands to get around on them.

upload To transfer a file from your local computer to a remote one. The opposite of download.

URL Uniform Resource Locator. This is the long-winded addressing system used by the World Wide Web. **http://mcp.com/~dclark/student.html** is a short example of a URL. (Try to say that ten times in a row.)

UUDECODE The changing of UUENCODED files back into their original state.

UUENCODE A method by which DOS and UNIX binary files (graphics, programs, spreadsheets, and so on) are transferred into ASCII characters. (Macintoshes use *BinHex* instead.)

Veronica   Stands for Very Easy Rodent-Oriented Netwide Index to Computerized Archives. (Yeah, I know, it's a stretch.) A UNIX utility used to search Gopher menu titles in gopherspace.

virus   A potentially damaging program that can be transferred from computer by shared floppy disks or via phone lines. These programs replicate themselves and spread. Virus scanning software and regular backups of your data can prevent you from becoming their victim.

VT100   The standard mode of terminal emulation used by many hosts. Also a product name of a DEC computer.

W3   A shorthand for World Wide Web.

WAIS   Stands for Wide Area Information Server. A system that allows for users to search a variety of databases on the Internet.

White Pages   An attempt to create a list of Internet users. Good luck using it.

Whois   A UNIX program used for searching for Internet users. Good luck using it, too.

World Wide Web   A system of navigating the Internet via pre-established links. The Web operates on a series of Home Pages set up by schools, governmental and commercial entities, and individuals (such as you and me) around the world. These pages include links to other Internet sites and resources.

WWW   See *World Wide Web*.

WYSIWYG   Stands for "What You See Is What You Get." The term originally referred to a program that showed you on-screen the exact result you would get when printing your data, for example, a word processing program that showed the various fonts on-screen that would print. Nowadays, the term has expanded to mean any user-friendly, graphical interface.

xmodem   A transfer protocol used to exchange data between computers via a modem.

ymodem   A transfer protocol used to exchange data between computers via a modem.

zmodem   A transfer protocol that includes error checking and crash recovery.